Marriage Disputes
in Medieval England

Marriage Disputes
in Medieval England

Frederik Pedersen

Hambledon and London
London and New York

Published by Hambledon and London 2000

102 Gloucester Avenue, London NW1 8HX (UK)
838 Broadway, New York, NY 10003 (USA)

ISBN 1 85285 198 8

A description of this book is
available from the British Library and
from the Library of Congress

Typeset from author's disk by Acorn Bookwork, Salisbury
Printed on acid-free paper and bound in
Great Britain by Cambridge University Press

Contents

Preface

Medieval people, lay and cleric alike, were surrounded by law and their associated legal systems: manorial law, feudal law, maritime law, merchant law, municipal law, roman law, royal law and canon law. The records of the medieval church courts have become one of the most fruitful sources for social and legal historians of the middle ages and have yielded valuable information about the way in which medieval people conducted their lives. By the thirteenth century the canon law of the church had established its jurisdiction over every case that affected the salvation of Christian souls and had thus become the one legal system that affected everyone who accepted the Roman pontiff as the successor of Christ, regardless of their social status. Cases came to be heard by ecclesiastical tribunals either because the litigation affected a member of the clergy or because its subject matter affected the salvation of Christian souls, and the most common among the latter group were cases about the validity of marriage.

With such a plethora of legal systems it should not be surprising that medieval people used the courts with a considerable amount of cunning. Anyone who has read *The Saga of Burnt Njal* will have been given a object lesson in how medieval people, like their modern counterparts, knew how to select the facts to present in a case and how to use the procedure of the courts to their advantage. The reader of *Njal's Saga* will also have learnt that litigation took place in a social space that allowed the litigants to proceed only according to a set of complex and rigorous rules that left little room to manoeuvre. Though Njal and his family are but one example of how the legal systems of the middle ages affected the parties involved in litigation, their example raises questions about the veracity of medieval legal sources. It therefore seems sensible to study in detail the way the courts and the laity interacted and to investigate the level of legal knowledge among the laity before using the legal records to extract details about social history.

This book studies the practice of one court – the ecclesiastical consistory court of York – during the first century of its documented

existence – the fourteenth. The choice of an ecclesiastical, rather than
a secular, court is deliberate, for only in marriage cases heard by ecclesiastical tribunals can the historian hope to hear the voice of one half
of the population. Women suffered a number of legal disadvantages in
the middle ages. Unmarried women appeared rarely, and married
women could not appear, as litigants in any other legal forum, so the
church court material has therefore been identified as a major source
for the history of women as well as for social history. Though litigation about benefices, tithes, breach of faith, defamation and jurisdiction is interesting in itself, it was felt that marriage cases – which as a
single group make up most of the surviving English litigation – offered
the most representative illustration of how medieval people interacted
with a legal system. Not only do the surviving documents illustrate
how the ecclesiastical court in York dealt with the individual cases,
but, since the law it interpreted was intended to be valid all over
Europe, there is reason to believe that the results of such an investigation will be of interest to scholars whose interests fall outside the
geographical boundaries of the diocese of York.

The overall conclusion – that the medieval archdiocese of York
provided a well-functioning system of justice in marriage cases that
conformed to the rules of European canon law – is perhaps not
surprising. But the following pages are so full of examples of attempts
to pervert the function of the court of York that it must be argued
that, though cases may demonstrate the outer limits of what the courts
were willing to accept as true, we cannot use the material without
establishing properly the parameters under which the litigation took
place on a case-to-case basis. In some cases, such as *Palmer* c. *Palmer
and Brune*, we must simply discard the York cause paper evidence in
the original case, in others, such as *Carnoby* c. *Monceaux*, we must
reconsider the context of the cases and draw conclusions about the
veracity of the evidence presented to the court. But in all cases we
cannot take the evidence of the material preserved by the courts as
anything but a collection of narratives, highly organised to fit specific
circumstances and suitable to further the argument of the litigant for
whose position they were produced.

It is inevitable that a book such as this has benefited from the help,
advice and the discussions I have had with many people over the
years. I therefore have a large number of people and institutions to
thank for help and inspiration in the preparation of this book. During
the ten year period 1985–95 I was fortunate enough to be able to raise

funding from private trusts for individual projects. I would like to acknowledge the financial aid of Carlsbergfondet, the World University Service of Canada and the Knud Højgaards Fond which supported me in the period 1985–91, Clare Hall for awarding me the Carlsberg-Clare Hall Visiting Fellowship 1991–92. The Cambridge Group for the History of Population and Social Structure granted me a three-month visiting fellowship in 1991 and Carlsbergfondet supported me financially from 1992–95.

Among the people I wish to thank are two of my supervisors in Copenhagen, Brian Patrick McGuire and Graham Caie, who introduced me to medieval studies and fired my imagination. Their work was continued by Michael M. Sheehan in Toronto, who was not only the most inspiring teacher I have had in a long career as a student but who also seemed to be able anticipate my pastoral needs during a very dark time in my life. I had hoped that Father Sheehan would have been my *Doktorvater*, but his untimely death shortly after my graduation from Toronto was a sad loss to me personally and to all those who study the history of the family. In his place, Charles Donahue, who was my external examiner in Toronto, has helped me often and generously. Our association began with the exchange of research notes in 1992, but I am convinced that Charles's continued letters of support for a number of research projects I have been involved in were instrumental in their success. Although I have used his notes for details in this book, I have always independently verified readings and interpretations. I must therefore emphasise that he is in no way responsible for errors I may have committed.

I also acknowledge the quality of the teaching and supervision in Toronto. In particular I received valuable lessons in Latin from Ann Dalzell and David Townsend, while Brian Stock and Giulio Silano introduced me to many aspects of canon law that I had never considered before. I also acknowledge my debt to other students and friends in Toronto, in particular Martin LeMaitre, Alfred Mackenzie, Lisa Marie Esposito, Ann Kuzdale, J.T. Stout, Jacqueline Murray, Timothy Haskett and Connie Rousseau, and to the inhabitants of The Grange in York (Charles Kightly, Simon Thompsett, Hilary Moxon and Sandra Barton) who took me in for a year when I was doing the ground work for my Toronto degree. For the past ten years I have lived in the UK and in that time I have benefited from discussions and support from a number of eminent scholars, among them: Larry Poos, Lloyd Bonfield, Roger Schofield, Richard M. Smith, Richard Wall, Peter Laslett, Jim Oeppen, Richard Helmholz, Paul Griffiths, Barrie Dobson, John Henderson, and Marjory McIntosh.

I owe thanks to the people and institutions who have helped me while writing this book in Aberdeen. I have been privileged to come to know Leslie MacFarlane, a brilliant scholar and mentor, and Angelo Forte. They have always taken the time to discuss academic matters with me and I have benefited enormously from their expertise. For the past year I have been on research leave as part of a rolling programme initiated by Professor Allan Macinnes in the History Department at the University of Aberdeen. Allan has also offered helpful advice during the year. I would also like to acknowledge the inspiration I have received from my colleagues at the History Department, which I believe is one of the most dynamic and forward-looking history departments in the UK. The University of York and the Borthwick Institute of Historical Research kindly appointed me Borthwick Institute Visiting Fellow for the calendar year 1999, so that I could take full advantage of the time I had off teaching. I have happily drawn on the expertise of the staff of the Borthwick, especially on the knowledge of David Smith and Chris Webb. Timothy Holman deserves thanks for sharing his wonderful flat with me during my sojourns in York. My wife, Sarah, combines two very rare things: a training as a medievalist from York and a successful career in publishing. She has read my manuscript several times, made me clarify obscure points and rewrite clumsy sentences. She has been a sounding board for my ideas to the extent that she now claims that she acknowledges Agnes of Huntington as the other woman in my life. I could not have written this book without her. The inspiration behind the last chapter is an anonymous reader who criticised me for not taking "secular developments" into account. The reason for this omission was obvious to me, but the comments spurred me on to write a version of the last chapter with which P.J.P. Goldberg took issue. I stand by my conclusions, but must also acknowledge the influence of these two individuals for the way in which they forced me to reconsider some largely subconscious decisions I made very early on in the composition of this work.

I have a final acknowledgement to make for which I must beg the reader's indulgence. Throughout my life I have had the benefit of the advice and patience of my father, Asger Pedersen. He died after long illness in the summer of 1998 and never saw this book finished. Like me, he came relatively late to his chosen field, cardiology and internal medicine, so he understood the importance of time in the maturation of thought. He often used to lament the current obsession with always having an answer to a problem regardless of the expertise or the time you have spent studying it. I learned from him that it takes time to develop insight and that it is worse to form a rash opinion than to resist outside pressure to be an expert. I always had strong support from him and his guidance in matters human as well as academic was always just right. He also embodied in himself the old-world values that that are contained in the words "gentle" and "cultured". His knowledge of the arts, especially of music, was almost as deep as his knowledge of his chosen fields. I can only hope that someday I may become as cultured as he was and that I can show as much love and acceptance of my son as he did to me. I dedicate this book in gratitude to his memory.

1

Medieval Marriage

Around the year 1140, Master Gratian of Bologna wrote his monumental attempt to reconcile the legal practice of canon law with the texts that had survived from the preceding millennium. With a felicitous choice of phrase that encompassed both the intended outcome of his work and his methodology, he called his work *Concordia discordantium canonum* (*The Harmony of Discordant Canons*), but it soon became known as *The Decretum of Master Gratian of Bologna* or simply the *Decretum*. His work set the stage for a rapid and decisive transition in the church's exercise of its jurisdiction. Gratian's work added a new dimension to the exercise of law in the west: the legal practice of the church had always been seen as built upon the logic of more than a thousand years of legal custom and teaching, but Gratian's *Decretum* demonstrated that it was possible to practise the law based on clear principles as well as on the authority of the church and its holy books. Gratian's work was swiftly disseminated and had a profound influence on the practice of law all over Europe.[1]

---

[1] Our perception of the identity of Master Gratian is constantly changing: until 1979 it was believed that Gratian was a Camaldolese monk from the monastery of St Felix and Nabor in Bologna, who was born in Tuscany or Umbria, that he taught law in Bologna until his death sometime before 1159 and that he single-handedly wrote the *Decretum* sometime before 1140: The *Catholic Encyclopedia*, vi (New York, 1907), s.v. Gratian, Johannes. Yet, in an examination of the evidence for Gratian's life, John T. Noonan, "Gratian Slept Here: The Changing Evidence for the Identity of the Father of the Systematic Study of Canon Law", *Traditio: Studies in Ancient and Medieval History, Thought and Religion*, 35 (1979), pp. 145–72, the known facts about Gratian were reduced to three: that he was probably Italian by birth; that he lived in Bologna in much of the 1130s and 1140s; and that he wrote most of the *Decretum* sometime before 1139. Recently Anders Winroth has sown even more doubt about Gratian's contribution to the composition of the text we now know as the *Decretum*, suggesting that Gratian circulated a preliminary edition of the text, which basically consisted of Gratian's *Dicta*, to a number of European centres of learning, before he (or his pupils) added the texts of the authorities to the text of the *Decretum*. Winroth furthermore suggests that Gratian may have died before the completion of his work in 1140, Anders Winroth, "The

But it was a text intended more for the classroom than for the actual practice of law, and nowhere is this clearer than in Gratian's discussion of what made a legal marriage. The clarification and revision of the *Decretum*'s canons on marriage became one of the main focal points of legal activity in the following century. Between the appearance of the *Decretum* and the publication of the *Decretals of Gregory IX* as the *Liber extra* in 1234, Gratian's discussion of marriage was interpreted in the works of the decretists and the decretalists who annotated, added to and analysed his work.[2] Gratian's basic discussion was also clarified by hundreds of decisions in marriage cases and published in decretal letters made by the ruling popes, most notably Alexander III (1159–1181) and Innocent III (1198–1216). With the publication of the *Liber extra* the consolidation of European marriage law was complete and it remained essentially the same until the Reformation.[3]

Gratian had set out two basic criteria for marriage, and these were never in doubt. The parties who wanted to marry had to be able to make an informed decision to marry and they had to be legally able to contract a marriage. Making an informed decision meant that the parties had to have reached the age of consent – usually twelve years

---

Two Recensions of Gratian's Decretum", *Zeitschrift der Savigny-Stiftung für Rechtsgeschichte: Kanonistische Abteilung*, 83 (1997), pp. 22–31.

[2] Decretists and decretalists are the words used to designate the early canon lawyers who commented on Gratian's *Decretum* (decretists) or the papal decretals (decretalists).

[3] The edition used throughout this book is the *editio romana* (with glosses) published in Venice 1591, *Decretum Gratiani emendatum et notationibus illustratum una cum glossis, Gregorio XIII Pont. Max. jussu editum* (Venice, 1591) and *Decretales domini Gregorii papae IX: V ae [sic] integritati una cum glossis restitutae ad exemplar Romanum diligenter recognitae* (Venice, 1591), henceforth referred to as *Glossa Ordinaria*.

The standard work on the development of canon law in sexual matters (including marriage) is James A. Brundage, *Law, Sex and Christian Society in Medieval Europe* (Chicago, 1987), which deals with the development of canon law from Gratian to the publication of the *Liber extra* on pp. 229–416. The same author's *Medieval Canon Law* (Harlow, 1996) is an excellent introduction to the general study of medieval canon law. Other studies include Stephan Kuttner, *Harmony from Dissonance: An Interpretation of Medieval Canon Law* (Latrobe, Pennsylvania, 1960); Manlio Bellomo, *The Common Legal Past of Europe, 1000–1800*, translated by Lydia G. Cochrane (Washington DC, 1995); and Harold J. Berman, *Law and Revolution: The Formation of the Western Legal Tradition* (Cambridge, Massachusetts, and London, 1983).

for girls and fourteen for boys – and that they had freely consented to the union.[4] The church realised that the parties could be under some pressure to marry, but as long as no undue force had been exercised to persuade them to marry – as long as the pressure was not of such a kind as to make "a constant man" change his mind – the church would allow it.[5] That the parties were free to marry meant that they were not related within the degrees forbidden by the church; that they had not previously contracted a legally valid marriage with someone who was alive at the time of the second marriage; and that they were not ordained in major orders or were professed in final vows.

Gratian's *Decretum,* for all its virtues, laid an imperfect foundation for the practice of law. Wishing to find a definition of the exact moment when a marriage became legally binding, Gratian introduced a distinction between *conjugium initum* and *conjugium ratum,* between the initiated and the ratified marriage. Both states of marriage created bonds of affinity – so that, for example, the groom could not marry the bride's sister or the bride marry the groom's brother – but only a ratified marriage created an indissoluble bond between the partners.[6] Thus it became necessary to find and define the distinguishing feature of the *conjugium ratum* and this distinguishing feature Gratian argued was the *commixtio sexuum,* which traditionally has been taken to mean the consummation of marriage.[7] Much of the legal discussion in Europe in the following century centred on solving this

---

[4] This rule was open to interpretation: the functional criterion for the age of consent was that the parties could procreate: "Quid si iste, qui iam compleuit quattuordecim annos, talis appareat, quod nullo modo possit generare, et contrahat, numquid tenet matrimonium? ... Contrarium credo quia nec est pubes ... nec in eo reperiuntur tria bona matrimonii, quae sunt fides, proles et sacramentum ... Iste non est talis, qui possit habere prolem." *Glossa Ordinaria,* ad X 4.2.3 "tardissime"). Compare also X 4.2.14 and *Glossa Ordinaria,* ad X 4.2.3 "generare").

[5] X 4.1.15. The Latin phrase is "metus qui cadere potest in constantem virum" (the fear that can fall upon a constant man).

[6] C. 27, q. 2, c. 11, 12, 14.

[7] C. 27, q. 2, c. 36. Compare John A. Alessandro, *Gratian's Notion of Marital Consummation* (Vatican City, 1971), pp. 1–2, and Brundage, *Law, Sex and Christian Society,* pp. 235–40. Both Alessandro and Brundage understand the phrase *commixtio sexuum* to mean straightforward intercourse. Lizzie Carlson, in a study of the influence of canon law on Scandinavian law, argues that the *deductio in lecto* – which Alessandro takes to be the occasion when intercourse took place – was a symbolic act, and did not necessarily mean that the parties had intercourse. Old Germanic law codes, she argued, required the *deductio in lecto* for the legal

problem. At the end of the hundred years a new and intellectually more satisfying definition had emerged. This definition – which was developed at the university in Paris and promulgated mainly by the decisions in marriage cases by popes Alexander III and Innocent III – removed the demonstration of consent to marriage from a visible exterior action, as understood from Gratian's *commixtio sexuum*, to an expression of interior consent. The Parisian model emphasised the need for this consent to be shown either in words or – if that was impossible – in deeds. Contrary to later belief, it did not require the presence of witnesses or a priest and it saw marriage solely as a voluntary contract between the parties.[8] Anyone free to marry could do so at any time and on any occasion; but if one or both of the parties had been coerced to contract the marriage it was invalidated.

The Parisian masters substituted a future/present distinction for Gratian's two stages of initiation and consummation as their way of reconciling the inconsistencies in the ancient texts. Thereafter, the focal point of any marriage case heard by an ecclesiastical court became the nature of the consent, whether it was a statement of an intent to marry here and now – which was known as a *verba de presenti* – or a promise to marry at some time in the future – which was known as a *verba de futuro*. The Parisian model argued that all that was required to establish a marriage was that two people of opposite sexes, who were free to marry and who were not related within the forbidden degrees, freely exchanged marriage vows which expressed their consent to marry at once. Neither the family's consent nor the presence of witnesses or of a priest was required. If they had exchanged their vows *verba de futuro*, some subsequent act showing consent was necessary before the contract was binding; but, like marriages contracted *verba de presenti*, such marriages also created

---

consequences of marriage to take effect but never depended on sexual activity to validate the union. Lizzie Carlson, *"Jag giver dig min dotter": trolovning och äktenskap i den svenska kvinnans äldra historia* (Lund, 1965), pp. 147–208 (German summary on pp. 259–67).

A better translation of *commixtio sexuum*, which retains the ambiguity of the original phrase, is "a mingling of the sexes", which can be taken to include cohabitation. This removes the unnecessary barrier to the understanding of Gratian's analysis of the marriage of Mary and Joseph in C. 27, q. 2, c. 40–45 created by both Alessandro and Brundage's approach.

[8] Christopher Lasch, "The Suppression of Clandestine Marriage in England: The Marriage Act of 1753", *Salmagundi*, 26 (1974), pp. 90–109.

legally binding unions without the necessity of a priest or even of witnesses.[9]

The result appeared needlessly complex to the great legal scholar Frederic Maitland, whose disparaging comment on the church's rules of incest was probably equally meant for the canon law of marriage in general:

> Behind these intricate rules there is no deep policy, there is no deep religious feeling; they are the idle ingenuities of men who are amusing themselves by inventing a game of skill which is to be played with neatly drawn tables of affinity and doggerel hexameters.[10]

Despite such modern criticisms, the decretists, popes and decretalists provided a system of law that emphasised a number of central tenets of the Christian faith while maintaining the law as a workable entity. First of all, it provided easy access to the married state for all (something that would have been inconceivable in the classical world where marriage was reserved for the noble classes). Secondly, it based itself on a logical set of rules, whose basic features could be comprehended easily by lay and cleric alike. Finally, from the end of the thirteenth century, the church began to provide a viable system of enforcement which provided for the laity's need of a comprehensible system of justice. The laity and the clergy embraced this system enthusiastically. The rationale behind the system was based on the fact that Christ charged the church with determining cases that caused conflict among Christians, and in particular with cases that had a bearing on the salvation of the souls of his subjects.[11] For this purpose every diocese operated a system of courts to hear cases that fell under its jurisdiction, either because of the persons involved or because the

---

[9] Jean Dauvillier, *Le mariage dans le droit classique de l'église, depuis de Décret de Gratien (1140) jusqu'à le mort de Clément V (1314)* (Paris, 1933), pp. 17–39 and pp. 76–139; Gérard Fransen, "La formation du lien matrimonial au moyen âge", *Revue de droit canonique*, 21 (1971), pp. 106–26.

[10] Frederick Pollock and Frederic William Maitland, *The History of English Law before the Time of Edward I*, revised by S. F. C Milsom (2nd edn, Cambridge, 1968), ii p. 389.

[11] Matthew 18:15. Innocent III's decretal *Novit* (X. 2.1.13) from 1204 quotes this text to justify papal interference in the dispute between King Philip Augustus of France and King John of England, but its application is clearly universal. See also Acts 15, where the leaders of the early church congregated in Jerusalem to determine whether Christians were bound by the Mosaic law, a question that was first raised by the church in Antioch.

matter was claimed under ecclesiastical jurisdiction because it touched on matters pertaining to the salvation of a Christian soul.

The rules contained in the *Liber extra* saw swift dissemination across Europe, and England was among the first countries to adopt its rules. Even before the publication of the *Liber extra*, English synods upheld the rules of marriage formation formulated by popes Alexander III and Innocent III and in some cases they were among the first to formulate them. Most important in the teaching of the church was the proposition that the voluntary consent of the parties was necessary for the legality of marriage. This principle was first seen in England as early as the ecclesiastical codes of Ethelred (1008), although his canon dealt with the rights of the widow freely to choose a new husband after a year of mourning.[12] The rule was repeated in the legislation of Cnut, who widened the canon's application to include all women.[13] By the time of the post-conquest Council of Westminster (1175), the English church fully embraced the principle that only the consent of the parties constituted marriage.[14] In 1215 Thomas Chobham, in his *Summa confessorum*, even went so far as explicitly to emphasise that the principle included those cases where marriage had been established without any formal ritual: in his analysis, neither the presence of witnesses nor the participation of a priest was required.[15] Thomas would probably have been seen as a radical by his contemporaries: it is clear that there was a large section of the church that thought that the consequence of the church's insistence on the consent of the parties identified by Thomas should rather be implied than made explicit: for

---

[12] V Atr 21 I in Fritz Liebermann, ed, *Die Gesetze der Angelsachsen*, i (Halle, 1960), pp. 242–43.

[13] II Cn 73 in Liebermann, *Gesetze*, i, pp. 360–61.

[14] David Wilkins, *Concilia magna Britanniae et Hiberniae a synodo Verolamiensi AD CCCCXLIV ad Londinensem AD MDC*, i (London, 1737), p. 477. The statement of this principle was by no means unique to England: it conforms to Gratian's statement in C. 30, q. 2, c. 1.

[15] Thomas Chobham, *Thomae de Chobham Summa confessorum*, edited by F. Broomfield (Leuven and Paris, 1954–67), p. 146. Jacqueline Murray, "Individualism and Consensual Marriage: Some Evidence from Medieval England", in *Women, Marriage and Family in Medieval Christendom: Essays in Memory of Michael M. Sheehan, CSB*, edited by Joel T. Rosenthal, and Constance Rousseau, Studies in Medieval Culture, 36 (Kalamazoo, Michigan, 1998), pp. 121–51, traces the acceptance of the idea of consensual marriage in English confessionals of the later middle ages.

the position taken by Thomas made it easy for the parties later to "discover" impediments or simply to deny that they had ever entered marriage. Consequently, the Canterbury synod of 1213–14 and its derivatives forbade these private unions and prescribed proper public forms for the entry into matrimony. If the marriage did take place without the proper public celebrations, the synod demanded that the marriage should only be admitted at the special dispensation of the bishop.[16]

The generations after the Fourth Lateran Council (1215) saw much legal activity in the church in England and on the Continent, especially in the provision of rules for marriage. Some thirty-four English synods held in the period 1213–89 dealt with the issue and all of them provided not only a clarification of the church's rules of marriage but also for their dissemination to the laity by means of sermons and in the confessional. And, as a corollary, the local churches began to provide fora for the resolution of marriage disputes.

The foundation for separate church courts had been laid soon after the Conquest with the grant of a separate jurisdiction to the church by William the Conqueror.[17] The very broad powers of this grant were defined more closely by the statute *Circumspecte agatis* (1286–87) in the late decades of the thirteenth century.[18] There is very little evidence for the church's exercise of this jurisdiction before the late thirteenth century and it is clear that formal courts held by deputies of the bishop at regularly assigned days were a new development of the thirteenth century.[19] Only the most sporadic evidence of the church's exercise of its jurisdiction exists from the end of the twelfth century, when ecclesiastical disputes were decided in the much more formal

---

[16] I Canterbury 51; I Salibury 85 (1228 X 56?); Constitutiones cuiusdam episcopi 59 (1225 X 30) ; and Durham peculiars 59 (1241 X 49), printed in F.M. Powicke and C.R. Cheney, eds, *Councils and Synods with Other Documents Relating to the English Church*, i (Oxford, 1964), pp. 34, 88, 190 and 444.

[17] Dorothy Whitelock, Martin Brett and C.N.L Brooke, eds, *Documents Relating to the English Church, AD 871–1204* (Oxford, 1981), pp. 623–24.

[18] F.M. Powicke and C.R. Cheney, editor, *Councils and Synods with Other Documents Relating to the English Church, 1205–1313* (Oxford, 1964), pp. 974–75.

[19] For the early history of the church courts, see C. Morris, "From Synod to Consistory: The Bishop's Court in England, 1150–1250", *Journal of Ecclesiastical History*, 22 (1971), pp. 115–23, and Jane Sayers, *Papal Judges Delegate in the Province of Canterbury, 1198–1254* (Oxford, 1971), pp. xx-xxi.

diocesan synods or in local chapters of archdeacons and rural deans.[20] During the thirteenth century, however, a member of the bishop's household, the bishop's official, gradually took over responsibility for the exercise of the church's jurisdiction. This process took place slowly at first but more quickly as the thirteenth century wore on. The official was intended to act as the bishop's substitute in his absence and this made the official's remit as much administrative as judicial. Consequently, he did not have to have trained as a lawyer nor did he preside over a regular court.

Following the Fourth Lateran Council (1215) and publication of the *Liber extra* in 1234, regular courts with their own personnel and procedure developed rapidly in England, as in the rest of Europe. At the latest in 1270, possibly a decade or two before, the court of the diocese of Canterbury had developed as a distinct institution with its own body of records and its own personnel.[21] The diocese of York followed the same path at roughly the same time and English ecclesiastical courts, both on diocesan and provincial level, soon recruited their members from among the graduates of the two English universities, Oxford and Cambridge, who also began to include training in both canon and civil law in this century.

The two provincial courts in Canterbury and York have left very different evidence for their early activity. Canterbury's archives reach almost a century further back in time than those in York but the Canterbury survivals are concentrated in four specific periods and consist mainly of *sede vacante* litigation, while the York material shows a steadily increasing volume of survivals from 1301 onwards covering the ordinary dispensation of the canon law. The York survivals will be analysed in detail below, but a brief summary of the Canterbury archives will provide a useful foil to the York material. The first large survival of some ninety documents dates from the later years of the pontificate of Hubert Walter (1193–1205), the following group documents the chapter's exercise of the bishop's justice *sede vacante* 1240–45, the next large deposit of records coincide with the *sede vacante* period between the death of Boniface of Savoy and the

---

[20] For examples, see C.R. Cheney and B.E.A. Jones, eds, *English Episcopal Acta* (London, 1986), no. 47a (1174 x 1181); E. Searle, ed., *Chronicle of Battle Abbey* (Oxford, 1980), pp. 126–27, and G.R. Elvey, ed., *Luffield Priory Charters Part 1* (Northampton, 1968), no. 67a.

[21] Norma Adams and Charles Donahue Jr, "Introduction", in *Select Cases from the Ecclesiastical Courts of the Province of Canterbury, c. 1200–1301*, Selden Society, 95 (London, 1981), p. 25.

appointment of Robert Kilwardby (1270–73). The final large survival of cases heard in Canterbury dates from the vacancy between Archbishop Pecham (d. 1292) and the consecration of Archbishop Winchelsey 12 September 1294.[22]

The early deposit of some ninety documents relating to the court's business from the last years of Hubert Walter's pontificate does not provide a very detailed picture of the court's activity, but it allows us to surmise that some sort of legal tribunals were already functioning and that laity and clergy alike took their cases before them. The sixty or so cases preserved from this period 1240–45 show that a court was already functioning according to canonical procedure by this time but contain no depositions or pleadings, perhaps as a result of an unresolved dispute over the right to exercise the archbishop's jurisdiction *sede vacante* between the prior and chapter of Canterbury and the bishops of the southern province. The period 1270–73 saw a revival of this dispute when the prior and chapter appointed one of their number to function as "official of the Court of Canterbury *sede vacante*". In what appears to have been an attempt to record the fact that they actually possessed this right, the prior and chapter collected some sixty rolls documenting their court's activity during that period. These cases are similar to the fourteenth-century survivals from York in the way each roll normally refers to one case only and contains a variety of documents composed in a format recognisable from contemporary treatises of legal procedure.[23] But in contrast to York, these Canterbury cases also mainly document the Canterbury court as an appellate court and during a period of disputed jurisdiction. Finally, the surviving documents from the period 1292–94 appear to show a much more smoothly functioning court with little challenge to its exercise of jurisdiction. The surviving documents are largely *processus* transmitted to the Canterbury court at the request of the official, though some cases contain some documents from the original case. Thus the surviving documents of the Canterbury court show some of the court's early history, but little about the exercise of its ordinary jurisdiction. For this we must turn to the northern province.

The two archdioceses divided England between them and the archdiocese of York administered the canon law in a geographical area

---

[22] B. L. Woodcock, *Medieval Ecclesiastical Courts in the Diocese of Canterbury* (London, 1952), pp. 7–29.

[23] Adams, and Donahue, "Select Canterbury Cases", p. 16. These different kinds of documents produced by medieval courts are described below p. .

of substantial size. To the south, the archdiocese bordered on the dioceses of Lincoln and Coventry and Lichfield, to the north west it met with the diocese of Carlisle and to the north with Durham. As episcopal sees, Carlisle and Durham held their own jurisdiction, but in cases of appeal they came within the cognisance of the archdiocese of York. Like everywhere else in medieval Europe, the archdiocese of York itself was littered with jurisdictions that were largely exempt from the archbishop's jurisdiction, either through ancient use or because of grants of exemption. Among these so-called peculiar juris-dictions were a large number of powerful religious houses and collegiate establishments which answered directly to the apostolic see. These included the Benedictine abbeys of York, Selby and Whitby; a large number of Cistercian abbeys such as Rievaulx, Kirkstall, Meaux, Byland, Furness and Fountains; and the collegiate establishments of Beverley, Southwell and Ripon.[24]

The archdiocese of York was divided into five archdeaconries – York (the West Riding), Cleveland, the East Riding, Nottingham and Richmond. These five archdeaconries were further subdivided into twenty-four rural deaneries which were distributed as follows: under the archdeacon of York fell the deaneries of the Christianity of York, Ainsty, Craven, Doncaster and Pontefract; and under the East Riding came the deaneries of Buckrose, Harthill, Holderness and Pickering; the archdeacon of Cleveland administered the deaneries of Bulmer, Cleveland and Rydale; the archdeacon of Nottingham administered the deaneries of Bingham, Newark, Nottingham and Retford; and, finally, the archdeacon of Richmond administered the deaneries of Aumundbury, Boroughbridge, Catterick, Copeland, Furness, Kendal, Lonsdale and Richmond,. Additional to these jurisdictions, the archbishop also possessed personal jurisdiction outside the diocese in St Oswald's in Gloucestershire and in Hexhamshire in Northumber-land.[25]

The geographical boundaries of the province of York, and hence of the jurisdiction of the *Curia Eboracensis*, had been settled since the

---

[24] William Brown and A. Hamilton Thompson, eds, *The Register of William Green-field, Lord Archbishop of York, 1306–15, Part 1*, Surtees Society, 145 (Durham, 1931), p. xiv.

[25] In practice the peculiars were not entirely exempt from archiepiscopal jurisdiction. Cases were heard by the consistory court on appeal from the peculiars of St John's, Beverley, and Chester.

late twelfth century when York's dispute with Canterbury about supremacy over the Scottish church was decided by Pope Celestine III. He had ruled that the Scottish church – except for the south-western diocese of Whithorn which could decide for itself – was answerable to the Roman pontiff directly.[26] In the fourteenth century the province of York consisted of the dioceses of Durham, Carlisle and York. The diocese of Whithorn recognised the supremacy of the diocese of York until 1355 when it transferred its allegiance to the Scottish church.[27] Among other things this meant that the courts in York held appellate jurisdiction over these dioceses as well as over the peculiars that still held jurisdiction from the archdiocese. After the loss of Whithorn, the northern province preserved its unity until 1541, when a parliamentary decree determined that the archdeaconry of Richmond was to be under the supremacy of the new diocese of Chester. Having first been designated a part of the province of Canterbury, Chester was transferred to the province of York by parliamentary decree in 1542.[28]

Within the geographical boundaries of the archdiocese, the archbishop's court dispensed the church's justice. The court and its personnel had a considerable level of expertise built up through legal practice and academic study. In addition there was an emphasis on tradition in the court which ensured that the cases were treated consistently. The laity recognised the court's expertise, and litigants willingly – or indeed enthusiastically – embraced the opportunity the church courts offered them to pursue their grievances and settle their disputes.

Although the court dispensed one archbishop's justice, it functioned as three separate courts: the consistory court, the court of the exchequer and the archbishop's special court of audience. There was there-

---

[26] The original bull from Pope Celeistine III dating from around 1192 granting the Scottish church a special status as the apostolic see's *filia specialis* has now been lost, but it was confirmed in a later bull issued by Pope Honorius III, Leslie Macfarlane, "The Primacy of the Scottish Church 1472–1521", *Innes Review*, 19 (1968), pp. 111–29. Honorius III's bull has been translated many times, but the most easily accessible translation can be found in George W. Greenaway, *English Historical Documents, 1042–1189* (London and New York, 1981).

[27] K. F. Burns, "The Medieval Courts", vol. 1 of "The Administrative System of the Ecclesiastical Courts in the Diocese and Province of York", unpublished manuscript, Leverhulme Research Scheme (York, 1962), p. 3.

[28] D.M. Smith, *A Guide to the Archive Collections in the Borthwick Institute of Historical Research*, Borthwick Texts and Calendars: Records of the Northern Province (York, 1973), p. 1.

fore no system of appeal within the York courts. Under exceptional circumstances, a case could be re-evaluated to investigate whether errors had been made in the conduct of the case, much like a judicial review today, but the next level of jurisdiction was the apostolic see, to which appeals to be made, unless successful objections could be made about the conduct of the case in York. The York courts, however, also heard cases as the appeal court for the peculiar courts which owed allegiance to the archbishop. The court thus received cases on appeal from lower courts geographically within its boundaries. These cases came mostly from Durham, Richmond and Beverley.

The court that dealt with the largest volume of work was the consistory court. The education of its personnel and its structure will be dealt with in detail later, but it is useful for the reader to know some details about it and some of the ways in which it differed from the other two courts before the analyses in subsequent chapters. The personnel of the courts were well trained: the official and his commissary general, who functioned as *ex officio* judges, had at least a university degree in either canon or civil law, as did the advocates of the court. The requirements for the education of the proctors who represented the litigants in the court room appears not to have been as high as for the judges and advocates, but their knowledge and understanding of the legal system in York were assured by a one-year "apprenticeship" which they and the advocates had to undertake before being allowed to practise in the court.

Ethical standards demanded of the members of court were high, though not unusually high for England: their aim was to see that justice was done, not to win their cases.[29] The members of the court were reminded annually of this duty by their oath of office, which they recited at the first meeting of the court every year. The oath required them to abandon cases they did not believe in and the 1311 statutes of Archbishop Greenfield ordained substantial punishments for those members of court who prosecuted a case which they knew to be unjust. Access to the law was guaranteed to almost every subject of the archbishop: Greenfield's statutes fixed the price of the services provided to litigants by the court and stipulated that those in need could approach the court and conduct their litigation free of ordinary charges.

---

[29] R. H. Helmholz, "Ethical Standard for Advocates and Proctors in Theory and Practice", in *Canon Law and the Law of England* (London, 1987), pp. 41–58.

The consistory court might meet on every day except Sunday during the four court sessions of the year: the Epiphany session convened on the first court day after 6 January while the Easter session began on the first Monday after Easter. The Trinity session lasted from the first court day after Trinity Sunday until on the last court day in July. The Michaelmas session began on the first court day after the feast of St Matthew (21 September). In all sessions – except for the Trinity session, which rose on the last court day in July – the court rose on the last court day in the Ember weeks. The Easter and Michaelmas terms were thus of fixed length – six weeks and three months, respectively – while the length of the Epiphany and Trinity terms varied with the date of Easter. In all, this meant that the court could meet on around 200 days out of every year. Surviving act books from 1417–30 show that these dates left the court with ample time to conduct its business: in no year were all consistory days taken up with business. The number of days when the act books inform us that "nothing was done on this day" varies from eleven (1417) to thirty-five (1425). Thus it is not very surprising that the number of court days was reduced to three days a week at some time between 1433 and 1484.[30]

The archbishop's exchequer was that department of his household which concerned itself with the financial affairs of the archdiocese. Although it eventually acquired jurisdiction over both spiritual and temporal matters, its primary concern continued to be the finances of the archbishop's household. During the early years of the existence of this court the exchequer's function was to receive and to account for all cash payments which were due to the archbishop. The exchequer also made payments on the archbishop's instructions to officials on archiepiscopal business, passed on payments to papal tax-collectors and looked after day-to-day payments in the archbishop's household. In 1374, when Master Thomas Gothmundham was appointed receiver general of the exchequer, the exchequer was granted the power to hear cases of probate in the *Curia Eboracensis*.[31]

---

[30] The number of court days in the fourteenth century follows the holidays laid out in X 2.9.5. Compare C. R. Cheney, "Rules for the Observance of Feastdays in Medieval England", *Bulletin of the Institute of Historical Research*, 34 (1982), *The English Church and its Laws; 12th-14th Centuries*, item no. 10, Variorum Collected Studies.

[31] Burns, 'The Medieval Courts', *p. 233*.

The court of the exchequer did not usually hear marriage cases, but in one instance, *Appleton* c. *Hothwayt* (1386), we find that the receiver general of the exchequer, Master Roger Pickering, functioned as a judge in a marriage case.[32] Appealing on procedural grounds the appellant, Thomas Hothwayt, challenged the court of exchequer's jurisdiction. The cause paper file records the case as it was heard at the consistory court and does not contain transcripts of the case before the exchequer court. In its decision, however, the consistory court confirmed the personal right of Master Roger Pickering to hear this case, but in such terms that it did not authorise the exchequer's general jurisdiction over marriage cases.[33]

The archbishop's court of audience could intervene in cases heard by the consistory court and the court of the archbishop's exchequer. Although in theory it was possible to transfer a case from the lower courts to this court at any time in the proceedings – or even to bring it before the archbishop in the first instance – this court is rarely seen to be active in the cause papers.[34] Only *Huntington* c. *Munkton* (1345–46) – a divorce case which began as a plea for the restoration of marital rights – has left substantial documentation from the archbishop's court of audience.[35] Even this case was eventually referred to the consistory court after a period of six months. In general, the archbishop's court of audience heard cases on the grounds of the importance of the issues involved or cases arising out of contempt of court in the archbishop's other courts. The court of audience also dealt with spiritual offences, such as heresy or apostasy, and criminal cases. In contrast to the consistory court, which was held in a fixed place in the *locum consistorii* in York Minster, the archbishop's court of audience was held wherever the archbishop

---

[32] *Appleton* c. *Hothwayt*. CP, E 150 (1389). Throughout this book cases are referred to by naming first the plaintiff in the original case. Consequently, in appeal cases the appellant is often named last (as is the case here).

[33] For a fuller treatment of *sub poena nubendi* cases and some comments on this case, see R. H. Helmholz, "Abjuration *Sub Poena Nubendi* in the Church Courts of Medieval England", in *Canon Law and the Law of England* (London, 1987), pp. 145–56, and the same author's *Marriage Litigation in Medieval England*, Cambridge Studies in English Legal History (Cambridge, 1974), pp. 172–81 (with examples: pp. 208–12). The York *sub poena nubendi* cases will be analysed below.

[34] Burns, 'The Medieval Courts', p. 201.

[35] *Huntington* c. *Munkton*. CP, E 248 (1345–46). See below, Chapter 2.

happened to be in the diocese. During his absence, the court of audience was presided over by the archbishop's vicar general.[36]

Broadly speaking, a case came before an ecclesiastical court for one of two reasons: either because of the persons involved or because of the subject matter of the case. A large number of people could claim the benefit of a hearing by the ecclesiastical courts in the fourteenth century. Most important among these were clerics, who, being members of the church, could claim the benefit of clergy if they were cited before a secular tribunal. By the same token they were also required by canon law not to attempt to settle their claims at a secular court but to bring it before the church courts. This rule protected clerics not only from prosecution in criminal cases, such as for theft, rape and bodily harm, but also in disputes over lands or movables belonging to them.[37]

Clerics figure rarely as litigants in the medieval matrimonial cause papers. The validity of a sentence passed by William Alman – a special commissary in a marriage enforcement case in 1389–90 – was challenged because Alman was said to be a bigamist. His contemporary, William Cawod (who served as the dean and chapter official during the vacancy of 1397 and as the archbishop's official from 1414–17), doubtless advised his daughter in her suit in 1391 when the court tried to establish which of two men she had married first. Being a member of the court, William Cawod probably estimated that the fact that his daughter had three independent witnesses to her exchange of vows was enough to secure a sentence favourable to her. Despite his being present at the exchange of vows, he did not testify in the case. All three witnesses heard, however, confirmed their existence.[38] One case, though originally about the sexual relations between two monks of the monastery of Furness and two women of that town, was heard in York as a challenge to the right of the archdeacon of Richmond to excommunicate the culprits.[39]

---

[36] Burns, 'The Medieval Courts', pp. 216–17.

[37] C. B. Firth, "Benefit of Clergy in the Time of Edward IV", *English Historical Review*, 32 (1917), pp. 175–91.

[38] Alman was challenged in *Appleton c. Hothwayt*; Cawod in *Garthe and Newton c. Waghen*. CP, E 150 (1389) and 245 (1391). It should be pointed out that although these cases included clerics among the people concerned with the case they were not heard as benefit of clergy cases: both were heard because their subject matter (challenge of commission and enforcement of marriage vows) fell under the jurisdiction of the church.

[39] CP, E 31 (1336–37).

Other people also had the right to plead in the ecclesiastical courts. Students (*scholares*) were allowed this privilege, as were crusaders,[40] but no one claims this privilege in the surviving cause papers. More important was the claim that widows and orphans had to be protected by the archbishop. Though these privileges were not explicitly invoked, at least three cases among the cause papers E series were heard under the tutelage of the archbishop: *Hiliard* c. *Hiliard* was a dispute over the validity of the marriage of Peter Hiliard's stepmother, Katherine, to his father, John Hiliard, which had been referred to the court in York from the King's Bench; *Hopton* c. *del Brome* was a dispute over the validity of vows exchanged under duress between a young widow and the ten-year-old son of her guardian; while the defendant in *Marrays* c. *Rowcliff* – Alice, daughter of Gervase de Rowcliff – was assigned a guardian by the court because she claimed to be under the age of consent.[41]

Most cases that were not conducted by virtue of the persons involved fell, however, under the jurisdiction of the church courts because of their subject matter. The church claimed jurisdiction over all cases that fell under the general heading of spiritual cases. In practice this meant that the church claimed the right to hear and determine all cases that touched on matters of faith, such as oaths, the administration of the sacraments, defamation and disputes over testamentary bequests. The consequences of sentences passed by church courts, elections for ecclesiastical offices and all disputes over benefices also formed part of the courts' jurisdiction.

The *Curia Eboracensis* dispensed the archbishop's justice throughout the northern province. In practice, this meant that the consistory court in York heard appeals in cases which originated in the archdeaconries, but that it also functioned as the first court to hear those cases which arose in the archbishop's own bailiwicks and in the city of York.[42] By

---

[40] Paul Fournier, *Les officialités au moyen âge: étude sur l'organisation, la competence et la procédure des tribunaux ecclésiastiques ordinaire en France, de 1180 à 1328* (Paris, 1880), pp. 77–78.

[41] *Hiliard* c. *Hiliard*, *Hopton* c. *Brome* and *Marrays* c. *Rowcliff*. CP, E 108 (1370); 62 (1348); 89 (1365–66).

[42] The archbishop had four bailiwicks – estates run under the supervision of a bailiff appointed by and directly responsible to the archbishop – in Yorkshire: Sherburn, Beverley and Ripon, and a special liberty in the port of Hull. The archbishop had four more bailiwicks outside Yorkshire: two in Nottinghamshire (Southwell and North Soke) and one each in Northumberland (Hexham) and Gloucestershire (Churchdown). Finally, the archbishop had special liberties in Westminster that

far the largest number of cases were heard as first instance cases – 222 cases of the 256 fourteenth-century cause paper files originated in the archbishop's courts. Seventy-one of the eighty-eight marriage cases which were brought to the cognisance of the archbishop's courts in York were first instance matrimonial litigation. The remaining seventeen matrimonial cases were first initiated at a lower court and later transmitted to York.[43]

By the beginning of the fourteenth century the extent and geographical limits of courts in York's jurisdiction had been determined and remained largely stable throughout the century. The statutes of Archbishop Greenfield from 1311 provided a maximum of thirty members of the courts, twenty of whom were to be advocates or proctors. It appears that the maximum number was never filled. The consistory court included a registry to preserve and copy the written decisions and other documents produced in connection with litigation in the court. This department of the court has left us with a large selection of legal documents from the cases conducted at the *Curia Eboracensis*. These documents offer an unrivalled opportunity to analyse the way in which a medieval court applied the rules of canon law in the area of its jurisdiction. Through time the majority of the documents – probably in the order of 98 per cent – have been lost, but the Borthwick Institute of Historical Research in York preserves what remain. The oral presentations of libels, and the consultations between advocates and judges that we know took place, have been lost forever. The archive nevertheless contains documents that cover almost all other aspects of court business, from procedural documents presented to the courts by the litigants, such as libels, positions and interrogatories, to documents produced by the court itself, such as letters and transcripts of earlier cases from officers appointed by the court to investigate the facts of a case in the field, and the sentences of the court.[44] What sets the York files apart from most other eccle-

---

were also administrated by a bailiff. Brown and Thompson, *The Register of William Greenfield, Lord Archbishop of York, 1306–15, Part 1*, p. xxvi.

[43] I have included the six surviving *sub poena nubendi* cases among these seventeen cases. Strictly speaking these cases were first instance cases in which the plaintiff petitioned the *Curia Eboracensis* to enforce a conditional marriage which had been imposed on the litigants by a lower court. I have included them in this group because they are directly dependent on the preceding litigation.

[44] A concise introduction to medieval procedure can be found in Adams and Donahue, "Select Canterbury Cases", pp. 37–72. A number of technical terms for

siastical archives in England is that they include a large number of depositions heard by the court. Among the 256 fourteenth-century cause paper files are eighty-eight files documenting litigation over marriages.[45] These eighty-eight matrimonial cases contain the depositions of more than 580 people. The depositions are an unusually vivid collection of narratives told to the court by the witnesses as recorded by the court scribes. Among them we find descriptions of marriage negotiations, nocturnal fights over women, leisure activities, daily work and events that occurred in the markets or in the courts. They contain stories of domestic happiness and of relationships that went sour; stories about the daily existence of paupers and rich men alike. Not only do they provide the historian with a rich mine of anthropological detail, they also allow the facts of the case to be weighed and the application of the canon law of marriage in the diocese of York to be discussed. The cause papers are by no means complete, but they are one of only two series of litigation files in England to consistently preserve enough of the documents produced in court to allow the modern historian to analyse not only the subject matter of the case but also how the case was argued and which strategies the litigants employed to win their cases. The other comparable survival is the series of thirteenth-century ecclesiastical suits identified in Canterbury.[46]

The E series is the earliest surviving series of cases from the diocese of York. The first case dates from 1301 and the series continues to 1400. This book has followed the modern catalogue division into

different types of marriage litigation will be used in this book. A full explanation of these terms can be found in Helmholz, *Marriage Litigation*.

[45] Calculating the number of marriage cases in the Borthwick Institute, I have followed the classifications found in D.M. Smith, *Ecclesiastical Cause Papers at York: The Court at York, 1301–1399*, Borthwick Texts and Calendars, 14 (York, 1988), which lists eighty-seven cases as "matrimonial", "alimony", "validity of marriage" or "divorce" cases, to which I have added *Hiliard c. Hiliard*, a plea of dower transmitted from the King's Bench. CP, E 108 (1370). *Percy c. Neville* and *Colvill c. Darell*, which are listed by Smith as matrimonial, did not deal with marriage *vows* when heard in York: *Percy c. Neville* is a plea for the payment of a promised dowry to the *pars actrix*'s son after his wife died, while *Colvill c. Darell* is a dispute over whether Thomas de Colvill had paid alimony to his wife, Margaret Darell, who had previously obtained a *divortium a mensa et thoro*. CP, E 12 (1313) and 14 (1324). Two related cases, *Brereley c. Bakster* and *Litster and Sandeshend c. Brereley*, which Smith listed separately, are now kept together in the same file as CP, E 256. CP, E 255 (1383) and 256 (1389).

[46] Adams and Donahue, "Select Canterbury Cases", pp. 2–4.

centuries, which – apart from the beginning date of 1301 – is an arbitrary division of the papers according to century and a function of the reorganisation and indexing which Canon Purvis initiated during the Second World War.[47] For the purposes of the present study it was decided to limit the investigation to one century and to the papers that survive from that period in order to limit the material without jeopardising the statistical significance of the sample. The E-series consists of 256 files of varying sizes and in varying degrees of completeness. Some, for example *Devoine* c. *Scot,* consist of only one sheet of parchment containing depositions;[48] while others, notably *Huntington* c. *Munkton* and *Marrays* c. *Rowcliff,* are bulky and comprehensive transcripts of cases that are legally complex and suggest a deeply felt resentment between the litigants.[49] The cause paper E-series contains the first cause paper file in existence at York, which dates from 1301. The case was an appeal from the sentence of the official of the archdeacon of Cleveland containing a copy of a matrimonial dispute conducted at that court between Andrew Le Cragger and Johanna daughter of Walter Chapelayn.[50]

Sixty-five decisions preserved among the cause papers were appealed to the Apostolic See and thirty-four of the total 256 cases were first heard in York as appeals against decisions made by lower courts. Sixty-six cases include an appeal to the official or to the archbishop against a decision made by a judge in the *Curia Eboracensis.* Among the 256 dossiers, eighty-eight – or just over one-third – deal with marriage. The remaining two-thirds deal with benefices (fifty-eight cases), tithes (thirty-four cases), defamation (twenty cases), disputes over testaments (nineteen cases), breach of faith[51] (fourteen cases) and jurisdictions (nine cases). Three cases do not fit in any of these categories. It has been impossible to identify the type of dispute in eleven cases. The eighty-eight matrimonial cause paper files in the E series contain depositions by more than 580 people who give information about some 120 marriages.[52]

[47] J.S. Purvis, *The Archives of the York Diocesan Registry: Their Provenance and History,* St Anthony's Hall Publications, 2 (London, 1952).

[48] CP, E 257 (1349)

[49] CP, E 248 (1345–46) and 89 (1365–66).

[50] Some depositions from this case are printed in Helmholz, *Marriage Litigation,* pp. 230–32.

[51] These cases were used to deal with debts and non-payments of dowry.

[52] Some cases involved more than two litigants.

The cause papers deal with a wide range of cases that fell under the jurisdiction of the church. The cases are almost all civil suits: only one case deals with a spiritual offence.[53] The cases fall into two major categories. One category concerns litigation among the clergy or between the clergy and the laity, such as disputes over benefices, jurisdictions and payment of tithes. Cases in this category make up about two-fifths of the surviving cause papers, disputes over benefices taking up almost three-fifths of this category. The remaining two-thirds of the cause papers show the laity involved in litigation over which the church had established its jurisdiction. These files include marriage disputes, testamentary litigation and breach of faith litigation.[54] This distribution of cases suggests that the jurisdiction of the *Curia Eboracensis* was well known among the population of the northern province, and that they did not hesitate to present their disputes for the court's arbitration.

Cases from the last quarter of the fourteenth century have been preserved in larger numbers. More than half the cases that survive originated in the last three decades of the fourteenth century. Curiously, if the cause papers are divided into two groups consisting of matrimonial and non-matrimonial cases, the matrimonial cases show an unbroken increase throughout the century while there is a sharp drop in the number of surviving non-matrimonial cases. A similar difference in trend for survival rates of matrimonial and non-matrimonial cases (but for a much smaller sample) can be observed in the decade 1320–29, when there is a steady rise in marriage cases but a stable trend for non-matrimonial cases. These trends cannot be explained by fluctuating population levels in the northern province: if they reflected these the court would have seen a noticeable drop in business during the famine years falling in the period 1310–20 and a sizeable drop in the decades which included outbreaks of the plague in the diocese of York in 1348 and 1366. The most likely explanation for these fluctuations are changes in the archival practices of the *Curia Eboracensis*, but the exact nature of these changes can only be guessed

---

[53] *Bolton c. Hakenays* was an appeal for the tuition of the court at York brought by Thomas Hakenays, a monk and former bursar of Whitby Abbey, who was accused of immorality, absconding from his monastery, misappropriation of goods and abandonment of his clerical habit by Thomas de Bolton, the abbot of the abbey. CP, E 164.

[54] A suit for breach of faith was the only recourse that a medieval merchant or loan-giver had within the courts. Hence most, if not all, the cases in this category are for the repayment of loans.

at. However, the composition of the remaining cases suggests that, for those years, cases involving litigation between clerics were kept in a separate file which has now been lost.

The eighty-eight marriage cases make up the largest single group of cases in the cause papers. Dividing the cases by their possible outcome, the cause papers fall into two groups. Just over half (forty-five) cases deal with the dissolution of a marriage (multi-party litigation, pre-contracts, annulments and separations), while the other half is made up of thirty-two cases concerning exchanges of promises to marry (enforcement and abjurations *sub poena nubendi*); two cases concerning alimony; two pleas for restitution of marital rights; and seven cases that do not fit any of these groups.

This neat division into two halves is slightly misleading: twenty-eight matrimonial and divorce cases should also appear among the cases that established the validity of marriages. A *causa matrimonialis et divortii* – as the cause papers themselves call this type of case – tried to determine the validity of a previous marriage. If the plaintiff was successful, the outcome was the end of one marriage and the enforcement of another. If the material is viewed in this way it can be said that, in contrast to modern courts, the *Curia Eboracensis* primarily investigated cases that were concerned with the beginnings of marriage rather than with its end.

We can only guess why some cause paper files were preserved while others were lost. The court, sitting in session for two hundred days of the year, must have conducted enough business to justify the large number of consistory days, and we know from internal evidence in the cause papers and from the archbishops' registers that other business was conducted. Without a doubt the entire cause paper E series represents a very small sample of the cases that the court heard. Some guesses can be made about the reasons for their survival.

The cases were not preserved because they were outstandingly difficult cases that had gone through every instance of the *Curia Eboracensis*. Only about a quarter of the cases were appealed in any decade of the fourteenth century. The trend of the survival of appealed cases remains constant at around five to ten cases for every decade, showing little increase or decrease. Further, it does not follow the trends of the survival rate of the total number of cases. This would seem to indicate a totally random survival of appealed cases. The same independence in trend shows when we look at the number of cases that were heard in York as appeals from lower jurisdictions. Given the figures just quoted, and the fact that sentences only survive in approximately half the cases, it is unlikely that the cases were kept to preserve a record of the decisions of higher instances of the court in York. Instead, the reasons for their survival must be found in another purpose. To find this we must consider the periods before and after the Reformation separately.

Before the Reformation it is likely that the cause papers were kept as records of the custom of the *Curia Eboracensis*. These could either be used to prove that the court held jurisdiction over certain types of cases or they could be consulted by new members of the court during their year of study and by older members for the study of procedure. There are numerous indications of this latter use in the cause papers themselves. Brief annotations are common, and these appear not to have been added by the scribe who originally drew up the documents: both handwriting and ink are different. None of the notes can be dated with certainty: they consist only of short entries which highlight the bare essentials of the most complex cases. Typically, they appear in cases with extensive depositions where the wording of a vow or the litigant's age is questioned.[55]

Based on an analysis of the contents of the cause papers, Canon Purvis suggested that they were precedence cases that had been kept for consultation by the members of the court. Individual cases were kept to illustrate different points of the law and, indeed, to a cursory eye they rarely overlap. Canon Purvis also speculated that large numbers of files had been lost in the reorganisation of the archives hinted at in the correspondence of the eighteenth-century Minster archivist, Mr Jubb:

> Much has been lost, no doubt, through accidents, through damage of various kinds, and through wear and tear. But much also seems to have been deliberately destroyed. The internal evidence of the group calendared as "Cause Papers, Precedents" appears to show that these are the remains of a much more numerous collection of files.[56] There seems to be evidence that they can best be explained by supposing that about the year 1740 someone, who was probably Mr Registrar Jubb, decided to make a selection of original papers which would be useful as precedent forms, for which there is always a demand in the Registrar's Office. He therefore

---

[55] Compare *Marrays* c. *Rowcliff* where the annotator has written the age of the actrix in the margin every time a witness answered the question about her age, or the drawing of a hand that points to the statement that says that Master Ivo Lardman was suspended from office for participating in the clandestine marriage of Katherine and John Hiliard in *Hiliard* c. *Hiliard*. CP, E 89 and 108.

[56] The present cause papers series E–J.

took a large number of files or bundles of papers, mainly of the second half of the seventeenth century, chose out those which seemed to him most characteristic or useful for his purpose, and destroyed the rest of the files or bundles.[57]

In her study of the history of the collection of ecclesiastical papers housed in the Borthwick Institute, Katharine M. Longley points out that the archiepiscopal archives were dispersed during the Reformation: some of York's cartularies reached the collections of Sir Robert Cotton where they can be consulted in the British Library;[58] some records were removed from York by members of the clergy for safekeeping during the Civil War and Interregnum; whilst others were removed to London after the fall of York to the parliamentarian army, first to Guerney House, Old Jewry, and then to the Excise Office in Broad Street.[59]

Although Purvis is not therefore the only historian to speculate about the losses to the archives, upon a closer examination of the survivals it becomes clear that it is impossible to make the categorical statement that the survivals are precedence cases: it is not possible to fit every surviving cause paper into a group where it would illustrate one point of law only. Instead, the cause papers constitute a comprehensive selection of the legal problems that the court might encounter. Although we cannot be sure that they are a totally random sample of the court's business, they can be said to be an unbiased sample of the actual cases that came before the courts in the fourteenth century.

This must be kept in mind when using the cause papers for a historical study. Although the cause papers offer us an unrivalled window into the minds and mentalities of the litigants in the court of York in the fourteenth century, they do not represent what the average person could expect from marriage at that time, nor can they be made to yield significant statistical information on what people thought about marriage in the northern province. The cases that remain for the historian's use illustrate a liminal experience of marriage in fourteenth-century England. The litigants did not appear before the court unless their marriage was unusual: a large group of them were highly visible members of society whose marital practice did not tally

---

[57] Purvis, *York Diocesan Registry*, p. 5.

[58] They are indexed in G.R.C. Davies, *Medieval Cartularies of Great Britain: A Short Catalogue* (London, 1958), pp. 125–27.

[59] K.M. Longley, "Towards a History of Archive-Keeping in the Church of York: II. The Capitular Muniments", *Borthwick Institute Bulletin*, 1 (1976), p. 103.

with that expected of them, another large group consisted of those members of society whose wealth made them particularly conscious of the legal implications of their marital arrangements, and some appeared before the court in York because their marital practice had already been the subject of scrutiny by the courts in their local community.

2

Romeo and Juliet of Stonegate

A dispute that was brought before any ecclesiastical court had to be presented in a way that made it possible to argue the case within the framework of canon law. This often means that a case which is seemingly about one thing is really about something quite different. It is rare for the historian to be able to demonstrate not only that such a transformation took place, but also how a dispute was transformed when it was argued in a church court. However, a number of the cause papers can be used for this purpose. Here the longest surviving fourteenth-century cause paper in York will be analysed to show how a dispute, although really about the rights over land which a woman brought into her marriage, was mutated into a case concerning the legality of her marriage. This was done so that the woman could preserve control over the lands she inherited on her father's death in order to delay or prevent her husband's sale of these lands. Although such a case might have been argued at the secular courts, with some difficulty, the woman would have had to continue sharing her house with a husband whom she regarded as increasingly dangerous and whose violent outbursts were an increasing public scandal from which some of her relatives and friends wished to protect her. She therefore presented the court with a plea for a *divortium a mensa et thoro* (divorce from table and bed).[1]

When tension in a marriage rose above acceptable levels in fourteenth-century York, a woman had few ways of enforcing her rights against her husband. Although the church exhorted spouses to treat each other with "marital affection", church courts were unwilling to accept that a marriage had broken down beyond repair. Litigation before church courts offered the only way in which spouses could legally separate, and these courts could only grant a legal separation or an annulment under certain narrowly defined conditions. When Canon Purvis compiled the first hand-list of the York

---

[1] Today we would call such an arrangement a marital separation.

cause papers during the Second World War he gave the name "Romeo and Juliet of Stonegate" to the longest and most dramatic of the eighty-eight preserved marriage cases. It chronicles the fortunes of the marriage between a strong-minded and independent woman and an equally strong-minded and increasingly violent man, both of whom came from the top echelons of York society. Although the litigation only lasted from August 1345 to November 1346, the case produced sixty-two documents containing some 40,000 words. Not only is the case unusual for its length, we are also fortunate that the will which provided some of the female litigant's wealth is preserved in the probate register of the dean and chapter, whose registers begin almost forty years before the probate register of wills in the archiepiscopal archives. The same probate register includes the wills of her uncle, who functioned as her guardian, and of her aunt by marriage, while the York Memorandum Book in the York City Archives contains the will of the father of another actor in the case, John Bristol, and a short entry in the Public Record Office in London suggests that at a later date the male litigant in the case – Simon Munkton – had remarried, presumably after the death of his first wife. Although wills can never provide more than a glimpse of the real wealth of the person making the bequests, since they only record one-third of the dying man's movable goods (and never record his holdings of land, which were a matter for the secular courts), they provide a unique insight into their level of wealth.[2] In the case of Agnes Huntington, the surviving wills suggest that she was very well provided for by her father. The course of the case between Agnes Huntington and Simon Munkton can therefore be reconstructed, issues touched by the case identified and educated guesses can be given about what happened to the principal actors after the case had been abandoned by the archbishop's court.

When Richard Huntington, a rich merchant who lived in the Petergate area of York, drew up his will on 22 June 1333 he provided for a magnificent funeral for himself. He wanted to be buried in the Minster, providing ten marks to pay for his epitaph, twenty pounds of silver for masses to be said for his soul and the souls of all faithful Christians, forty pounds of wax to be made into candles to be burned around his body on the day of his burial, and ten marks to be spent on

[2] Michael M. Sheehan, *The Will in Medieval England: From the Conversion of the Anglo-Saxons to the End of the Thirteenth Century*, Studies and Texts, 6 (Toronto, 1963).

bread to be distributed among the poor. But he did not forget his family. Apart from the bequests providing for his funeral, Richard Huntington left money and movables to Isabella, his wife,[3] and for his under-age children, Selda, Richard, William and Agnes. To Isabella he left twenty-four marks, the contents of her room in their house, twelve spoons, a silver plate and a chest made of maple. To Richard he left only a few things: his ceremonial armour, his silver robe, a chest and twelve spoons and the sum of ten marks. To his daughter, Selda, he left his pots, a legacy which may have been more valuable than is immediately obvious, and one hundred shillings.[4] To the other children, he left equally large legacies. On coming of age, his son William was to receive the rent of a tenement house "with all its buildings and grounds" which Richard, senior, held in Petergate,[5] while his daughter Agnes was left a legacy of twenty pounds silver. All the bequests were to be looked after by his executors – his wife Isabella, Hugh Miton and, especially, his brother William Huntington. Agnes Huntington was therefore well provided for when her father died, and her uncle took good care of her fortune while she was under-age. She was probably even wealthier than appears in her father's will, for a will only disposed of movable goods and incomes from rent. Real estate was not included, but the preserved papers in the marriage case she initiated in 1345 make it clear that Agnes owned holdings and tenements in Huntington and Earswick not listed in the will.

In the following six years Agnes lived with her family in York and on the estate they owned in Huntington. Isabella, Richard Huntington's widow, met another York merchant, Hamo Hessay, who became Agnes's stepfather. Hamo Hessay was one of York's dignitaries: he represented the city in parliament four times, in 1337, 1339, 1352

---

[3] Due to a scribal error she is referred to as *Isolda, uxor eius* in the will.

[4] Selda may have died before she came of age for neither she nor her two brothers were mentioned in the court case that was initiated in 1345. When Richard Huntington's brother, William Huntington, who was given the vessels "for the use of my daughter Selda", made his will in 1362, he in turn passed on all *his* pots and vessels to his wife, Emma. We cannot say for certain what Richard Huntington traded in, but his brother described himself as a "citizen and apothecary of York". Considering the legacy of his pots to his daughter, it is likely that he, too, traded in spices.

[5] The ownership of this house, which Richard had bought from the executors of the rector of the church of St Gregory in Fishergate, was to be hotly disputed by its tenant, John Helperby, who claimed that his mother had the right to the house. The dispute was not settled until thirty years later. Copies of some of the pleas from the King's Bench in this case are preserved in CP, E 248.

and 1353, and served as a witness to numerous transfers of property in the city in the period 1330–60. Though Hamo Hessay owned a number of houses in York and in Huntington, he moved into the house called "Mulberry Hall" in Petergate ward which had previously belonged to Richard Huntington, where he shared his household with Agnes and her mother. Although he had married Agnes's mother, Hamo Hessay appears not to have interfered much in her life except when she first began to think about getting married. Agnes's strong will and her independent choice of husband were to cause problems for the family, especially for her equally strong-willed mother.

Although the essential rules of marriage had been formulated in papal decisions concerning individual cases in the century following the publication of Gratian's *Decretum* around 1140, the rules were only published as a collection with papal authorisation in 1234.[6] The rules of canon law were thus relatively new and their implementation by ecclesiastical courts in the diocese of York even more recent. Canon law was adamant in its insistence on two things: the right of the individual freely to choose a spouse and the primacy of the spoken word in the making of a marriage. Only the voluntary exchange of vows which indicated the consent of a man and a woman, who were legally free to marry, could create a valid marriage. The church allowed no exception to the rule that the parties must consent to the marriage and insisted on the consent being spoken in most cases.[7] The exchanges of vows could take a number of forms if they were to create a legally valid contract. The most important distinction was between consent indicating an intent to marry in the future and consent with an intent to create a marriage at once. These two types of consent became known in legal language as *matrimonium per verba de futuro* and *matrimonium per verba de presenti*. Likewise, the courts recognised that certain conditions – such as the need to obtain the permission of parents – could be imposed on a contract of marriage.[8] The

---

[6] The history of the development of the church law on marriage is traced in James A. Brundage, *Law, Sex, and Christian Society in Medieval Europe* (Chicago, 1987). The English contribution to the development of the canon law of marriage and the synodal legislation enforced in England is investigated in Michael M. Sheehan, "Marriage Theory and Practice in the Conciliar Legislation and Diocesan Statutes of Medieval England", *Mediaeval Studies,* 40 (1978), pp. 408–60.

[7] In the case of mute people, the consent could be indicated by signs and gestures.

[8] For a full discussion of conditional marriages, see R. H. Helmholz, *Marriage Litigation in Medieval England*, Cambridge Studies in English Legal History (Cambridge, 1974), pp. 47–57.

church's decision that two people could marry by exchanging vows, and that the presence of witnesses was desirable – but not necessary – to establish a legally binding marriage, handed a powerful tool to young people who wanted to marry against the wishes of their parents. Where young people previously had no means to assert their will if their wishes were different to those of their parents, they now had recourse to the church courts. The law also offered a way to settle disputes over the legal force of the words used when a marriage was proposed: a vow *per verba de presenti* took precedence over a vow *per verba de futuro*, and a conditional contract did not create a legally binding marriage until the conditions were met. This rule was to remove an potential stumbling-block to the marriage of Agnes Huntington and Simon Munkton.

The manner in which Agnes tried to enforce her choice of marriage partner against her parents' wishes demonstrates both the strengths and the weaknesses of the relatively new rules of marriage. On the one hand, canon law provided an avenue for Agnes to mount a serious challenge to her parents' authority in her choice of marriage partner; on the other, canon law could not protect her against her parents' pressure to marry a man of their choice. It might be said that, because the law demanded a stubborn dedication to their cause on the part of the person trying to enforce a marriage, the law was therefore protected against frivolous claims on its time. In early February 1339 Agnes Huntington had decided that she wanted to marry John Bristol, junior. Financially and socially, John Bristol was not a bad catch. His father – John Bristol, senior – had been a freeman of the city since 1314, a bailiff in 1334–35 and had served as a member of parliament for the city in 1335, a position that Agnes's stepfather filled for the first time two years later in 1337. He was also a successful businessman who owned houses in Lop Lane, Petergate and Jubbergate. But for some reason Agnes's parents did not like John Bristol, junior, and Agnes's mother fiercely opposed the proposed marriage between Agnes and John. Whether Agnes knew her rights under canon law or not, she was not easily dissuaded. Either her relationship with John was of such long duration and of such notoriety in Petergate ward that it had come to the attention of the dean of the Christianity of York, whose tasks included supervising the morals of the people under his jurisdiction, or Agnes's mother and stepfather reported the couple to him. As a preparation for a proper meeting of the dean's court, the dean appointed three clerics to investigate John and Agnes's relationship to determine if they had exchanged words that created a legally binding marriage or if the couple should be forced to forswear their relationship.[9] These three clerics – Gilbert Pocklington, David Ledes and John Couthorp (the last being a kinsman of the Huntington family) – met Agnes's parents, her uncle William Huntington and John Bristol's parents in Mulberry Hall on Monday 7 February 1339.

Long before this meeting, Agnes's parents had made their disapproval of John Bristol clear to the servants of the household. On the morning of 7 February the matron of the household, Margaret Foxholes, was caught in a conflict of loyalties as Agnes and John tried to use her in their attempt to create a legally binding marriage, using the canon law rule that spoken consent was enough. Margaret described herself as a close friend of Agnes and said they had been close for about four years. She was originally employed by Agnes's mother around 1335 "to carry her keys" and during her term of employment she shared her bed with Agnes in York and in Huntington, a fact that made her privy to most of Agnes's secrets.[10] That morning Margaret had gone to see why the door of the house called the Sandhous in Mulberry Hall's garden facing Grapcuntlane was open.[11] In the doorway of the Sandhous she found Agnes and John embracing each other.

---

[9] The legal foundations for the dean's supervision of morals is explored in R. H. Helmholz, "Abjuration *Sub Poena Nubendi* in the Church Courts of Medieval England", in *Canon Law and the Law of England* (London, 1987), pp. 145–56, and R. H. Helmholz, *Marriage Litigation in Medieval England*, Cambridge Studies in English Legal History (Cambridge, 1974), pp. 172–81 (with examples, pp. 208–12).

[10] "Et dictam Agnetam primo novit ad festum Pentecostem ultimo preterito fuerunt decem anni elapsi, pro eo quod tunc venit ad matrem dicte Agnete, cum qua stetit, ei deserviendo et claves suos portando, circa quatuor annos tunc proximo sequente. Et per totum tempus quo dicta Margareta stetit in servicio [illa] et prefata Agneta singulis noctibus in uno lecto simul jacuerunt aliquando apud Ebor' et aliquando [apud] Huntingtoun juxta Ebor." CP, E 248–23.

When a witness admitted to being a *socia in lecto* it usually meant that they claimed to have a detailed knowledge of the inner life of their bedfellow. In the case of Nicholas Cantilupe and Katherine Paynell, the witness Margaret Halgton made this clear to the court: "Preterea dicit quod a tempore quo dicta Katherina fuit subtracta a uberibus matris sue et quasi singulis noctibus ipsa Katherina fuit consortia istius jurate in lecto et ideo voluit revelare sibi omnia secreta sua, ut dicit." *Paynell* c. *Cantilupe*, CP, E 259–16 (1368); see also *Marrays* c. *Rowcliff*, CP, E 89 (1365–66).

[11] The present-day Grape Lane.

The witness said to Agnes, "Alas, alas, what are you doing here?" To which Agnes answered, "This past night you chastised me for a deed of mine. Now you will see what will be done and made." The said Agnes took the said John by his right hand, saying thus, "Here I take you, John, son of John of Bristol, as my man, to have and to hold, for better or for worse, for fairer and for grimmer for the duration of my life and to this I give you my pledge".[12]

Margaret Foxholes had been caught in a conflict of loyalties between her employer and her friend. Her first reaction was to run from the scene. John tried to stop her, catching hold of her saying, "Wait, hear some more!" But Margaret replied, "No, by Saint Mary, I am distressed that I heard as much as I heard", and walked away from the Sandhous. Agnes ran after her and pleaded with Margaret "with her arms raised in the air". She managed to persuade Margaret to return and listen to what John Bristol had to say. Standing at the door of the Sandhous, John said: "Agnes, behold my oath that if your family does not give me one penny I hold myself satisfied by you to have you as my wife". To which the said Agnes said, "I shall have those things which my father left me for the enemies of my family".[13]

In the end, Margaret Foxholes did not witness a *mutual* exchange of vows and for this reason Margaret's testimony could only be used to

---

[12] "Ibi invenit dictos Johannem et Agnetam simul stantes et brachiis suis adinvicem amplectantes, cui Agnete ipsa jurata sic dixit, ut dicit, 'Heu, heu, quid facis hic?' Cui ipsa Agneta respondit 'Hoc exsterna nocte redarguisti me de uno facto. Iam videbis quod erit factum et statutum.' Ipsa Agneta cepit dictum Johannem per manum dexteram, sic dicendo, 'Hic accipio te, Johannem filium Johannis de Bristoll, in virum meum habendum et tenendum, pro meliori et peiori, pulcriori et deformiori ad terminum vite mee et ad hoc do tibi fidem meam'." CP, E 248–23.

[13] "Statim post prolationem dictorum verborum per prefatam Agnetam ipsa jurata a prefata domo incepit recedere, et tunc idem Johannes cepit dictam juratam per gremium et dixit ei, 'Expecta, plus audies'. Cui ipsa jurata respondit, 'Non, per sanctam Mariam, penitet me quod tantum audivi quantum audivi'. Et sic ipsa jurata a prefata domo recessit et Johannem et Agnetam supradictos in prefata domo solos dimisit ... Et dicta Agneta sequebatur eam et elevatis manibus dixit sic, 'Margareta, rogo vos, vadatis ad ostium aule et loquamini cum dicto Johanne'. Et statim ipsa jurata adivit ostium predicte aule versus stratam regiam in Petergat Eboracensis et ipsa Agneta ea [sic] sequebatur prefatam juratam. Et statim cum venissent prefate Margareta et Agneta ad dictum ostium, dictus Johannes de Bristoll intravit per idem ostium et cepit dictam Agnetam per manum dexteram, sic dicendo: 'Agneta, ecce fidem meam si amici tui non dederunt michi unum denariatum [sic] in bonis, ego reputo me contentum de te ad habendum in uxorem meam'. Cui ipsa Agneta respondit, 'Hec quod pater meus michi legavit habebo inimicis amicorum meorum'." CP, E 248–16.

substantiate the *presumption* of marriage, not the actual existence of it. However, it was clear that Margaret had understood the implications of the actions of Agnes and John and that she was unwilling as the events unfolded to be a witness to their vows. The fact that Margaret walked away towards the house halfway through the exchange of vows shows that all three people present knew that the situation might end in actions that had legal validity: but Margaret may have known that if she did not hear both Agnes and John pronounce their vows in words that indicated present consent her testimony would only support the allegation that Agnes and John *intended* to marry on the morning of the tribunal's meeting. Although, by itself, Margaret Foxholes' testimony could not prove that a mutual exchange of vows had taken place, Agnes produced three other witnesses before the archbishop's court of audience six years later to prove that an unconditional exchange of vows had taken place on the day the tribunal met at Mulberry Hall. These witnesses, however, did not appear before the dean of the Christianity's court in 1339.[14]

At the meeting of the dean's tribunal on 7 February John and Agnes tried to persuade Agnes's parents to consent to their marriage. John repeated his willingness to marry Agnes, even if it meant losing the inheritance left to her by Richard Huntington which was still being looked after by her uncle William. He even offered the money to Hamo Hessay if only he would agree to the union.[15] But Agnes's mother was adamantly opposed to the marriage. Gilbert Pocklington, one of the three clerks of the dean's court present at the meeting, said that:

> He heard the said Agnes's mother say threateningly that she would draw a maternal curse upon herself if she swore to any [marriage] contract unless it be a conditional one, namely [on condition that] her parents agreed.[16]

[14] The three witnesses who testified to Agnes and John's unconditional contract were Agnes's uncle's friend William Joveby, his wife Mariota and Juliana Baker. When their evidence was presented to the court, Simon entered a series of exceptions to their evidence. William Joveby in particular may have perjured himself in 1345.

[15] "Et ad hoc faciendum ulterius dicit se velle remittere eidem jurato [Hamo Hessay] quicquid predicte Agnetam legatum fuit in testimonio patris sui, presentibus tunc et premissa audientibus Johanne de Munkgat, clerico, dicto Johanne filio Johannis ac ipso jurato et non pluribus quod ipse scit, ut dicit." CP, E 248–19.

[16] "Dicit etiam idem juratus quod audivit matrem eiusdem Agnete sibi dicere comminandam quod inferret sibi maledictionem maternam si aliquem contractum faceretur nisi conditionale, videlicet si parentes dicte Agnete consentirent." CP, E 248–23d.

By a mixture of intimidation and persuasion Agnes's mother and Hamo Hessay managed to keep evidence of an unconditional contract out of the court of the dean of the Christianity when it met a week later. They even went so far as to threaten one of the officers of the court. After the preliminary meeting in Mulberry Hall, John Couthorp, a clerk of the court of the dean of the Christianity and a kinsman of Agnes, continued to investigate the case and found evidence that John and Agnes *had* exchanged unconditional marriage vows on several occasions. John, Agnes and Margaret Foxholes confessed this privately to him and John Couthorp decided to confront Agnes's mother with this information. Her reaction was prompt: if John Couthorp did not stop associating with John Bristol, Agnes's mother would have his legs broken.[17]

A week later, the dean of the Christianity's court, presided over by Master William Yafford and his scribe, John Munkgate, convened in front of the altar of the Virgin Mary in the undercroft in the Minster. Before Agnes and John gave their evidence, John Bristol, senior, got up and warned his son that he would bring his father's curse upon himself if he testified falsely about the contract. Agnes's mother made Agnes kneel and also warned her that she would be cursed by her mother if she tried to conceal the true nature of the contract. Then the court required Agnes and John to swear on the Gospels and give evidence. Agnes told the court that the contract had been conditional on her parents' consent, while John stated that the contract had been unconditional. As there was no supplementary evidence heard by this court, John and Agnes were dismissed to their consciences and were pronounced free to marry when and where they would.[18] It was a common occurrence for church courts to dismiss the parties "to their consciences". By doing so, the court acknowledged that it could have been misled by the evidence and left it to the parties themselves to implement its findings: if a litigant was still convinced that he or she was married to the other party, the litigant was supposed to remain faithful to the alleged spouse and not to marry another for the duration of their lives.

Agnes's hopes of marriage to John Bristol had been quashed by her fear of her mother. Her resolve had failed her at the crucial moment

---

[17] "Audivit etiam idem juratus matrem dicte Agnete cominare eidem jurato quod dimitteret societatem dicti Johannis vel frangi faceret crura eiusdem jurati." CP, E 248–23d (John de Couthorp).

[18] CP, E 248–19, Richard Snaweshill and Hamo de Hessay.

in court when she could have sworn to an unconditional contract and have expected the church court to uphold her marriage to John Bristol. But she had learned a vital lesson about marriage: she now knew that if she stood up for her right to marry and produced convincing evidence showing that she had exchanged vows with a man and did not succumb to her fear of her parents, she could count on the ecclesiastical courts to uphold her marriage to her chosen partner. Her new choice was to be Simon Munkton, the son of the goldsmith Roger Munkton. Like John Bristol, Simon Munkton was a neighbour. He lived and worked in Stonegate where his father had a workshop. The exact date of their first exchange of vows is uncertain, because that date became the subject of subsequent litigation when Agnes sought the help of the courts in 1345 and the matter was never satisfactorily resolved by the court. Agnes claimed that she met Simon after the meeting of the dean of the Christianity's court in 1339 and at first Simon agreed. However, later he claimed that they had married as early as September 1338, before Agnes and John Bristol had even met. This issue became the focus of a number of confusing (and confused) depositions and it remains impossible to this day to say which of the dates was the real date of their first meeting. If the re-examination of two witnesses which Simon produced to prove the 1338 marriage are to be believed (and both of them had previously given contradictory evidence to the court), there was one obstacle that had to be cleared before Simon and Agnes could marry. This, however, proved easier than it was later to prove in the case of Agnes and John Bristol. As part of the final stages of the case, John Marschall and Emma Munkton (who was not related to Simon) claimed to have been present at an exchange of marriage vows between Simon and Agnes some time between 29 September and 11 November 1338.[19] Emma Munkton explained to the court that she had seen Simon and John Marschall standing in the garden of Mulberry Hall and that Agnes had been standing in the window above the garden in her step-father's house. Simon and Agnes had been seeing each other for a while at that time, but Simon's father had decided that his son ought to become a cleric and had announced this to Simon and Agnes sometime earlier. Agnes was upset and determined to prevent Simon from joining the priesthood. According to Emma Munkton, Agnes said:

[19] Emma de Munkton's deposition states that she was born in Richmond but had lived in York for the last ten years. Simon was born in York.

Simon, I understood that your father wants to make you enter religion and this cannot happen because you know well that we are engaged to each other and I want to have you and no one else as my man.[20]

The other witness, John Marschall, reported that Agnes had been more determined,

I want you and no one else to be my man, so much so that if you were to join the church, I shall call you back from it.[21]

Agnes and Simon knew of the church's rules of marriage and their solution to the dilemma was to marry at once. John Marschall, a witness whose trustworthiness is questionable, described the scene to the court in great detail: with Agnes standing in the window of her room in her father's house and Simon Munkton standing in the garden below, she and Simon contracted marriage by exchanging words *de presenti*, thus creating a legally valid marriage at once. That the exchange was intended to create the bond was emphasised by their actions:

and because the said window was so far from the said garden that the said Simon and Agnes could not touch each other with their hands, the said Agnes extended her hand and kissed it. Which hand she extended as far as she could towards the said Simon standing in the said garden (as the witness says) and the said Simon immediately kissed his own hand and reached as far as he could upwards by reaching above towards the said window, so that this extension of his arm could replace a kiss by the said Simon, just like the extension of the said Agnes's arm was made to Simon below as a sign of a kiss given to the said Simon.[22]

---

[20] "Simon, intellexi quod pater tuus vult facere te religionem ingredi et hoc fieri non potest quia bene scis quod sumus adinvicem affidati et volo te habere in virum meum et nullum alium." CP, E 248–4.

[21] "Volo te in virum meum habere et nullum alium ita quod si ingressus esses religionem aliquam ab eadem te revocarem." CP, E 248–4.

[22] "Et quia dicta fenestra distabat a gardino predicto ita quod ipsi Simon et Agnes se invicem manibus tangere non potuerunt, ipsa Agnes brachium suum extendebat et manum suam osculatum fuit, quam porrexit dicto Simone in dicto gardino stante quatenus potuit, ut dicit. Et idem Simon statim osculatus fuit manum suum propriam et ipsam porrexit superius quatenus potuit brachium suum extendendo superius versus fenestram predictam, ut eiusdem brachii sui extentio esset loco osculi ex parte eiusdem Simonis sicut extentio brachii dicte Agnetis stantis in fenestra predicta facta fuit dicto Simon inferius in signum osculi eodem Simone dandi, ut dicit." CP, E 248–18.

John Marschall added that later that same day he had seen Simon throw a ring across the garden fence to Agnes in her room. Agnes had often since then showed the ring to John "as a sign of the love she had towards the said Simon".[23] These depositions must, however, be taken with a large pinch of salt: John Marschall and Emma Munkton's depositions are the last preserved documents in the case and may have been produced in an attempt to satisfy the court that the marriage of Agnes and Simon was valid after the two litigants had reached an out-of-court settlement.

Agnes and Simon had exchanged words that created a marriage in the estimation of John Marschall and Emma Munkton; and in the eyes of the law the words carried enough force to create a legally binding bond between them. Although Simon and Agnes were married from the moment they had exchanged these words, Simon's witnesses added extra evidence to show that Agnes and Simon had performed certain symbolic acts to show that it was also their *intention* to marry. Since a legal bond had allegedly been created by Simon's and Agnes's vows, a subsequent solemnisation of the marriage in church was not legally required. Simon and Agnes, however, made sure that their marriage was made known publicly through a church ceremony in their parish church, St Michael le Belfrey, on 25 November 1340. The ceremony was attended by around one hundred people and both Agnes's and Simon's parents were among those present.[24]

In the years following their vows, Agnes and Simon's marriage gradually fell apart. For the first couple of years the couple lived happily with Simon's family in Petergate and their relationship showed no signs of strain. After a year or two Agnes gave birth to a son, whom they named Hamo after Agnes's stepfather, and Agnes's mother died leaving Hamo Hessay to marry again. The couple also took possession of Agnes's lands in Huntington and Earswick, hired servants and set up their own household in Huntington. However, the period was characterised by a gradual deterioration of the relationship between Agnes and Simon, who for some reason became increasingly violent. On 25 June 1345, Simon attacked Agnes in their home in Huntington because she would not consent to the sale of lands she had received from her father. He had already confirmed the transfer of

---

[23] "Quemquidem anulum dicta Agnes eidem jurato pluries ostendit in signum dilectionis quam habuit erga Simonem predictum, ut dicit." CP, E 248–18.

[24] CP, E 248–18, 248–32, 248–3. The three witnesses were the assisting priest at the ceremony, Simon's father and one of the wedding guests.

the land to the steward of Lord Richard Neville and urgently needed
Agnes to consent to the transfer of property.[25] When she continued to
refuse, Simon evicted her from their house that evening. Agnes had
reached breaking point and sued for a divorce from Simon in the court
of the archbishop's official in York. Canon law did not allow divorce
in the form it is available today. Currently a marriage can be dissolved
leaving both partners free to marry, but in the fourteenth century
there were only two ways spouses could legally live apart. One was
what today would be characterised as a legal separation, a "divorce
from bed and board" (*divortium a mensa et thoro*), which allowed the
partners to live in separate households but not to remarry; the other
was a "divorce from the bond" (*divortium a vinculo*), an annulment of
marriage which left the partners free to marry another partner of their
choice. The former required the spouse suing for divorce to prove that
there was a serious breakdown of the marriage and that cohabitation
was no longer possible; the latter required the plaintiff to prove that
there was a technical flaw in the current marriage, for example that
one of the partners was already married before the present marriage or
that the partners were related within forbidden degrees of consanguinity.[26] During the course of the litigation Agnes was to plead for both
a separation and – by changing her story about the marriage to John
Bristol – for an annulment of her marriage to Simon.

Agnes initiated divorce proceedings some time between 26 and 29

---

[25] "Requisitus de exheredatione facta per dictum Simonem prefate Agnete, dicit quod
presens fuit apud Huntington inter festa pentecost' et sancti Johannis baptiste vel
circiter, ubi et quando vidit et audivit predictum Simonem libere seisina Johan' de
Flete, senescallo domini Ricardi de Nevill, de omnibus terris et tenementis que
fuerunt dicte Agnete in Huntington et Ercewyk, et per hoc credit idem juratus
quod ipse Simon dictam Agnetem exheredavit." CP, E 248–34, William de Joveby.
Two other witnesses, Nicholas Franteys and John Snaweshill, confirm the transfer
of land to Lord Nevill in the same document. For an outline of women's property
rights, see A.W.B. Simpson, *A History of the Land Law* (Oxford, 1986), and
Michael M. Sheehan, "The Influence of Canon Law on the Property Rights of
Married Women in England", *Mediaeval Studies*, 25 (1963), pp. 109–24. Many
witnesses testified to Agnes's unwillingness to endorse Simon's use of her wealth
and the presence in the file of two writs from the king to the sheriff of York
concerning some of Agnes's land from that same year (CP, E 248–12, 248–13)
shows that she was actively engaged in the management of her own property
matters.

[26] Helmholz compared the function of the the ecclesiastical judge in divorce *a mensa
et thoro* cases to "a rather heavy-handed marriage counsellor", a description which
is not far off the mark, Helmholz, *Marriage Litigation*, p. 101. Helmholz outlines
the sometimes confusing rules governing divorce, ibid., pp. 74–111.

July 1345 before the court of the archbishop's official in York.[27] Agnes's original plea has not been preserved, so it is not possible to tell which kind of divorce she sought. Agnes entered her plea just before the court rose for its summer recess, and this afforded her the prospect of a long rest period to recover from a violent attack by Simon a few days earlier. Because the official's court was not due to reconvene until 29 September, Simon initiated legal proceedings before the archbishop's court of audience in August to find a speedy solution to his embarrassing inability to finalise the sale of Agnes's inheritance. If he was successful in his plea, Agnes would have no higher English ecclesiastical court to appeal to, as the archbishop's court of audience had the power to override the proceedings of the official's court. In order to make a plea at the archbishop's court of audience, Simon had to present the case as one of spousal abandonment and consequently he declared to the court that his marriage to Agnes was well known and attested to in the city of York: Agnes and he had entered into marriage and had solemnised it at the church of St Michael le Belfrey after the proclamation of banns and they had cohabited for several years in Petergate. As further evidence of their marriage, Simon mentioned their son, Hamo. But, Simon said, without proper reason "because of her inborn fear", Agnes had left him and was now living apart, "robbing him of his belongings due to him by marriage".[28] Simon's remarks about Agnes "robbing him of his belongings due to him by marriage" underlines that he was in a financial predicament and that the speedy decision offered by the archbishop's court of audience, which could allow him quickly to sell her family lands in Huntington and Earswick, was a clear priority for him. Although the common law held that the husband held and administered the wife's land, the husband only held the land in trust and had to be able to give an account of his use of the land at the death of either spouse or at the dissolution of the marriage. This sale could not go through without Agnes's consent. The earliest dated document in the case is the letter from the archbishop of York,

---

[27] A letter from the commissary general dated 30 October 1345, which quotes a writ of supersedence from the archbishop dated 20 September 1345, says as much: "Quia vero, sicut intelleximus, ad instantiam dicte Agnetis fecistis dictum Simonem, auctoritate nostra, ad dictam curiam nostram Eboracensis super federo matrimonii inter eos contracto coram vobis ad judicium evocari." CP, E 248–37.
The court rose for its summer recess on the last court day of July. In 1345, 31 July fell on a Sunday and the court did not meet on a Saturday.

[28] "Ipsum a possessione sua conjugale indebite spoliando." CP, E 248–51.

William la Zouche, dated 21 August, which summoned Agnes to appear before the archbishop's court of audience on 16 September as a result of Simon's accusation that she had left him without proper authorisation from the church.[29] The archbishop's letter was phrased in almost the same words as Simon's original complaint of a couple of days earlier and commanded Agnes to renew her cohabitation with Simon.[30] A further letter was sent to the dean of the Christianity of York commanding him to cite Agnes to appear before the archbishop's court of audience which convened in Ripon on 16 September.[31]

When the court met at Ripon on 16 September 1345 Agnes sent her proctor, John Lacer,[32] who produced a letter to the archbishop explaining that Agnes dared not leave the safety of the city of York:

> because of the likely threat of death – which could fall upon a constant woman – which was brought forward and threatened by the said Simon and his accomplices and because of the pain of her body and the excessive cruelty committed against her by the said Simon and his accomplices (which she fears they will likely commit against her in the future) and because of the plunder that will surely happen if she falls into the hands or power of the said Simon, which she believes to happen if she goes outside the city of York in person.[33]

---

[29] CP, E 248–51. This letter would have been preceded a couple of days earlier by a presentation by Simon to the archbishop's court of audience, so it is likely that Simon first appeared before the court some time during the week 14–21 August.

[30] CP, E 248–52 [undated]. A return of a mandate to the dean of the Christianity of York, dated 8 September, contains a copy of the original mandate to cite Agnes before the court, dated 21 August 1345 (CP, E 248–42). Taking into account the speed with which the archiepiscopal chancery normally worked it is possible to assume that CP, E 248–52 was written in the week prior to that date.

[31] CP, E 248–42.

[32] John Lacer was established as her proctor, two days earlier, on 14 September 1345. CP, E 248–42.

[33] "Propter verisimilem mortis metum (quem cadere poterit in constantem mulierem) per dictum Simonem et suos complices sibi comminantem et inferendam ac propter cruciatum corporis sui et mimam [sic] sevitiam per eundem Simonem et suos complices sibi illatos quos verisimiliter sibi inferri timet in futurum necnon propter exheredationem quam verisimiliter intraret, si in manus sive potestatem dicti Simonis incideret, prout incidere credit, si extra civitatem Eboracum personaliter laboraret." CP, E 248–40.

The letter is endorsed *Proponitum die Martis*, which presumably refers to the Wednesday before the first session of the court on 16 September 1345, that is 14 September.

John Lacer presented the court with three witnesses who gave evidence about Agnes's fear of Simon.[34] They explained that on 25 July 1345 Simon and Agnes had had an argument over the sale of her lands in Huntington and Earswick. Simon wanted to sell but she had refused to consent and for this reason Simon had attacked her and beat her "so much that blood poured out both by her nostrils and ears".[35] Simon believed her to be dead and took refuge in the cemetery of the local church, but not before asking a neighbour called Nicholas Franteys to go to their house to see if Agnes was still alive. She *was* still alive, but in such a bad state that, after washing her face in a well in the garden, Nicholas and his fellow witness William Joveby carried her still bleeding to her neighbour John Snaweshill's house. William Joveby added that Simon had expelled Agnes from their house that very evening "vowing that she would never have any good from him nor any lands or tenements".[36]

Simon's explanation of the discord between him and Agnes was that she had disobeyed an order not to associate with certain people who worked against Simon's and Agnes's interests. He added that he had been without murderous intent and had only castigated Agnes "lightly and without danger of death or mutilation of any limb, as he may castigate her according to the law", because she disobeyed him and because:

> she had had conversation with certain men in suspect places against the will and prohibition of the said Simon, the said Agnes's husband. And she conducted herself in a suspect manner on several occasions against the said Simon and irreverently spoke disgraceful words against the said Simon.[37]

[34] CP, E 248–39 and more fully in CP, E 248–34. Both documents are undated, but CP, E 248–39 was clearly heard at the meeting of the court in Ripon on 16 September 1345 since the judge interrogated the witnesses directly and each witness was asked "whether he believed that the said woman dared come to Ripon today for her defence" ("Requisitus an credit quod dicta mulier audebat accidere ad Ryponem isto die pro defensione cause sue dicit quod..."). An interrogation of these witnesses is mentioned in the *acta* under the second meeting of the court in Ripon. The *acta* do not date this meeting.

[35] "ita quod sanguis exivit tam per nares quam aures eiusdem". CP, E 248–33.

[36] "Asserens quod [nuncquam] aliquod bonum ab ipse nec de terris et tenementis predictis haberet." CP, E 248–33.

[37] "[Castigatio] facta fuit per deviatis et malegestis eiusdem Agnetis, que prius cum quibusdam hominibus in locis suspectis colloquium habuit et tractatum contra voluntatem et inhibitionem eiusdem Simonis, mariti eiusdem Agnetis, et suspectam erga eundem Simonem in pluribus se redidit ac verba probrosa contra eundem

Three days later Simon produced three witnesses to prove his alternative interpretation of events. These witnesses told the court about events that had taken place almost two months before Simon's alleged attack on Agnes in Huntington and presented Simon as a cuckolded husband. They explained that on 5 May 1345 Simon and Agnes had a row not over lands or money, but because Simon had heard that Agnes was sleeping with a squire called William Morthyng. The confrontation had escalated, according to Johanna Houson:

> and because the said Agnes spoke disgracefully and answered him irreverently, the said Simon boxed her on the ear with a stroke of his hand, a gentle one, though – according to this witness – and in order to castigate and not to be violent, in her opinion.[38]

Johanna Houson and another witness, Robert Kyng – both of whom were domestic servants in Agnes and Simon's household – added that Agnes had done public penance for her adultery with William Morthyng. Simon's alternative version of events raised dangerous possibilities of failure for Agnes. If Agnes succeeded in having the marriage dissolved through either kind of divorce she could look forward to the church court overseeing the restitution of her property. If, however, Simon succeeded in showing that she had been an adulteress, he would retain both his own and her portion of their goods in marriage.[39] Based on Simon's original plea and on the witnesses heard so far, on 20 September the archbishop sent a writ of supersedence – a letter from one court ordering another court not to proceed with a case until it has been heard (and in some cases decided) by the court issuing the letter of supersession – to the official's court where Agnes's plea of divorce was due to be heard the following day.[40] Acknowledging the severity of the claimed violence, however, the archbishop's court overturned its previous decision and

---

Simonem irreverenter protulit, absque periculo mortis seu mutiliatione membrorum, leviter ut sibi de jure licuit castigando." CP, E 248–31.

[38] "Et quia eadem Agnes protulit probrosa et irreverenter respondit eidem dictus Simon dedit ei [sic] alapam cum pugno mano, lenem tamen, ut dicit ipsa jurata, et causa castigationis et non violentie, ut credit." CP, E 248–30, Johanna Houson.

[39] X. 4. 20. 2, 3 and 4, compare Sheehan, "The Influence of Canon Law", pp. 110, 114.

[40] The original letter does not survive, but the official's commissary general acknowledged receipt of the writ on 30 October. CP, E 248–37.

permitted Agnes to live separately while the case lasted, thus deciding against Simon's claim for immediate restitution.[41]

Even when hiding inside the York city walls, Agnes had good reason to fear for her safety. Acting on his understanding of the archbishop's decision, Simon turned up at William Huntington's house in Petergate in York around suppertime on 25 September 1345, nine days after the meeting in Ripon, to persuade Agnes to come with him. It is unclear what happened at first. Simon probably tried to persuade Agnes to come with him to their own house and, when she refused, lost his temper and tried to force her to come with him. It was at this point that witnesses were called to the scene by Agnes's screams. Witnesses were heard for both sides but they disagreed on the severity of the violence. Not unsurprisingly, Simon's witnesses claimed that the fracas had been relatively mild. Henry Galtres – a resident of Stonegate – explained that

> having heard this [clamour] this witness went to the window of his house in the said neighbourhood and saw the said Agnes lying and the said Simon standing over her in the the said neighbourhood, with the intention, in the witness's opinion, that he might lead her to this Simon's house as his wife without any harm being done to her, as the witness firmly believes.[42]

Witnesses heard on Agnes's behalf described events more sinister. Obviously disgusted with Simon's behaviour, Thomas Esoby – another resident of Stonegate – explained to the court that he saw

> Simon throw Agnes, with whom we are dealing, to the ground – and in a very smelly place, as the witness says – and sit upon her stomach. But whether Simon hit the said Agnes then, he does not know for certain, as the witness says. And when these two, Simon and Agnes, thus were lying on the ground, John Midelton, a tailor living in the said neighbourhood, came and took the said Simon by his head and pulled him towards himself away from the stomach of the said Agnes, as the witness says. Indeed, this Simon then drew his knife, but did not strike anyone with it, as far as the

---

[41] CP, E 248–37, dated 20 September 1345.

[42] "Quo audito, idem juratus accessit ad fenestram domus sue in vico predicto, et vidit dictam Agnetem jacentem et dictum Simonem [stantem] super eam in eodem vico, ea intentione, reputatione sua, ut eam posset duxisse ad mansum ipsius Simonis ut uxorem suam sine aliqua molestia eidem inferenda prout firmiter credit." CP, E 248–54.

witness might know, as the witness says. He also says that John said to the former Simon, "*Unthriandman*, if you had some right before, you have lost it now".[43]

Juliana Aldeburgh, a neighbour who nursed Agnes after the attack, added that Simon kicked and hit Agnes so badly that she had to remain in bed for a fortnight and that it had seemed to her that Simon wanted to kill Agnes when he drew his knife, while John Snaweshill said that Simon had broken two of her ribs.[44]

Despite Simon's attack of 25 September on Agnes, the case continued to be heard by the archbishop's court of audience. In all, the court devoted eleven sessions in Ripon, Cawood, Cowthorp and Bishop's Burton by Beverley to the case in the period from September 1345 to February 1346. Every session of the archbishop's court of audience took place outside York and Agnes never appeared before the court in person, preferring to send one of her proctors. Throughout the seven months from late July 1345 to February 1346 Agnes remained in hiding in York, despite the best efforts of the archbishop's officers. As late as 28 January 1346 the archbishop's sub-treasurer, John Arme, sent a letter in reply to a commission by the archbishop on 23 January by which the archbishop had charged him to cite Agnes to appear before the court of audience in Cawood on 30 January 1346. The sub-treasurer explained that he had been unable to find Agnes though he searched everywhere in the city of York "secretly, diligently and on several occasions, even in your archiepiscopal palace there and in the secret dwellings in that palace and in other houses of her uncle William Huntington in that city".[45] This effort in searchng for Agnes and forcing her to attend the archbishop's court of audience was to be the last. Both Simon and the archbishop's court of audience

[43] "[Vidit Simonem] prosternere Agnetam, de qua agitur, ad terram et in loco valde fetido, ut dicit, et super ventrem eiusdem Agnete jacere, sed an eandem Agnetam idem Simon tunc percussit nescit pro certo, ut dicit. Et ipsis Simone et Agnete sic jacentibus accessivit Johannes de Midelton, cissor, manens in vico predicto et cepit ipsum Simonem per caput et ipsum ad se traxit de ventre dicte Agnete, ut dicit. Qui quidem Simon cultellum suum tunc extraxit, sed neminem cum eidem percussit, quod sciat ipse juratus, ut dicit. Dicit etiam quod idem Johannes prefato Simoni sic dixit, 'vnthriandman, si primo aliquod jus habuisti, illud iam amisisti'." CP, E 248–26c.

[44] CP, E 248–39.

[45] "In civitate Eboracensis et in palacio vestri archiepiscopale ibidem et in domibus secretis eiusdem palatiis et aliis domibus Willelmi de Huntyngton, avunculis sui, in civitate predictam diligenter, secrete et pluries quesivi." CP, E 248–29.

seem to have accepted that the case would be long-lasting and that Agnes and Simon did have severe marital problems. For this reason, the court prepared to return the case to the official's court where it would receive attention as an ordinary case of annulment of marriage. As a consequence, Simon produced three new witnesses after the archbishop's court of audience's winter break.[46] These gave evidence from 17–25 January 1346 stating that a marriage had been solemnised between Simon and Agnes on 25 November 1340 at the church of St Michael le Belfrey.[47] The assistant priest at the ceremony, Simon's father and one of the wedding guests testified that the ceremony had been attended by a large number of people and that Agnes's mother, Isabella, and her step-father, Hamo Hessay, and Simon's parents were among the guests. All three witnesses agreed that Simon and Agnes had cohabited and that the couple had produced a child, who died after a year or two. The case was now seen as a simple case of broken marriage vows and on 26 January it was agreed to transfer the case to the court of the archbishop's official, who convened his court inside the city walls of York. An additional benefit to this decision was that Agnes would now be able to attend the meetings of the court in person without fearing for her life. Thus Agnes had managed to delay the case and the sale of her lands for more than seven months and Simon had been unable to proceed at all.

Simon had pleaded his own case before the archbishop's court and conducted his case without the aid of a proctor and continued to do so for most of the duration of the case. In contrast, as the case grew in complexity, Agnes employed more proctors and, by April 1346, when the first dated document comes from the official's court, she was employing the services of three proctors. By using the services of so many of the courts proctors – only six proctors practised at the court – Agnes may in fact have tried to block Simon's access to legal assistance. Since one of her neighbours in Petergate was William Snaweshill, whose brother, John, was another proctor of the court, Simon was thus left with only two proctors to choose from. It was therefore only almost three months later, on 3 April 1346, after hearings about Simon's attack on Agnes had ended, that Simon finally appointed a member of the court, Robert Rampton, to act as his proctor.[48] Agnes,

---

[46] The court rose for its Christmas break on 13 December 1345 and reconvened on 6 January 1346.

[47] CP, E 248–18, 248–32, 248–33.

[48] CP, E 248–27.

on the other hand, had taken full advantage of whatever legal expertise she could find. On 4 November 1345 she established John of Beverly as her second proctor to act with John Lacer,[49] and on 2 February 1346 John Lacer used the power Agnes had given him in her commission of 14 September 1345 to establish a third proctor, Peter Couthorp, to act with him and John of Beverly for her case in court.[50]

The strategies of the two litigants became clear when the case was transferred to the official's court in February 1346. After seven months of ligation it seemed that Agnes had the upper hand in the conflict, at least as long as the case was heard by the archbishop's court of audience, where she could successfully delay the case by claiming that she was in fear of her life without entering into an argument about the legal substance of matter: whether she and Simon actually were married. Simon had hoped to regain control of Agnes's person and her lands but had not met with much success. Agnes had successfully argued that her person was in danger from Simon and through her argument had frustrated any hope Simon might have had for a speedy decision, and her ability to remain in hiding in York (even as the neighbour of the brother of a member of the court) had clearly shown the shortcomings of the power of the court. With her connections in York, she could remain in hiding for as long as she wanted and the archbishop's officers were powerless to apprehend her. As long as she was unwilling to appear before the court, Simon realised he would not be able to engage the main issue of the case: whether Agnes could legally live by herself. Simon had tried every legal – and sometimes illegal – means at his disposal since July 1345 when the marriage broke down. His refusal to take legal advice and his misunderstanding of the consequences of the archbishop's order to Agnes to resume cohabitation had led to an escalation of the violence in the case and ultimately frustrated his hopes of a speedy decision. Almost every meeting of the archbishop's court of audience was taken up with the production of evidence on the issue of whether Agnes did have good reason to fear Simon. On balance, the court granted Agnes the right to live apart from Simon at least while the case was being heard by the official's court. In contrast to Simon, Agnes seems to have taken all the legal advice she could get. She appointed proctors to act for her

[49] CP, E 248–38.

[50] CP, E 248–35. Although Peter Couthorp shares his surname with John Couthorp, who was a proctor at the dean of the Christianity's court six years earlier, there is no evidence that the two proctors were related.

in the case and these proctors conducted her case well. They managed to persuade the archbishop's court of audience that it was not the right forum for the case and that Agnes had a legitimate case against Simon which should be heard at the ordinary forum for those kinds of cases, the official's court.

Although Agnes had claimed from the beginning that she was married to John Bristol at the time of the solemnisation of her marriage to Simon,[51] and her witnesses at the very first meeting of the archbishop's court of audience in Ripon had quoted her fear of bigamy as a contributing factor to her leaving Simon, the hearing of this plea was delayed until the official's court decided whether her fear of Simon's violence was justified.[52] The archbishop's court of audience had been told about Simon's attack on Agnes in Huntington almost as soon as the case began and, in the course of the four months from February to June 1346, the official's court learned the details of Simon's second attack on her in Petergate.[53] During the period from 1 February to 26 June 1346, only one witness gave evidence about the substance of the marriage case. No documentary evidence shows that a verdict was reached about the violence in Petergate and Simon's clear transgression against the authority of the courts, but the attack may have influenced the court to overturn its initial order to Agnes and allow her to live apart from Simon, once again frustrating Simon's hopes of gaining control over their lands in Huntington and Earswick.

Simon and Agnes finally joined issue on the problem of whom Agnes had married first in May and June 1346.[54] Agnes claimed that she and Simon were married in 1340, while Simon's witnesses at first claimed they were married in October 1339. As we shall see, this date was

---

[51] CP, E 248–49.

[52] CP, E 248–39: William de Joveby, John de Snoweshull, Gervase de Rowcliff and Willliam de Huntington.

[53] See p. .

[54] The chronology of events during the period from April to November 1346 is unclear since no *acta* survive after 2 February 1346 and only a few documents are dated. But from the dated documents it is possible to construct a chronological outline which can be fleshed out by internal evidence in the remaining undated documents. The dated documents tell us that the witness John Marshall was heard in support of Simon's case on 10 May 1346 (CP, E 248–18) and Agnes produced nine witnesses to her pre-contract with John of Bristol on 19–30 June (CP, E 248–23–d). Margaret Foxholes, was heard for Agnes's case on 1 July (CP, E 248–23d). Further depositions were taken down on 9 October, 17–18 November and 24–26 November 1346. The depositions of late November 1346 are the last dated documents in the case.

later moved earlier to counter Agnes's claimed marriage to John in February 1339. The three witnesses heard for Simon's case before the archbishop's court of audience on 27 January had testified with varying levels of detail to a solemnisation of vows in St Michael le Belfrey on 25 November 1340, to cohabitation after that date and to the birth of a child whom both parents acknowledged as theirs. They had been unable, however, to prove that any vows had been exchanged before that date. Agnes, in her first response to Simon's allegations before the archbishop's court of audience, had claimed that she had married John Bristol almost a year before that. But it was not until almost a year after Agnes's initial decision to litigate that the court saw substantial evidence about her marriage to John Bristol. Simon produced the first witness, John Marschall, before the official's court on 10 May 1346. John Marschall was there to testify to Agnes's and Simon's earliest exchange of vows, but his testimony had one flaw: Agnes could assemble a large group of witnesses to testify that she had married John Bristol before the date of the alleged exchange of vows between Simon and Agnes. John Marschall explained that on 12 October 1339 he had seen Agnes stand in the window of her room in her father's house and Simon Munkton standing in the garden below. The two of them contracted marriage with a standard *verba de presenti* formula. In an attempt to add credence to his story John Marschall added numerous details designed to demonstrate that it had been Simon and Agnes's intent to marry. He also testified to the solemnisation of the contract between Simon and Agnes on the 25 November 1340 in St Michael le Belfrey, which he said had taken place in the presence of many people, including Simon's and Agnes's parents.[55]

Agnes had used the period from the production of Simon's witnesses on 27 January 1346 to mid-June to assemble a strong case showing that she had married John Bristol long before she met Simon. She proposed to present eleven witnesses to testify about her relationship with John Bristol, three of whom would confirm that an unconditional exchange of vows had taken place as early as February 1339, eight

---

[55] At his first production as a witness John Marschall only testified that Agnes and Simon had told him that they had actually married "more than a year" before the exchange of kisses and a ring, which was alleged to have happened on St Wilfred's Day (12 October) 1339: "Dicit etiam se didicisse ex relatu dictorum Simonis et Agnete quod per unum annum et amplius ante dictam diem in festo Sancti Wilfridi ipsi Simon et Agnes matrimonium contraxerunt." CP, E 248–18.

months before the date alleged by Simon's witness. She would also argue that John of Bristol was still alive and a further seven witnesses would confirm that John of Bristol swore to the dean of the Christianity of York's court that the contract he had made with Agnes was unconditional. Faced with the prospect of further obstacles, Simon once again tried to settle the case out of court. Like his previous attempt, his intervention was dangerously close to violence and ultimately unproductive. This attempt only came to the attention of the court four months later when Agnes tried to have the court disregard the evidence of one of Simon's witnesses, Robert Tayergrave, with the argument that the witness was disqualified by excommunication because he had broken the peace of the church by assisting in her physical abduction from the Minster. Three witnesses explained to the court how Robert Tayergrave had assisted Simon in abducting Agnes from a Corpus Christi procession within the precinct of the Minster on 14 June 1346. Gervase of Rawcliff testified that Robert and Simon had carried her off against her will, Simon holding Agnes's head and Robert her feet. The abduction was witnessed by many dignitaries of the city, among them the mayor John Sherburn, Agnes's stepfather, Hamo Hessay, and Thomas Grantham.[56] Gervase Rawcliff was the only witness produced by Agnes who had been present in person and seen the events as they unfolded. Emma, the wife of William Joveby, had heard about events from others. She confirmed Gervase Rawcliff's version of the story, adding the detail that "the said Agnes shouted to them that she could walk on her feet to wherever they were taking her. The said Simon and Robert, heeding her request, led her to the house of Roger Munkton".[57] Afterwards, she said, Robert and Simon had returned to take part in the Corpus Christi procession. Her husband, William Joveby, told the same story, but like her he had not been present in person. Simon replied that the abduction had been without violence and that Robert Tayergrave had only wanted to help reunite the two spouses. Simon also claimed that they had all participated in the Corpus Christi procession later that day.

Regardless of whether the events of 14 June were an abduction or a somewhat heavy-handed attempt at reconciliation on Simon's part, the outcome of his actions did not change Agnes's resolve. She persisted with the case and produced the proposed eleven witnesses on 19 June,

---

[56] None of these three were interrogated about these events.
[57] CP, E 248–14.

26–27 June and 30 June, adding a twelfth witness, Margaret Foxholes, who happened to be in York on 1 July 1346. The first three witnesses, two of whom had been servants in her parents' household, confirmed that they had overheard a mutual exchange of valid vows between Agnes and John on 7 February 1339, the day of the meeting of the tribunal of the dean of the Christianity of York. This put their marriage twenty-two months before the solemnisation of marriage between Agnes and Simon in St Michael le Belfrey.[58] Their exchange of vows took place in front of the three witnesses near the outhouse called *Sandhous* in Agnes's father's house in Stonegate. Agnes and John had been standing on either side of the fence that separated Richard Huntington's house from the neighbouring house in Grapcunt lane. All three witnesses testified to the same occasion and another eight witnesses, most of them clerics, testified that they had heard John Bristol swear on at least three separate occasions of varying degrees of formality that his contract with Agnes had been uncondi-tional.[59] One of these witnesses, Adam Warhum, claimed to have met John Bristol only two weeks before giving evidence.[60]

The central point in Agnes's argument was that she and John Bristol had exchanged vows on 7 February 1339 and, consequently, Simon's reply to Agnes's impressive list of witnesses concentrated on the four witnesses who claimed to have been present at such an event. His attack on Margaret Foxholes did not need much substance since there was no other witness who confirmed her story that John Bristol had pledged his faith to Agnes on the morning of 7 February 1339. He questioned the legality of her interrogation, because she was heard after he and Agnes had agreed not to produce any more witnesses and because she was interrogated in Simon's absence by Master John Hakkethorp, who, Simon claimed, was hostile to Simon's case.[61] Juliana Baker was challenged on a minor detail in her testimony: she

---

[58] CP, E 248–23d.

[59] CP, E 248–23d: William Grene, William Cotingham, Gilbert Pokelington, David Ledes, John Couthorp, Adam Warhum, Thomas Octelay, and Walter Kyllingbek.

[60] The non-appearence of John Bristol, junior, as a witness is puzzling. No attempt was made by either party to call him as a witness. It suggests that Agnes and Simon feared that John's testimony might decide the case and that they were not inter-ested in a decision either way: instead the delays in the sale of Agnes's lands intro-duced may have been of major benefit to both parties.

[61] The inclusion of her testimony was in great part due to the fact that she happened to be in York on a day when her testimony could be taken down: "dicit quod ob aliam causam venit ad civitatem, et tempore quo venit ad eam nescivit de [ventila-

could not possibly be speaking the truth in that part of her testimony where she said that she was present seven years ago in a place called the "Sandhous" or in "Mowbraihalle" since there was no such place in Stonegate and never had been. Strictly speaking Simon was right: there was no "Mowbraihalle" in Petergate ward. In her deposition Juliana mentions "Moubrayall". The difference is slight, but only an officer of the court with a good grasp of the local geography of Stonegate would catch the subtlety of Simon's argument, which was literally true but based on an obscure point of spelling and pronounciation of local York place names. Simon continued his exception by confounding the issue even more: there was a place called "Moubingate" in York, but it was not situated in Petergate. His exception against William Joveby of Huntington was more substantial: William had denied detailed knowledge of marriage between Agnes and John Bristol when he was interrogated by the archbishop's court of audience on 16 September the previous year, a statement that did not tally with his assertion that he had been present at an exchange of vows. Against Emma Munkton, he argued that she was living scandalously with William Huntington.[62] Perhaps it is not surprising that most of his initial exceptions had no effect.[63] Instead, Simon produced a more substantial counterclaim on the last court day before the summer recess on 29 July 1346. Simon intended to prove that Agnes's and John's contract had been conditional upon the consent of their parents and that before Agnes and Simon married the dean of the Christianity of York had heard their case and pronounced them free to marry whom they wanted.[64] When the court had reconvened after its summer recess, Simon produced four witnesses – Master Thomas Doncaster, Richard Snaweshill, Agnes's stepfather Hamo Hessay and Robert Tayergrave – on 9 and 11 October 1346 in evidence of this version of the events.

Master Thomas Doncaster told the court that some time between 23 June and 1 August 1338 he had overheard Simon and Agnes exchanging vows in her father's house in Stonegate. Agnes said:

tione] istius cause antequam fuit citata ad perhibendum testimonium veritati in causa predicta". CP, E 248–16.

Her testimony was taken down on a separate piece of parchment which was sewn onto the testimony of eleven other witnesses heard for Agnes before the whole roll containing the depositions was presented to the court.

[62] CP, E 248–2, 248–20.

[63] CP, E 248–2, 248–21, 248–20, 248–15.

[64] CP, E 248–43, 248–44.

"Simon, behold my pledge that I shall have you as my husband." And [the witness] heard the said Simon say to the said Agnes, "Agnes, behold my pledge that I shall have you as my wife".[65]

Such a vow was open to interpretation: it could either refer to Agnes and Simon's intention to marry in the future (in which case a legal marriage could be established by their having sexual intercourse) or it could signify their present consent to marriage. Thomas Doncaster added that he left Simon and Agnes alone in the room immediately after having heard this, but only after he heard her say to Simon, "When a woman wants a man so much for herself, he can do little except to kiss her".[66] Master Thomas said that he did not know whether they had had sex, but his choice of words to describe how he left them is redolent of the formula that the court always used to describe intercourse: he left them "naked man with naked woman" (*solus cum sola*) with ample time to consummate their union. As a chaplain Thomas Doncaster would be familiar with the formulas of speech used in court and his insinuation would probably not have gone unnoticed by the court.

Agnes's witnesses of 19 June to 1 July had testified about an actual exchange of unconditional vows which predated her marriage to Simon by six months. The second and third of Simon's witnesses – Hamo Hessay and Richard Snaweshill – told the story of the meeting of the court of the dean of the Christianity of York in the crypt of York Minster when Agnes swore that she had married John Bristol conditionally. Hamo Hessay added a long and flowing narrative about John Bristol's unsuccessful attempt to gain Isabella Huntington's and his own permission to marry Agnes by offering to give them the money Agnes's father had left her. Hamo added that every time he had asked Margaret Foxholes about the alleged contract between John of Bristol and Agnes she had denied any knowledge of the matter. The fourth witness, Robert Tayergrave, was heard last but his deposition has not been preserved in the file. This loss is doubly unfortunate as his evidence seems to have been important: the admissibility of the evidence of Thomas Doncaster and Robert Tayergrave became the

---

[65] "'Simon, ecce fidem meam quod habebo te in virum meum.' Et eundem Simonem statim post audivit dicta Agneta sic dicere, 'Agnes, ecce fidem meam quod habebo te in uxorem meam'." CP, E 248–19.

[66] "Quando una mulier optulit se tantum uni homini, modicum posset ipse facere nisi osculare eam." CP, E 248–19.

object of fierce dispute in the last two months of the case. Thus the witnesses for Simon, who testified to an exchange of vows between Simon and Agnes before her vows with John Bristol, were John Marschall (who had been interrogated in May), Thomas Doncaster and presumably Robert Tayergrave. When the court rose for its summer recess on 31 July, John Marschall's testimony had not been substantiated by another witness, so Agnes chose to concentrate her attack on Thomas Doncaster and Robert Tayergrave and to leave her stepfather's testimony about the solemnisation of her marriage to Simon unchallenged.

At a meeting of the court three weeks later, Agnes's proctor focused on the two witnesses most damaging to Agnes's case.[67] He claimed that both Thomas Doncaster and Robert Tayergrave had been in major excommunication at the time of their deposition. Thomas Doncaster had never been absolved of the excommunication which had been pronounced against all thieves in possession of stolen goods by the chaplain of St Michael le Belfrey seven years earlier, when Thomas had stolen an axe from a carpenter called John Hoby. Robert Tayergrave had infringed the liberty of the church when he helped Simon violently abduct Agnes from York Minster during the Corpus Christi procession four months earlier, some days before Agnes produced her main witnesses in the case.[68] Simon could not deny that something resembling an abduction had taken place. Instead he objected that Agnes had agreed to the abduction afterwards and that Robert Tayergrave's only aim had been to restore the couple to each other and that he had been without any intention of trespassing on the liberty of the church.[69]

Agnes produced at least five witnesses to prove her exceptions to Simon's witnesses on 17 and 18 October.[70] Three of them – Emma Munkton, William Huntington and Gervase Rawcliff – spoke about how Robert Tayergrave had assisted Simon in abducting Agnes from the Corpus Christi procession within the precinct of the Minster on the Wednesday of Corpus Christi week. A fourth witness, Master John, a chaplain in St Michael le Belfrey, supported Agnes's claim

---

[67] CP, E 248–16.

[68] CP, E 248–16, 248–7.

[69] CP, E 248–5, 248–3.

[70] The roll CP, E 248–14, containing the depositions presented to the court, is not complete. Stitch marks at the bottom of the membrane indicate that more than five witnesses were heard.

about Thomas Doncaster's excommunication in general terms: he did not remember excommunicating Robert Tayergrave or Thomas Doncaster as such, but three times a year he routinely excommunicated anyone in possession of stolen goods. Therefore, on the Sunday following Trinity Sunday seven years earlier (16 May 1339), he had excommunicated all those implicated in the theft of an axe from John Hoby.[71] The fifth witness was John Hoby himself, who explained to the court that he had asked of Thomas Doncaster whether he had the axe in his possession and Thomas had explained that he had had it once but that he had pawned it to a certain carpenter who was at that time incarcerated in the archbishop's prison. John Hoby had then bought back the axe from the prisoner by paying Thomas Doncaster's debt "with difficulty".[72] William Huntington confirmed this story.

The main flaw in Agnes's argument was that John Hoby had recovered his axe long before he was interrogated by the court. Thomas Doncaster was therefore no longer under a sentence of excommunication. Consequently, Simon directed his attention to those three witnesses who had given evidence about the abduction from the Minster: Emma Munkton, he claimed, was living scandalously with Agnes's uncle William Huntington, Gervase Rawcliff was related to her and Agnes's uncle William Huntington was the attorney in a case concerning a piece of land which William Legister had brought against Simon and Agnes before the commissary general.[73]

The final six witnesses in the case were heard for Simon on 24–26 November 1346. Two of them, Thomas Beford and Master John Brian, the registrar of the court, were officers of the court. They testified that Robert Tayergrave had been absolved from any sentence of excommunication he might be under before his deposition was heard by the court, while John Marschall testified to the general good character of Robert Tayergrave. Additional evidence about the recovery of John Hoby's axe was provided by Thomas Lonsyng, who had been present on 2 November 1346 when Simon had gone to the

---

[71] CP, E 248–14.

[72] "Cui incarcerato idem juratus solvit octo denarios predictos et eidem jurato dictus incarceratus dictam securim cum difficultate liberavit, ut dicit." CP, E 248–14.

[73] The official's commissary general had claimed jurisdiction over this case which therefore was heard at an ecclesiastical court. Simon produced two documents in the case which confirmed his claim that William de Huntington was his and Agnes's attorney in the case. CP, E 248–12, 248–13.

village of Wigington to question John Hoby about the stolen axe. The combined evidence would have removed any doubt about the admissibility of the testimony of Robert Tayergrave and Thomas Doncaster, leaving Simon free to pursue the main argument of his case: that his contract of marriage to Agnes Huntington preceded the contract with John Bristol.

Simon brought two witnesses to give evidence about an exchange of vows between Simon and Agnes "sometime between the feasts of St Michael and St Martin" 1338.[74] Both witnesses had been interrogated by the court before. John Marschall had been heard on 10 May when he had told the story of the exchange of vows between Agnes standing in her window and Simon on the ground in the neighbouring garden. He then dated this event to October 1339, after Agnes's supposed marriage to John Bristol in February 1339. The other witness, Emma Munkton – who had given evidence about Simon's abduction of Agnes to the court only eight days before – now appeared as a witness for Simon. Although Simon had thus found a witness to corroborate John's story, some adjustments had to be made to John's deposition of 10 May. Emma Munkton claimed to have been present at an exchange of vows between Simon and Agnes which took place sometime between the feasts of St Michael and St Martin eight years earlier (29 September and 11 November 1338). The circumstances surrounding this exchange of vows were almost identical to the circumstances described by John Marschall in his first deposition: Agnes was standing by her second floor window across the garden from Simon, who was at ground floor level with John Marschall, but different words were exchanged and the new vows were open to interpretation. Although presumably they were speaking about the same event, Emma and John did not hear the same words: Emma heard a reciprocal promise to marry while John Marschall reported more cautiously this time; he only heard Simon say to Agnes that he wanted her as his wife. In contrast to Emma, John did not report any reply from Agnes. Both agreed that they were the only witnesses to the exchange of vows, but Emma added that she had not heard any neighbourhood rumour about the event. Emma also added that she had heard Agnes swear that she was not married to John Bristol because their contract had been conditional and had been entered into after she and Simon engaged themselves. On 10 May John Marschall had said that he had seen Simon and Agnes contract with each other on 1 October 1339,

[74] 29 September to 11 November 1338.

but this time his memory was not as precise: he now only remembered a vague time span "between the feasts of St Michael and St Martin eight years ago" (29 September and 11 November 1338), which of course put the exchange long before any contract between John Bristol and Agnes.

These witness accounts are the last document in the surviving file. We will never know what the outcome of the case was or why the case broke off here. 26 November 1346 is too early for the litigants to have died in the plague and the procedural documents have only survived for the period before the case was transferred to the commissary general's court and therefore tell us nothing about this problem. Simon's witnesses are in no way conclusive and there is good reason to think that the case could have gone on for many more months.

It is, however, highly probable that a compromise was reached in the case. Agnes and Simon appear to have had another son, called Thomas, after the case. This Thomas owned land in Huntington, which William Huntington rented. Thomas died young, for when William Huntington died in 1362 he referred to the land as "the land in Huntington which once belonged to Thomas, son of Simon Huntington".[75] There is no mention of any member of the Huntington family called Simon in CP, E 248, nor of a son called Thomas. It is natural to expect the Simon Munkton's surname would change to Huntington if he had lived in Huntington for a large part of his life. Agnes is not heard of again, but Simon was alive in 1357 having remarried and appears to have taken up selling spices like William Huntington.[76] John Bristol died soon after the case, very possibly in the plague which hit York some nine months after the case was abandoned. In a will, proved on 15 December 1349, his father left six marks for divine service to be celebrated for himself, his wife and for "his dead boys", one of whom was the John of Bristol who wanted to marry Agnes Huntington.[77] Both William Huntington and John Bristol maintained a strong faith in the officers of the church, even after their encounters with the legal system: William Huntington left the ultimate responsibility for the sale of his house in Petergate

---

[75] "Illa terra in Huntyngton que quondam fuit Thome filii Symonis de Huntyngton, quam terram habeo ex dimmissione ad firmam ad terminum annorum." York Minster Library Dean and Chapter Probate Register, vol. 1, fos 37v-38r.

[76] W. Paley Baildon, *Feet of Fines for the County of York from 1347 to 1377. 21–51 Edward III*, Yorkshire Archaeological Society (London, 1915), p. 59.

[77] York City Archives, York memorandum book, year book fol. 11–11b.

and the use in pious deeds of the money raised in that way to the official or the commissary general "whoever they may be at the time".[78] John Bristol provided even more detailed instructions for the sale of his goods: on the death of his wife Joan, his houses were to be sold within four months by the official with the advice of two senior advocates of the court. Of the money thus realised, the official was to receive 40s. and the two advocates each 20s. If the official and advocates did not wish to perform this task, the dean and senior penitentiary of the Minster should sell the tenements and each should receive two marks of the money thus realised.[79]

The canon law of marriage was not published to protect women's property rights, but with a combination of skill and determination it could be used for that purpose. The case of Agnes Huntington and Simon Munkton shows how one woman went about the task of protecting her land from the mismanagement of her husband. But because the church courts could only intervene if it was a dispute over marriage, the parties turned it into a dispute over the legality of their marriage. Agnes Huntington sued for a divorce from Simon while, in the hope of a speedy decision over the sale, Simon approached the archbishop's court of audience to ask for a restitution of his conjugal rights. Because Simon had argued that Agnes had no legal reasons for leaving, his approach to the archbishop allowed Agnes the opportunity to delay the case for almost a year before entering into a discussion of the main point of canon law: whether she was married to another man when she married Simon. When Agnes finally presented her evidence it was weak and based on the evidence of only three witnesses, one of whom had previously told the court that he had no knowledge of a prior marriage. When Simon presented his witnesses, who would probably have been given more credence than Agnes's witnesses by the court because of their higher social status, Agnes had to revert to exceptions to the admissibility of their evidence rather than to substantive exceptions against the content of their testimony. Her case seems to have collapsed when her exceptions were shown not to be sustainable in court.

---

[78] "Et si contingat predictum Robertum sine herede de corpore suo legitime procreato in fatum decedere tunc volo quod totum predictum edificium cum suis partium per officialis curie Ebor' et eius commissarium generalem, qui pro tempore fuerunt, vendatur et quod tota pecunia inde levanda in celebratione diorum ac aliis operibus pietatis totaliter convertatur." Dean and Chapter Probate Register, vol. I, fol. 37v.

[79] York City Archives: York memorandum book, year book fol., 11b.

Litigation does not only take place in a court room and not all factors that influence the course of the litigation are documented by the courts. The historian is rarely able to gain an insight into the considerations external to the conduct of the case, such as intimidation or the possibility of a compromise, or internal to it, like a consideration of the likelihood of a favourable outcome. However, "Romeo and Juliet of Stonegate" allows exactly that. We do not have all the evidence, but enough has been left in the surviving documentation to show the constant interaction between what went on in the court room and events that took place outside the court. Agnes's original decision to litigate in York was taken because of Simon's attack on her on 25 July 1345. She would have had very little time actually to compose a plea to the official's court since the court rose for its summer recess only four days later. Because the official's court was not scheduled to meet for another seven weeks, Simon approached the archbishop's court of audience and asked to be reinstated in his marital rights, which would once again allow him to put pressure on Agnes to sell her lands in Huntington. When Simon thought that he had successfully approached the court of audience and obtained a letter from the court which ordered her to resume cohabitation, he tried to force Agnes without the aid of any officials of the court. His attempt went wrong and ended in violence in Petergate: according to several witnesses, Agnes was so badly beaten up that she required rest for an extended period of time. Through his own actions, Simon thus delayed his case, allowing several months to pass with procedural wrangling. Towards the end of January 1346, after six months' litigation, the court of audience accepted that it did not have the means to force Agnes to attend court outside the city walls and a decision was made to transfer the case to the official's court which convened in the Minster in York. The official's court was initially most interested in Simon's illegal attack on Agnes in Petergate, spending almost two and a half months investigating this before witnesses were presented about Agnes's alleged precontract with John Bristol, junior. Once again, violence preceded Agnes's appearance in court. Four days before she was due to produce her witnesses she was abducted during a Corpus Christi procession by the Minster. She appears not to have come to any actual bodily harm on this occasion, but it was clear that Simon wanted urgently to prevent the appearance of her witnesses. In the event, he was unsuccessful. As Agnes had managed to time the production of witnesses to just before the court rose for its summer recess, she gained another six weeks of relative security from Simon. Simon, however, had also produced witnesses toward the end of the court term and must therefore have been relatively untroubled by this. Instead, he seemed more unsettled by Agnes's exceptions to two of his witnesses. These exceptions raised the possibility that their evidence had been inadmissible. Agnes produced witnesses to their excommunication on 17–18 November 1346, but their depositions were weak. Simon produced the final witnesses in the case from 24–26 November 1346.

A medieval woman had few means at her disposal to protect her interests against her husband, who could appear before any secular court to alienate property under his authority, whether it had been acquired by recent purchase, originated in his own family or in the possessions brought into the marriage by his wife. Agnes Huntington's attempt to gain a divorce from her husband correctly identified the one weapon that a woman in her condition had left to protect her belongings in land. Although we have no conclusive evidence about the outcome of the case, the surviving documents bear witness to Agnes Huntington's determination and to her ability to use a legal system, which had been formulated to protect the salvation of her soul, to protect her secular interests – at least in the short term.

3

Lay Knowledge of the Law of Marriage

The previous chapter described how Agnes Huntington and Simon Munkton attempted to use the church courts for their own purposes – Simon to gain control of his wife's land and Agnes to protect her ownership of this land. It raises a number of issues about the representativeness of the case: the case *Huntington* c. *Munkton* may simply have been extraordinary or the litigants unusually well informed about the law. The rest of this book will focus on some of the questions about the laity's use of the courts suggested already. Throughout the book, individual cases will be examined. While, by necessity, these analyses may appear impressionistic since they focus only on individual cases, this method of close reading and relating the contents of the cases to the law is essential for an understanding of how the law was perceived and used by the laity in fourteenth-century England. This chapter will look at evidence of the level of knowledge of canon law among ordinary people. Litigants actively sought out the courts, and they demonstrated a knowledge of the basic rules of marriage in their use of the legal system and had faith that the courts would attempt to dispense justice evenhandedly. Later chapters will demonstrate that the qualifications of the court personnel gave the laity good reason to place their trust in the courts. It will also be shown that the laity had excellent opportunities to familiarise themselves with the law in the course of their lives and had the opportunity of receiving good legal advice should they decide to litigate.

The implementation of the canon law of marriage by the medieval church has been seen as one of the major turning points in the history of western Europe.[1] It opened up the married estate to all Christians and gave new and far-reaching powers to the individual in the choice of their partners. It provided the means to settle diputes over the validity of marriage and settled once and for all the question about the

---

[1] Michael M. Sheehan, "Marriage Theory and Practice in the Conciliar Legislation and Diocesan Statutes of Medieval England", *Mediaeval Studies,* 40 (1978), pp. 408–60.

legitimacy of offspring. It also provided fora for the populace where they might find a solution to their marital problems.[2] The teaching of the church on marriage, particularly in England, is well understood and some comparative studies of its development and application have begun to appear. The development of the canonical theory of marriage has been described by James Brundage in his magisterial monograph *Law, Sex and Christian Society*, and the development of a papal policy of marriage has been outlined in numerous studies by Charles Donahue.[3] The translation of the papal decisions on marriage into conciliar and synodal legislation in England has been described in detailed studies by Michael Sheehan,[4] while the function of the ecclesiastical courts when dealing with marriage cases has been studied by R. H. Helmholz.[5] In an article published in 1988 Sheehan argued that the ideology of marriage proposed in the ethical teaching of the medieval church since the third century, allowing former slaves to marry, had penetrated to all levels of society and that even the poorest members of society were willing to stand up for the right to marriage that was allowed them by the church. This development, he argued,

[2] The subject has accumulated a large bibliography in the last forty years. A good analytical bibliography of the literature to 1990 is found in Michael M. Sheehan and Jacqueline Murray, compilers, *Domestic Society in Medieval Europe: A Select Bibliography* (Toronto, 1990).

[3] James A. Brundage, *Law, Sex, and Christian Society*; Charles Donahue, Jr, "The Policy of Alexander the Third's Consent Theory of Marriage", in *Proceedings of the Fourth International Conference of Medieval Canon Law*, edited by Stephan Kuttner, Monumenta Iuris Canonici, 5 (Vatican City, 1976), pp. 251–81; Charles Donahue, Jr, "Proof by Witnesses in the Medieval Courts of England: An Imperfect Reception of the Learned Law", in *On the Laws and Customs of England: Essays in Honor of Samuel E. Thorne*, edited by Morris S. Arnold, Thomas A. Green, Sally A. Scully and Stephen D. White (Chapel Hill, North Carolina, 1981), pp. 127–58; Charles Donahue, Jr, "The Canon Law on the Formation of Marriage and Social Practice in the Later Middle Ages", *Journal of Family History*, 8 (1983), pp. 144–58.

[4] Michael M. Sheehan, "Theory and Practice: Marriage of the Unfree and the Poor in Medieval Society", *Mediaeval Studies*, 50 (1988), pp. 457–87; The development of the English synodal legislation which allowed the implementation of the Christian ideal of marriage is analysed in Michael M. Sheehan, "Marriage and Family in English Conciliar Legislation", in *Essays in Honour of Anton Charles Pegis*, edited by J. Reginald O'Donnell (Toronto, 1974), pp. 205–14, and in Michael M. Sheehan, "Choice of Marriage Partner in the Middle Ages: Development and Mode of Application of a Theory of Marriage", *Studies in Medieval and Renaissance History*, 1 (1978), pp. 1–33.

[5] R. H. Helmholz, *Marriage Litigation*.

had its origins not only in synodal legislation but also in the ideological indoctrination of church sermons and the establishment of a system of ecclesiastical jurisdiction which gave the church the means to enforce conformity with its ethical ideals and ensured that ordinary people were aware of the rules of canon law on marriage.[6]

These studies have concentrated on the development of a legal framework around marriage and on the way the courts understood and applied canonical doctrine. In contrast, comparatively little has been written about how these rules affected the medieval laity. In an article from the early 1970s, Michael Sheehan studied the matrimonial litigation preserved in the Ely consistory court register for the period 1374–82 and concluded that a fairly representative cross-section of the fourteenth-century Cambridgeshire population was aware of and used the court, with the possible exception of the highest status groups of that population.[7] Addressing the important question of variations in litigation patterns as a reflection of social reality, Charles Donahue investigated the marriage litigation preserved by some French courts and compared it to the litigation preserved by their English counterparts. He came to the conclusion that English parents were less successful than their French counterparts in enforcing their choice of marriage partner for their children.[8] Donahue's results were questioned by Andrew Finch, who found little support for Donahue's findings in the sources.[9] Jeremy Goldberg, on the other hand, sees the changes in litigation patterns in York as important indicators of changes in the medieval labour market.[10]

It is the purpose of this chapter to investigate another – and, it is suggested, central – problem in the exploration of the interaction of the laity and the law of marriage in the middle ages, namely the extent to which the laity who appeared before the church courts knew the

[6] Sheehan, "Marriage Theory and Practice in Conciliar Legislation"; Sheehan, "Marriage and the Unfree".

[7] Michael M. Sheehan, "The Formation and Stability of Marriage in Fourteenth-Century England: Evidence of an Ely Register", *Mediaeval Studies,* 33 (1971), pp. 228–63.

[8] Donahue, "Formation of Marriage and Social Practice".

[9] Andrew Finch, "Parental Authority and the Problem of Clandestine Marriage in the Later Middle Ages", *Law and History Review,* 8 (1990), pp. 189–204. Finch's understanding of the problem has been questioned in a robust reply by Charles Donahue, Jr, "Clandestine' Marriage in the Later Middle Ages: A Reply", *Law and History Review,* 10, (1992), pp. 315–22.

[10] P. J. P. Goldberg, *Women, Work, and Life Cycle in a Medieval Economy: Women in York and Yorkshire, c. 1300–1520* (Oxford, 1992).

law that these courts served to enact. The answer to this problem has important implications, not only for the legal historian but also for those literary scholars who study texts such as Chaucer's *Troilus and Criseyde*, in which a point of canon law can be raised as a problem in the interpretation of the text.[11] This chapter will support the conclusion H. A. Kelly drew in his discussion of *Troilus and Criseyde*: "there was an area of ambiguity about [clandestine] marriage, and it was precisely this ambiguity that Chaucer wished to exploit. He could reasonably rely on his readers from their own experience to be aware of the uncertainty that existed in all secret alliances".[12]

Two questions will be pursued in this chapter: whether a litigant could expect a favourable reception of her plea of marriage if it had been contracted with few witnesses;[13] and how the people who appeared before ecclesiastical courts applied the canon law of marriage to their own lives. To answer these questions cases have been chosen to show how litigants allegedly behaved *before* they came into contact with the courts, although, of course, some significant actions were taken as a result of the litigants' interaction with the courts.

It is natural that the documents that survive from a court illustrate the difficulties people had in applying the law to their own affairs. The rules of marriage were complex and sometimes the validity of a marriage depended on sophisticated analyses of the words and actions of the litigants. It may be that Richard Helmholz was right when he remarked that "ordinary people are simply not as careful with their words as the distinction [between a marriage contracted *verba de futuro* and *verba de presenti*] requires".[14] But even in cases that deal with the validity of marriage vows exchanged without the presence of a priest, the litigants sometimes showed a surprisingly sophisticated understanding of the law. In every case that was heard by the court in

---

[11] I refer in particular to the discussion arising from H. A. Kelly's assertion that Troilus and Criseyde were married, Henry Ansgar Kelly, *Love and Marriage in the Age of Chaucer* (Ithaca, New York, 1975), pp. 217–42, and the review of the book by Derek Brewer in "Review of Henry Ansgar Kelly, *Love and Marriage in the Age of Chaucer*", *Review of English Studies*, 28 (1977), pp. 194–97. See also David Aers, "Criseyde: Woman in Medieval Society", *Chaucer Review*, 13, (1979), pp. 177–200, reprinted in C. David Benson, ed, *Critical Essays on Chaucer's Troilus and Creseyde and his Major Early Poems* (Milton Keynes, 1991), pp. 177–200.

[12] Kelly, *Love and Marriage*, p. 240.

[13] I am using the feminine personal pronoun on purpose here: two-thirds of the eighty-eight marriage cases surviving in York were first brought before an ecclesiastical court by women.

[14] Helmholz, *Marriage Litigation*, p. 37.

York, at least one party in each case must have known something about the rules of canon law – enough to know that an exchange of promises, however ambiguous it might be, could form the basis of a litigation before a church court. Plaintiffs must also have been convinced that they had a chance of winning their case in a court of law. Otherwise it would not have been worth their while spending time and money to prosecute in York.[15]

A basic knowledge of the law is evident in all cases in the cause papers and a willingness to prosecute marriage cases is found at all levels of society. At a very basic level, *Schipyn* c. *Smyth* shows that a woman in the rural countryside had enough knowledge of canon law to assemble her case quickly and efficiently, even though she might not remember the correct formula for an exchange of marriage vows.[16] Maud Schipyn brought her case before the commissary general in November 1355, at most six weeks after an alleged exchange of vows. She claimed that she had contracted marriage with Robert Smyth on 17 October of that year. On 22 December she brought two witnesses to their union: William Theker and his wife Margaret. These two witnesses agreed about the main events that led to marriage, but Margaret's testimony contains the most detail. She had been "somewhat ill" on 17 October and had stayed home with her husband in the basement of Robert Smyth's house in Bolton Percy:

And she saw through the door of said basement how said Robert pushed and pulled the said Maud into his house towards a place which is called "Kowbos" in English, and there he attempted to know her carnally. And then the said Maud said, "*Our goddes forbode* that you should have the power to know me carnally unless you will marry me". The said Robert answered, "Behold my oath that if I take anyone to be my wife I shall take you if you will yield to me". The said Maud answered, "Behold my oath that I will be at your disposal". And the said Robert took her in his arms and threw her to the ground in "le Kowbos" and knew her carnally.[17]

This exchange of vows was even more ambiguous than that between Troilus and Criseyde. Where Criseyde answered, "I am thyn" (*Troilus*

---

[15] Only in the nine surviving *sub poena nubendi* cases can it be argued that the litigants did not know about the law at the time of their first contact with the courts. We shall see, however, that in two of these cases the litigants were clearly aware of the law *after* their encounter with the courts.

[16] *Schipyn* c. *Smith*. CP, E 70 (1355–56).

[17] "die sabbati ultimo preterito fuerunt viii septimane elapse, ipsa jurata fuit aliqualiter infirma et jacuit secrete super lecto suo in celario dicti Roberti apud Bolton

and Criseyde, iii, line 1512), Maud Schipyn answered, "Behold my oath that I will be at your disposal", but her case shows that she knew that she and Robert Smyth could contract marriage without the help of a priest. She also believed that they had contracted such a marriage, despite the ambiguous form of their exchange. Indeed, according to the rules of most English synods in the fourteenth century, any intercourse subsequent to a conditional or future contract indicated to the church that the parties waived any conditions, including the wish to postpone the legal consequences of marriage, and that the union therefore would be held to be legally binding in a court of law. Therefore Maud Schipyn assumed that her exchange of marriage vows with Robert Smyth constituted a legally valid marriage.

The rule that subsequent intercourse created the presumption that the parties had consented to marriage removed the necessity for the courts to determine whether the parties actually *had* waived the conditions in the internal forum. The courts only needed to establish that intercourse had taken place – with or without the intention to marry – before they could impose the consequences of marriage on the parties. The rule of the presumptive marriage was first formulated in England by canon 55 of Stephen Langton's provincial synod for Canterbury, from 1213 or 1214.[18]

Maud Schipyn quickly followed up her case at the court in York. It started in the month of November and lasted until some time in March the following year. There is no surviving sentence among the cause papers in York, so we cannot know whether her claim was successful, but her legal argument should have won her the case. Robert seems to have been so advised and, consequently, concentrated

---

Percy (anglice *in le boure*), et vidit per hostium dicti celarii qualiter dictus Robertus duxit et traxit dictam Matildam in domum suam ad quemdam locum (qui dicitur anglice *kowbos*) et ibi nitebatur ipsam carnaliter cognoscere. Et tunc dixit dicta Matilda, '*Our goddes forbode*, quod tu habeas potestatem me carnaliter cognoscendi, nisi tu velis me ducere in uxorem'. Qui Robertus respondit, 'Ecce fides mea, quod si aliquam ducam in uxorem meam, ducam te, si tu velis esse ad voluntatem meam'. Que Matilda respondit, 'Ecce, fides mea quod ego volo esse ad voluntatem vestram'. Et statim dictus Robertus cepit eam inter brachia sua et misit eam deorsum in *le kowbos* et cognovit [eam carn]a[li]ter." CP, E 70–6.

[18] "quia si talem fidem carnalis copula subsequatur, *ecclesia pro matrimonio hoc habebit*, et faciet tanquam matrimonium observari" [my emphasis]; Michael M. Sheehan, "Marriage Theory and Practice in the Conciliar Legislation and Diocesan Statutes of Medieval England", *Mediaeval Studies*, 40 (1978), pp. 408–60 (pp. 413, with text in n. 24, cf. also pp. 429–30).

on proving that Maud's two witnesses were somewhere else at the time of the alleged intercourse. Richard Helmholz is correct in pointing out that neither Robert Smyth nor Maud Schipyn exhibited due care over the distinction between *verba de futuro* and *verba de presenti*; but it is clear that Maud Schipyn knew that *words* could make a marriage. She may also have known that a subsequent sexual union made such a marriage legally binding. Her legal problem was that she was not careful enough to make Robert Smyth pronounce the right words and that correct vows were not consciously pronounced *in front of witnesses.*

An example of litigants' more sophisticated knowledge of the rules of canon law is found in a case from the last decade of the fourteenth century. Lovers' talk ending with two statements that were close to an exchange of promises to marry formed the basis of litigation in *Greystanes* c. *Dale*.[19] But it is clear from the depositions that, at the time of the exchange of words, the man, Thomas Dale, wished to establish a bond *de futuro* with Margaret Greystanes, who eventually sued him at the court of the bishop of Durham to have their marriage enforced. Although the witnesses did not say so, either Thomas was aware that the exchange of vows was *de futuro* or – more likely – he was subsequently forced by parental pressure to marry Emma Corry, a woman they had chosen for him. He certainly did not jeopardise his position as a spouse *de futuro* by having intercourse with Margaret Graystanes, despite the desire he expressed for her.

The case was initiated by Margaret Graystanes, who had Thomas Dale cited before the bishop of Durham in late 1394. Their case was transmitted on appeal to the court in York in early 1395. The alleged marriage had been preceded by some talk of espousal, but hardly the kind of detailed marriage negotiations which occurred in some of the cases to be investigated later. Thomas Dale had gone to the house of his uncle, Thomas Cokefield, on Sunday, 3 March 1394. There they were joined by Margaret Graystanes. But it was not until the evening when everyone had gone to bed that Thomas and Margaret had the opportunity to talk seriously about marriage. Emmota, Thomas's aunt, explained that, when night fell, Thomas and his uncle went into one bed, while she shared a bed with Margaret. But Thomas got up from his uncle's bed and came naked into their bed wearing only his

---

[19] *Greystanes* c. *Dale*, CP, E 215 (1394–95).

breeches, and there he said to Margaret:

> "By my faith, I wish that you and I had the same thing in mind!" And
> Margaret responded, "What is on your mind?" To which Thomas said, "In
> faith, the thing that I want to speak about is as far away as the width of
> two hands of a man, namely between your heart and my heart". To which
> Margaret answered, "What is in your heart?" To which Thomas answered,
> "In faith, in the future when I plan to have a wife, I intend to take you as
> my wife". To which Margaret answered, "I am an exceedingly poor wife
> for you because I do not have enough possessions to match your wealth".
> To which Thomas said, "I will make you the mistress of the goods I have,
> and [I shall teach you] to look after them if you do not know". To which
> Margaret said, "I would gladly learn". And then Thomas said, "It is a
> wonder that a man must make a woman understand such intimate things
> about his heart and will, and that he knows nothing [about the feelings] of
> the woman".[20]

Thomas and Margaret continued their conversation along these lines,
declaring their love for each other, until they finally exchanged words
that constituted a marriage by *verba de presenti*.[21] Thomas left the bed
after this exchange and they did not have intercourse that night.
Emmota Cokefield claims that intercourse took place some five weeks
later, but only once. She was the only witness to this exchange of

---

[20] "Et in nocte dictus Thomas et maritus inierunt unum lectum et ista testis et
Margareta in alium lectum. Surrexit vero Thomas predictus de lecto mariti sui et
veniebat in lectum earum nudus ... brachis suis, et dixit predicte Margarete, 'Per
fidem meam, vellem quod tu et ego essemus in uno, et eodem proposito'. Et
respondit Margareta, 'Quod est propositum vestrum?' Cui Thomas dixit, 'In fide,
propositum de quo intendo loqu[i est] in latitudine duarum palmarum hominis,
videlicet inter cor tuum et cor meum'. Cui Margareta dixit, 'Quid est in corde
vestro?' Cui Thomas respondit, 'In fide, in posterum cum intendo habere uxorem
propositum meum [est ducere te i]n uxorem'. Cui Margareta dixit, 'Sum nimis
pauper uxor pro vobis quia non habeo bona sufficentia facultatibus vestris'. Cui
Thomas dixit, 'Bonorum que habeo faciam te magistram et si nescivis [docebo te]
regulare illa'. Cui Margareta, 'Libenter addiscerem'. Et tunc dixit Thomas,
'Mirabile est, quod vir facere debet mulierem scire tam intima de corde et
voluntate suis, et quod ipse nichil sci[t de voluntate] mulieris'." CP, E 215-2.

[21] "Cui Margareta respondit: 'Ad quid sciretis plus de corde meo quam vos scitis,
quia, si intima cordis mei scrutentur et sciretis ea, in posterum me dirideretis et
declinare velitis a materia de [aspiratione] mea'. Cui Thomas dixit, 'Per fidem,
Margareta, hoc nuncquam faciam, quia, per fidem, nullam mulierem in ista patria
tantum diligo habere in uxorem sicut te, si in tanto diligeres me habere in maritum
[tuum'. Et Margareta respondit:] 'Per Christum diligo vos habere in maritum

vows which had set up a marriage by *verba de presenti*. Her husband did not testify in court. Margaret Graystanes' reply, "I am pleased to have you as my husband", is as ambiguous as Criseyde's "I am thyn", and it formed the basis for her litigation in Durham. The evidence of Emmota Cokefield with the supporting evidence of neighbourhood rumour of the existence of marriage formed the basis on which Margaret Graystanes won her case in Durham.

Thomas successfully blocked the marriage by further litigation in York. Bringing a new aspect into the case, Thomas argued that he was married to a certain Emma Corry. For, despite Thomas's assurances to the contrary, he did find another wife who was closer to him in social status only two weeks after his exchange of vows with Margaret – or his family found her for him. This time Thomas publicly entered into a marriage after negotiations had occurred and after a celebration of the engagement in Emma Corry's father's garden on 20 March 1394. The marriage settlement called for the payment of twenty marks as a dowry, and the parties swore that they did not have rights (*jus*) to any other partner. Banns were read in the parish church of Staindrop on three consecutive Sundays before marriage was celebrated in front of the doors of the church early in the morning of the Wednesday after Easter (10 April 1394). One witness added that he believed that Thomas and Emma had agreed to marry even before negotiations were initiated.

Despite its apparent legality, the witnesses were clearly aware that the marriage between Emma Corry and Thomas Dale was not without its legal problems. All three of them described the marriage negotiations of 20 March in great detail, telling the court where they took place, who was present, and that the parties' exchange of vows was guided by the chaplain John Alwent, a kinsman of Thomas. They also named a chaplain who published the banns between them – Master William Horne, a chaplain of the parish church of Stabyll – and supplied the names of the people who had witnessed the solemnisation. However, when they were pressed to answer the question of who had presided over the marriage solemnisation and at which church the

---

meum ultra omnes homines in patria ista sicut et vos me econtra'. Cui Thomas, 'Margareta dicis tu verum?' Et ipsa Margareta respondit 'Ita, in fide mei'. Cui Thomas dixit, 'Hoc vellem ego'. Cui ipsa 'In fide sic facio'. Cui dixit Thomas, 'Margareta, placet mihi, per fidem meam, habere te in uxorem meam'. Et ipsa respondit et dixit, 'Placet mihi habere te in maritum meum'. [Et postea osculabantur] multotiens." CP, E 215–2.

rites were performed, they refused to answer the court.[22] If they had named the priest and the marriage of Thomas and Margaret was declared valid, the priest who officiated over the marriage of Thomas and Emma Corry was liable to be suspended from his office. That this was not an idle threat is seen in the case of Master Ivo Lardmand, who was suspended for three years for presiding over the marriage of Peter and Katherine Hiliard.[23]

There can be little doubt that to Thomas the marriage to Emma Corry was more advantageous financially. This can be seen from Margaret Graystanes's surprised protestations when Thomas proposed to her and by her admission of her inability to look after his estate. She also initially appeared before the official in Durham without the advice of an advocate and presented her libel orally, which suggests that she was not able to pay for the advice of a proctor before initiating the case. Emma Corry, on the other hand, brought with her a dowry of twenty marks. If we are to believe the evidence of Emmota Cokefield, Thomas had waived his conditions to marriage to Margaret by having intercourse with her once and must therefore be presumed to be married to her. But her testimony was not confirmed by anyone else. Thus, if it can be assumed that the outcome of the case would be the same as in other cases in York where there was only one witness to

---

[22] The depositions of Thomas's witnesses quite clearly state that they wilfully withheld information from the court. The deposition of John Helcott reads "Non tamen vult exprimere, ut dicit, in quo loco nec in qua ecclesia huiusmodi matrimonium fuit contractum nec quis capellanus solempnizavit matrimonium predictum". The witness John Corry, who claimed not to be Emma's kinsman "having been diligently examined did not care to say" (diligenter examinatus non curat exprimere) who or where. A final witness, Henry Caberry, also refused to answer the question: "sed in quo loco vel ecclesia nec quis presbyter solempnizavit matrimonium predictum non vult deponere, ut dicit". (All three deposition are contained in CP, E 215–8). The fourteenth-century cause paper files contain no other examples of such clear refusals to say where the marriage was celebrated or by whom. The logical conclusion must be that these witnesses knew that something was wrong with the contract and were trying to protect the officiating priest who was liable to three years suspension if the marriage was deemed to be clandestine, or worse, to have been celebrated in the knowledge that there might be an outstanding marriage to be determined. Two people are likely candidates as the priest who officiated over the solemnisation: John or Adam Alwent. Both were Thomas's kinsmen, both were chaplains, and both were present at the marriage negotiations between Thomas's and Emma's parents.

[23] This punishment is in agreement with the synodal legislation in force at the time; see Sheehan, "Marriage Theory and Practice in Conciliar Legislation", pp. 427–29. For more details of this case, see below, p. 166-168.

a marriage contract, the court in York would have passed sentence for Thomas and Emma Corry. Circumstantial evidence presented before the court in Durham, however, which included three witnesses heard for Margaret, substantiated the presumption of marriage in the neighbourhood. For this reason (and presumably also because it had not heard about the marriage of Thomas and Emma), the court in Durham had held for a marriage between Thomas and Margaret Graystanes. We can only speculate about the outcome of the case since a sentence from the consistory court in York is not preserved among the cause papers. The case exhibits many irregularities: Margaret Greystanes' evidence was weak and she was unable to produce the usual two witnesses to her marriage to Thomas; on the other hand, Thomas produced witnesses whose refusal to answer the question about the officiating priest must have presented the court with a serious problem about their credibility. It may be surmised that the fact that Thomas's three witnesses refused to name the officiating priest may have undermined his case to such an extent that it was decided to abandon it before the sentence or, perhaps more likely, that some out-of-court settlement was agreed between the parties.

Graystanes c. *Dale* shows that ordinary people could have real difficulty in understanding the intricacies of canon law rules of marriage, at least before they came into closer contact with the legal system. But the litigants knew that they *could* contract marriage with their words. Thomas Dale seems to have believed that his contract with Margaret Graystanes was a contract by *verba de futuro* which could be broken in accordance with the rules of canon law. There was enough evidence, however, to support a sentence by the court of Durham in favour of marriage until Margaret Graystanes's plea was contradicted by that of Emma Corry in York.[24] It is even possible that the case was settled out of court: if the officiating priest was one of Thomas's two kinsmen he would be in grave danger of suspension. The case thus probably ended in a deadlock: Thomas's side in the case may have decided not to risk the career of one of their family to prove the solemnisation of the more advantageous marriage to Emma Corry.

---

[24] The special commissary of the bishop of Durham, Master John Hakkethorp, passed sentence for marriage between Margaret Stayndrop and Thomas Graystanes. According to the surviving *processus* sent to York by the Durham court, this sentence was based solely on the first-hand evidence of Thomas's aunt Emmota Cokefeld, and on the evidence of another witness who reported that there was neighbourhood rumour to the existence of a marriage. It was only at the appeal stage that Emma Corry claimed Thomas in marriage at the court in York.

It can be argued that a proctor who was familiar with canon law could have instructed witnesses on what to say and how to say it before they gave their testimony in these cases. Although the depositions do not usually allow us to judge whether they are actually telling the truth, there are some exceptions. Two examples will be examined here. One case recorded the immediate physical reaction of a witness, the other the testimony of a mentally retarded witness, which makes it unlikely that the witness *could* be instructed.

Margaret Foxholes, who appeared as a witness for Agnes Huntington in the phenomenally complex case preserved in *Huntington* c. *Munkton*, was clearly distressed when her employer's stepdaughter tried to force her to witness an exchange of vows with John Bristol.[25] Margaret clearly understood the implications of the actions of Agnes and John, and she was unwilling, as the events unfolded, to be used as a witness to their vows. It is significant that Margaret walked away towards Mulberry Hall halfway through the exchange of vows: she seems to have known that if she did not hear *reciprocal* vows her testimony would only support the allegation that there was neighbourhood rumour to the marriage. All three actors in this incident were clearly aware of the rule that marriage could be established without the participation of a priest, and Margaret Foxholes was keen not to be used as a pawn in the couple's conflict with Agnes's parents. Margaret's flight from the scene of the exchange of vows demonstrates that she knew that by her actions she could make her deposition less valuable to Agnes and John.

The other instance in which we can dismiss the possibility that a witness was coached is in CP, E 92 (1366–67). The witness William Bridsall demonstrated that he knew the basics of the canon law rules for marriage, despite the fact that he was "more stupid than wise", to use one witness' description of his mental capacity. William Bridsall was heard by the court as a witness for Alice Redyng, the plaintiff. By his own description he was a beggar and a day-labourer during the harvest season. According to Alice Redyng's opponent, John Boton, he was a drunkard and a beggar (*ebrius et mendicus*). William was one of two witnesses to overhear an exchange of vows *de presenti* between John de Boton, a chapman, and Alice Redyng in the village of Scamston.

Alice Redyng had brought the evidence of William Bridsall and

[25] CP, E 248 (1345–46). See Chapter 2 above.

Thomas Fouler to prove that she had exchanged vows with John on 27 December 1366. John, who was the nephew of their landlady, had been conducting a long-lasting love affair with Alice Redyng. On that particular day, the two had gone into a tannery in the house to discuss their relationship. William Bridsall overheard Alice Redyng press John for a commitment to marry her:

> "John, you should not tell me anything except what you will observe, because I have been deceived before. And if you want me as your wife, tell me". And to this John answered, "Truly, yes, I want to have you as my wife. And behold my oath: I shall take you as my wife". And then Alice said to said "John, *Placet* (or in English, "I vouchessauf") what you said then. And I want to have you as my husband". And both of them bound themselves, one to the other, to do so by their oath.[26]

Thomas Fouler overheard the same exchange standing in the door to the tannery. He added that when he and John Boton had some wine together in Scarborough only three weeks before the court appearance, John had sworn that he had had sex with Alice Redyng. On the same occasion John had attempted to make Thomas promise not to give evidence about the exchange of vows between himself and Alice. Thomas, however, had admitted this in confession, and his confessor had enjoined him to go to the court and give evidence on pain of excommunication.[27]

Legally, the case was simply about a vow to marry, contracted *verba de futuro* with subsequent intercourse. John Boton concentrated his defence on the reliability of Alice's witnesses. He claimed that William

---

[26] "Et die Sancti Johannis apostoli ... predicti Johannes et Alicia stabant infra bercariam dicti Ricardi modicum infra hostium et ipsa Alicia tunc dixit prefato Johanni: 'Johannes, non dicas mihi aliqua nisi ea quae velis servare quia ante hoc tempora ego fui decepta. Et si velis habere me in uxorem tuam, dicas mihi.' Et cui ipse Johannes respondit: 'Fideliter, sic. Volo habere te in uxorem meam et ecce fidem meam, ego ducam te in uxorem meam.' Et tunc ipsa Alicia dixit 'Johannes, placet (anglice *i vouchessauf*) quod tunc dicis. Et ego volo habere te in maritum meum.' Et uterque eorundem alteri ad hoc faciendo astrinxerunt fide sua." CP, E 92–13 (1366–67).

[27] "Dicit ulterius requisitus quod dictus Johannes Botoun die Sancti Thome ... ultimo preterito fuerunt tres septimane elapsi et iste juratus simul potaverunt vinum in quadam camera bassa infra stepta fratrum minorum de Scardeburgh' situata, sedentes super quodam lecto. Et dictus Johannes rogavit istum juratum quod non revelaret alicui verba matrimonialia in dicta bercaria, ut prefertur, per eum prolata et quod iret ad fratrem Thomam de Essay de ordine minorum pro confessione

Bridsall was not *compos mentis*. Five of John Boton's six witnesses concentrated on this issue. The witnesses disagreed about the extent to which William Bridsall was to be characterised as mentally deficient. Robert Webster, for example, said that William was a "faithful and discerning man" and that he liked an occasional drink,[28] whereas Geoffrey Raynston explained that William was "more stupid than wise" and that he had often seen him beg for bread from door to door.[29] Although they drew different conclusions about William Bridsall's reliability as a witness from the incident, these three witnesses and John, son of Ralph Pobethorp, also told the court of an occasion the previous autumn when William got so drunk that, having lost his overcoat, he had to be conducted to his home.[30] William Bridsall was thus considered to be a simpleton by every witness to his reliability. Despite this disadvantage, the court accepted his testimony that he was present at an exchange of vows.

In view of the fact that four witnesses testified that William was mentally retarded, it may be argued he was unaware he was overhearing a valid promise to marry and that he might have been instructed on how to testify. Three elements in his deposition imply that this was not the case. In the introductory preamble to his deposition (which usually told the court who the witness was, what his social position, age and income were, and that he was not a biased witness), he openly declared that he hoped that Alice would win her case "because he believes that she has justice in favour of her in her

habenda eo quod non revelaret predicta verba ... narravit sibi omnia premissa in confessione et dictus frater dixit isto jurato quod si non revelaret premissa esset excommunicatus et injunxit isto jurato quod non deberet premissa ullo modo tacere." CP, E 92–13 (1366–67).

[28] "Dicit quod Willelmus de Bridsall reputatur homo fidelis et decernis. Quod iste juratus novit in persona eiusdem Willelmi est quod est mendicus et aliquando vult inebriari. Et utrum aliunde sit mente captus vel non nescit iste juratus, ut dicit." CP, E 92–5 (1366).

[29] "Dicit quod novit Willelmum de Bridsall per aspectum corporis et reputat eum potius stultum quam sapientem quem sepius vidit ostiatim mendicare panem in parochia de Killyngtoun' sed nescit si corruptus vel informatus protulit suum testimonium in presenti causa." CP, E 92–7 (1366).

[30] "Dicit quod notorium est quod dictus Willelmus de Bridsale querit panem suum ostiatim mendicando, quem iste juratus novit per annum elapsum, et non vidit ipsum aliquam stultitiam medio tempore facere nec audivit, excepto quod fuit ita ebrius die Omnium Sanctorum ultimo preterito quod amisit armilansam suam." CP, E 92–7 (1366–67).

case".[31] In his deposition about the exchange of vows in the tannery, he was also at pains to point out that "both of them bound themselves, one to the other, *by their oath*", which shows that he knew that such an oath had an impact on the case. Finally, he claimed to have overheard another exchange of vows two days later in the garden of the house. The case is not strengthened by this event (there were no other witnesses to substantiate it). If anyone wished to instruct him in such a way as to help their case, it would have been enough to instruct him how to testify about the first exchange. Instructing him on a second exchange would have added immeasurably to the complexity of the task of instruction with no perceivable benefit to the case.

It is therefore safe to conclude that the deposition is a true expression of the way William understood canon law on marriage. He understood that marriage could be contracted by two people without the participation of a priest and that he had twice been present at an exchange of marriage vows. Whether he understood the difference between *verba de presenti* and *verba de futuro* is impossible to say from his deposition. The York consistory court never asked a witness for his or her legal opinion. Instead, depositions describe only those words or actions in the case which may have had legal consequences.

One way to avoid the uncertainty of a private exchange of vows was to make sure that a priest or notary public was present at the negotiations, or was summoned to overhear the exchange of vows. This ensured that the words used instituted the desired kind of union. A priest or notary public was called as a witness in twenty cases among the fourteenth-century cause papers. These priests and notaries prompted the parties with the words for their marriage, celebrated mass after the couple had exchanged vows, or were simply present at the subsequent wedding feast.[32]

The highly formalised marriage negotiations and the presence of a priest and an unspecified cleric found in a case from Doncaster in 1391 probably saved the innkeeper Alice Brathewell from an undesired

The witness Richard Pebete said that William Bridsall was generally sober: "excepto quod die omnium sanctorum ultimo preterito vidit eum ita ebrium quod non potuit ire solus de loco in quo fuit ad hospitium suum nisi cum auxilio istius jurati et aliorum". CP, E 92–5 (1366–67).

[31] "vellet quod optineret in causa, eo quod credit quod habet justitiam in causa pro ea". CP, E 92–13 (1367).

[32] CP, E 15, 25, 36, 62, 71, 82, 89, 102, 106, 108, 114, 126, 150, 188, 202, 211, 215, 248, 257 and 259.

marriage to William Dowson, but only just. Her case was heard in York as a *causa matrimonialis et divortii* because she claimed to have contracted a legally binding marriage to another man, this time from Pontefract, called William Roger. We will concentrate only on the events that lead to her alleged marriage to William Dowson. In court he produced two of his servants as witnesses whom Alice Brathewell claimed were lying. She conceded that she had conducted marriage negotiations with William but alleged nothing had come of them. In her defence she also argued that soon after the alleged contract she had contracted a binding marriage with William Roger. The details of the case are as follows:

William Dowson rode into Doncaster on Wednesday 11 May 1391, where he stayed at Alice Brathewell's inn. He decided that she might be the right woman to approach with a proposal of marriage, and he let his two servants, John Bukton and John Clerk of Grenhale, conduct the marriage negotiations for him. John Clerk of Doncaster, who appeared as a witness for Alice Dowson, explained to the court that:

> after dinner the said John Bukton declared to the said Alice that the said William Dowson was a very rich and fitting husband for her, inducing and enticing the said Alice to contract marriage with the said William as well as he could, when she declared that it was not her intention to have a husband within a year from the time of her husband's death.[33]

Although Alice showed an interest in continuing the negotiations, William's witnesses did not say that she agreed to marriage on this occasion. Instead, she wanted to have another meeting in which they would decide when and whether to get married. Her neighbours intervened at this point: they felt that having William stay with Alice while they were conducting marriage negotiations was not proper, so he was made to move to another house in Doncaster.[34] The neighbours' move

---

[33] "Et post cenam dictus Johannes Bukton asseruit dicte Alicie quod Willelmus Dowson predictus fuit multum dives et potens ac competens maritus pro ipsa, inducendo et allitiendo dictam Aliciam quatenus potuit ad contrahendum matrimonium cum dicto Willelmo, ipsa Alicia respondente quod non fuit intentionis sue habere maritum infra annum a tempore mortis mariti sui." CP, E 188–6 (1391).

[34] "Et ideo propter vitandi [sic] scandalum dicte Alicie predicti burgenses ville de Doncaster' fecerunt dictum Willelmum recedere de hospitio dicte Alicie et providederunt sibi in alia parte villa [sic] de hospicio aliunde, ut dicit iste juratus." CP, E 188–6 (1391).

may have been motivated by a desire to protect her from subsequent litigation. By their actions the neighbours made it much more difficult for William Dowson to argue that he and Alice Brathewell had intercourse after the marriage negotiations.

Marriage negotiations were continued on the following day in a croft belonging to Alice Brathewell, and the question of whether these negotiations ended in a marriage *per verba de presenti* or *per verba de futuro* was crucial to the outcome of the case. Alice's witness, John Clerk of Doncaster, described Alice's position to the court. John Bukton, he said, tried "in every possible way and manner he could" to persuade Alice to marry William Dowson. Although he was present, William kept in the background and let his servant conduct negotiations for him. Alice had said she was concerned about her reputation in Doncaster:

> and after great fuss had been made of the said Alice, Alice herself answered that the matrons of the village of Doncaster and her other neighbours would reproach her if she were to contract marriage so thoughtlessly to a stranger whom she did not even know before, in the presence of the said William Dowson, Master John Maltby, a chaplain, John Clerk of Grenhale, and this witness.[35]

John Clerk of Grenhale, who assisted in the negotiations for William Dowson, insisted that Alice and William had not only contracted a valid marriage on this occasion, but they had accompanied the exchange with the exchange of kisses while holding hands and that the whole party had immediately gone to Thomas Taverner's inn to drink ale. There, John Clerk of Grenhale said, Alice had admitted the existence of a contract in front of witnesses.[36] Alice argued that she

---

[35] "Et post magnam instantiam dicte Alicie factam, ipsa Alicia respondit quod matrones ville de Doncaster' et alii vicini sui multum de ea obloquerentur si ipsa contraheret matrimonium ita indeliberate cum uno extraneo cuius notitiam nuncquam prius habuit, presentibus Willelmo Dowson predicto, domino Johanne Maltby cappelano, Johanne Clerk de Grenhale et isto jurato." CP, E 188–6 (1391).

[36] "Ad primum articulum dicit quod ... in quodam stabulo infra mansum dicte Alicie in villa de Doncaster, contraxerunt dicti Ricardus et Alicia stantes sub hac forma, viro tenente mulierem per manum dexteram et dicente, 'Hic accipio te, Aliciam, in uxorem meam et ad hoc do tibi fidem meam', muliere econtrario respondente, 'Hic accipio te, Willelmum, in virum meum et ad hoc do tibi fidem meam', et traxerunt manus et osculabantur adinvicem presentibus isto jurato, Johanne Bukton, conteste suo, et Henrico Herthom. Et tunc incontinentes accesserunt ad domum Thome

had only agreed to consider the offer of marriage and told John and William that she would give her final answer six weeks hence.[37] But William and John were not satisfied with this outcome and returned later the same day to put further pressure on Alice to give an answer before the six weeks were up:

> And after a small interval of time said William Dowson and John Bukton came back after they had left and with great persistence succeeded in reducing the said term of six weeks to one month by the consent of said Alice, in the presence of this witness, John Clerk of Grenhale [and] Master John de Maltby, a chaplain, in the words of this witness.[38]

The commissary general's court in York held with Alice Brathewell and decided that a binding marriage had not been established at these negotiations. The court disregarded the depositions of William's two witnesses who said that a valid marriage had been contracted. Alice had argued that William's witnesses were unreliable since they were his servants. The court based its decision on Alice's three witnesses, one of whom was a priest and one of whom was a cleric of unspecified status.

There are therefore a number of actions which show that Alice Brathewell was familiar with canon law. Her neighbours' provision of another place for William Dowson to live during the marriage negotiations indicates that they were familiar with the rule that subsequent intercourse created a binding marriage. She lived in a neighbourhood where there was ready access to a priest and had taken the sensible precaution of employing this priest to be present when she conducted

---

Taverner, vicini sui, et biberunt cervesiam. Et ibi audivit dictam Aliciam recognoscere et fateri huiusmodi contractum matrimonialem in presentia dicti Willelmi, presentibus isto jurato, Johanne Bukton conteste suo, Henrico Herthom et aliis de quorum nominibus non recolit. Item requisitus dicit quod audivit dictum Willelmum et Aliciam tantum unica vice contrahere." CP, E 188–12 (1391).

[37] "predictus Johannes Bukton, Willelmus, et Alicia statuerunt terminum sex septimane proximo tunc sequente ad habendum finale [sic] responsum ipsius Alicie de matrimonio inter dictum Willelmum et Aliciam contrahendo". CP, E 188–6 (1391).

[38] "Et post modicum temporis intervallum dictus Willelmus Dowson et Johannes Bukton – post recessum ipsorum – redierunt et cum magna instantia dictum terminum sex septimanarum de consensu dicte Alicie usque ad unam mensem abreviari optinuerunt, presentibus isto jurato, Johanne Clerk de Grenhale, domino Johanne de Maltby, cappelano, ut dicit." CP, E 188–6 (1391).

her marriage negotiations. In the end, her precautions saved her from a marriage she did not want.

So far, cases have been chosen to demonstrate that the litigants had a knowledge of the basic facts of canon law rules of marriage. Both litigants and witnesses knew that words could establish a marriage, and they also knew that the quality of the words affected their legal consequences. But some litigants showed a more sophisticated under-standing and attempted to use the law for their own ends. Two cases will be considered, each demonstrating a different use of the law. One case shows that the plaintiff had an awareness that the rules regarding consanguinity could be used to procure an annulment of his marriage because he had had intercourse with his wife's cousin, the other shows an unusual and original solution to the problem of how to promise to marry a woman only if she conceived a child.

Some cases appear to have been initiated out of a wish simply to end a relationship that one of the partners no longer wished to continue, supporting Brewer's impression of the impermanence of marriage in the fourteenth century. But all of these cases show that the litigants were aware of the rules determining when a marriage was legally binding. Various stratagems were employed. One of the more sophisticated arguments employed was to use a previous affair with a kinsman of the present spouse as an excuse for annulment of the present marriage. In CP, E 33 there was ample proof of previous sexual intercourse between the defendant, John Boton, son of John Carthorp, and a certain Mariota Lasci, the second cousin of the plain-tiff, Johanna, daughter of Peter Acclum. The witnesses, who were all in their forties, agreed that there had been intercourse on several occasions between John and Mariota before John had contracted marriage with Johanna. Margaret Cloghton explained that the relationship between John and Mariota had lasted for more than a year and that they had been given a penance for this by their confessor. She clarified the nature of the relationship by saying that John: "often, whenever he wanted to, willingly knew her [Mariota] carnally as if he held her in concubinage".[39] All four witnesses heard

---

[39] The Latin text of the witness account implies that they shared a common confessor: "Requisita qualiter scit quod adinvicem carnaliter commiscuerunt dictis diebus lune et martis horis predictis dicit quod vidit eos adinvicem carnaliter commiscentes et ideo penitentia fuerat sibi ministrata a confessore suo. Et sepius pro libito voluntatis sui quandocumque voluerit eam carnaliter cognovit quasi eam tenuit in concubinatum per annum et amplius." CP, E 33–1 (1337).

in the case confirmed the consanguinity between Mariota and Johanna. Most of the witnesses added that Mariota was alive at least some time after the marriage between Johanna and John. A sentence does not survive in this case.

By far the most spectacular attempt to circumvent the spirit while remaining true to the letter of the law was performed by Robert Midelton of Bishop Burton around 1349. The case, which has the number CP, E 79, was first heard by the York consistory court in late November 1358. Alice Welewyk appeared before the commissary general claiming that nine years earlier she had contracted marriage by *verba de futuro* with Robert Midelton, son of the late Henry Midelton of Bishop Burton, that they had had intercourse, and that she had borne Robert Midelton a child. Robert de Midelton claimed to have contracted marriage with Elizabeth Frothyngham with proper rites and with preceding marriage negotiations eight years before the case was heard in York. Alice Welewyk produced two witnesses to her claim that her marriage to Robert was prior to that of Robert and Elizabeth. The two witnesses confirmed the existence of an unusual conditional oath of marriage, but only one of them had been present at the actual exchange.[40] The other witness reported events that took place a year later when Robert ended his relationship to Alice Welewyk.

Alice Harpham explained that, during her term of service to Alice Welewyk nine years earlier, Robert had frequently come to their house to implore Alice de Welewyk to let him have intercourse with her but Alice had always refused him. She would only consent to have intercourse with him if he made her a guarantee that he would marry her.[41] Robert was not prepared to give that assurance. He wanted to

---

[40] Alice's claim to have married Robert appears to have been true, even though the court held against her: Robert appeared before the court three weeks after the official passed sentence for Robert and Elizabeth Frothyngham's marriage and swore to the truth of Alice's allegations.

[41] "Ac eadem Alicia semper quando ipsi simul loquebantur de dicta materia, quotiens cumque ista testis audivit, semper [sic] respondebat sibi dicens quod ipsa noluit permittere eum ipsam carnaliter cognoscere nisi primo faceret sibi securitatem quod eam deberet ducere in uxorem. Et bene recolit, ut dicit, quod quodam die dicti temporis intermedii, videlicet in die lune proxime post diem dominicam in ramis palmarum proximo futuro erunt novem anni elapsi, predictus Robertus in modo quo prefertur fecit et loquebatur predicte Alicie in domo sua supradicta, situata in vico vocatur *Estgate* Beverl' et ipsa Alicia eodem modo respondebat sibi in modo quo prefertur dicens se nolle permittere ipsum Robertum eam carnaliter

determine whether they could have children before he exchanged vows with her. Demonstrating that he had a detailed knowledge of the canon law about marriage and displaying considerable cleverness in circumventing it, he explained that, because he wanted to make sure that she could conceive by him, he could not promise to marry her. If they exchanged a conditional vow before they had sex, they would be married as soon as they had intercourse regardless of any condition they included their vows. Instead, he suggested that he make the promise to someone else.[42] Alice agreed to this and called her servant to her to receive Robert's oath to marry.

Robert's and Alice's relationship lasted for just under a year. During that year Robert had met Elizabeth Frothyngham and initiated marriage negotiations with her family. The family was unquestionably wealthy: the marriage negotiations took place in Hamadus de Frothyngham's private chapel in the village of Frysmersk, and the solemnisation of the marriage three weeks later with more than one hundred guests was known about in all neighbouring villages.[43] The witnesses do not say how long it took for the parties to agree on a marriage contract, but – judging by Hamadus Frothyngham's relief when he finally sent for a chaplain – the negotiations were arduous. The parties came to an agreement on 2 March 1351. As in most other cases, the witnesses are silent on the contents of the contract: the court was satisfied to know about circumstances of the vows and the

cognoscere nisi faceret sibi primo securitatem quod eam duceret in uxorem. Ac idem Robertus incontinenti respondebat sibi dicens in hunc modum, 'Ego nollem ducere te in uxorem nisi scirem quod tu poteris de me concipere prolem et habere, et ideo si tu vis permittere me tecum coire [et con]tingat me prolem de te suscitare, pro certo volo te tunc ducere in uxorem et super hoc volo facere securitatem." CP, E 79 (1358–60).

[42] "'Sed etiam hec [nolo] facere ad presens, quia, si sic facerem et me tibi obligarem in forma qua prefertur, statim prima nocte postquam [te] cognovero deberes esse uxor mea licet prolem nuncquam conceperis et ideo volo facere securitatem [cum] alii cui volueris sed non tibi', ad quod dicta Alicia respondebat dicens se fuisse contenta." CP, E 79–12 (1358–60).

[43] The witness Richard de Wynestede explained this when asked how he knew that they had married: "Et hoc scit non quia interfuit, ut dicit, sed quia dicta solempnizatio fuit ita solempniter et notorie facta in presentia quamplurimi centum hominum quod non potuit alicui existenti in [dicta] villa vel in aliis villis propinque vicinis latere. Et istemet testis, ut dicit, fuit tunc presens in quadam villa vocata Wynestede que vix distat a dicta villa de Frysmersk' ad spatium unius miliarii." CP, E 79–13 (1358–60).

words that were used to finalise it.[44] Although this exchange of vows
had created a valid union which did not need to be confirmed, the
marriage was solemnised three weeks later in the parish church of
Frysmersk, after the publication of banns on three consecutive
Sundays in the parishes of Frysmersk and Burton. Alice seems to have
been present on at least one of these occasions, but she did not then
object to the marriage.

Alice's silence had been secured beforehand. According to William
Wetewang, a canon and the master of the hospital of St Giles in
Beverley, Robert and Alice had come to see him there on an unspeci-
fied day before Robert was due to solemnise his marriage to Elizabeth
Frothyngham. Robert was clearly in an apologetic mood and soon
began to speak:

> "Master William, we come to you as the best friend Alice has here apart
> from the prior of Warter, her kinsman. And you must know that I am very
> indebted to her for various reasons and therefore want to help her with my
> goods, as the agreement was between me and her. I will recite this agree-
> ment before you and see if you and she still will consent". To which this
> witness answered in this way: "Robert, certainly you are very indebted to
> her if it is like what I heard, because it has been said to me that previously
> you promised that you should take her as your wife if it happened that she
> conceived by you – as indeed she did – and that you knew her carnally,
> and that in her presence you gave your pledge to Alice de Harpham, who
> was her servant then, that you would have done these things under that
> condition which has now been met."[45]

Robert did not contradict William about his obligation to marry Alice.

---

[44] Et habito consensu mutuo inter eos tandem, istemet testis misit pro quodam
capellano, vocato domino Ricardo de Wynestede, ut eosdem Robertum et Elizabetham simul affidaret. Qui quidem dominus Robertus statim postquam ibi venerat
et intellexerat causam adventus sui, informavit dictas personas per que verba ipsi
seinvicem mutue affidarunt, dicentes in hunc modum. Primo predictus Robertus, ad
informationem dicti capellani, dixit sic: 'Ego accipio te Elizabetham in uxorem
meam tenendam et habendam usque ad finem vite mee, et ad hoc do tibi fidem
meam', ac ipsa Elizabetha eodem modo respondebat sibi dicens, 'Hic accipio te
Robertum in virum meum tenendum et habendum quousque mors nos seperaverit,
et ad hoc do tibi fidem meam'." CP, E 79–13 (1358–60).

[45] "'Domine Willelme, nos venimus hic ad vos tanquam ad meliorem amicum quem
ista Alicia habet in istis [partibus] preter priorem de Wartr', consanguineum ipsius
Alicie. Et debetis scire quod ego sum multum obligatus sibi ex diversis causis et
ideo volo iuuare eam cum bonis meis prout est conventum inter me et ipsam,
quam quidem contentionem volo recitare coram vobis et videre si vos et ipsa adhuc

In fact, he seemed genuinely distressed and promised to compensate her financially. The negotiations about this compensation took place between Robert and William while Alice was silently present in the room. In the end they agreed that Robert should pay her twelve silver marks over the next year. William commented that he did not know for sure why it was so important to Robert to make this covenant with Alice, but he believed that it was to make sure that Alice did not object to his marriage to Elizabeth Frothyngham.[46]

Both judges who heard the case ruled against Alice Welewyk. The evidence produced by Robert Midelton presented a convincing case: he was able to produce three witnesses to his marriage negotiations with Elizabeth Frothyngham, one of whom was the cleric who guided their exchange of marriage vows after marriage negotiations. But appearances were deceptive: although two judges had passed sentence in favour of Robert and Elizabeth's marriage, and although Elizabeth and Robert had five children, Alice persisted and appealed the case to the Apostolic See. Before the case could be transmitted to the Roman *Curia*, Robert was called to testify before the court in York and acknowledged the validity of his marriage to Alice Welewyk. A memorandum, dated 14 October 1359, was attached to the case reporting that he had confessed to an exchange of vows with Alice Harpham, subsequent intercourse, and the birth of his child by Alice Welewyk before his contract with Elizabeth.[47] Despite this admission,

velitis et velit consentire.' Cui iste testis respondit in hunc modum: 'Roberte, pro certo, si ita sit prout audivi dici, tu multis es obligatus sibi, quia dictum fuit michi quod tu ante hoc tempus promisisti quod tu deberes ipsam Aliciam ducere in uxorem, si contingeret eam de te prolem concipere – prout revera fecit – et quod tu, post huius promissionem, ipsam carnaliter cognovisti, et quod tu dedisti fidem tuam Alicie de Harpham, tunc servienti sue, in presentia sua, quod tu deberes premissa fecisse sub predicta conditione, que iam est impleta, ut dicitur'." CP, E 79–12 (1358–60).

I have used the English word "friend" for *amicus* in this translation, since Robert Midelton clearly distinguished between Alice's *consanguineus*, the prior of Wartre and her *amicus*, William de Wetewang.

[46] "Sed ob quam causam ista fecit sibi promissione pro certo nescit deponere iste testis, ut dicit, ... ibidem aliquam causa ibidem [sic] exprimere nisi quia dixit se multum teneri ipsi ... stia sua quod ipse predictam promissionem fecit illa de causa ne ipsa Alicia aliquomodo ... pnizationi matrimoniali quam fecit fieri inter ipsum et Elizabeth de Frothyngham." CP, E 79–12 (1358–60).

[47] "Memorandum quod xiiiito die octobris anno domini millesimo cccmo lixmo Robertus de Midelton de Burton, juratus et ex officio per dominum officialem curie Eboracensis interrogatus, fuit solutus a quocumque contractu matrimoniali

the court passed sentence in favour of the marriage of Elizabeth Frothyngham on 11 December 1359. The case was eventually appealed to the Apostolic See.

Robert's behaviour demonstrates that he had a sophisticated understanding of canon law. His legal summation was impeccable and shows that he was aware of that rule which Robert Smyth, the defendant in *Schipyn* c. *Smyth* had not known, according to which subsequent intercourse made a conditional marriage binding and made a marriage *de futuro* into a legally binding marriage.[48] He was able to devise a way of avoiding the consequences of intercourse which was logically, if not legally, sound. It is worth adding that Robert's solution seems to be unique to him: it does not appear to have been discussed in any contemporary treatises on the canon law of marriage. Robert Midelton must have had his reasons for his actions, but it is clear that he tried to do the right thing by Alice when he separated from her nine years earlier: he certainly did so when he confessed to his marriage to Alice after winning his case in the first instance at the consistory court in York. Robert had one child by Alice, and this child stood to inherit after Alice and Robert if the marriage could be shown to have been valid at the time of its birth. She was obviously willing and able to let her case be tested by the Apostolic See, so presumably she also had money to pay for this litigation. But Elizabeth Frothyngham had clearly been worth the effort of the arduous marriage negotiations: the scale of marriage celebrations mentioned by the witness Robert Wynestede, the bribe of twelve marks paid for Alice Welewyk's silence, and the insecurity that Robert Midelton must have felt for the nine years he was married to Elizabeth Frothyngham all point to that conclusion. We can only guess at his reasons for this unusual arrangement, but the wealth of Elizabeth's family must have played at least some part in Robert's decision to marry her.

---

cum Elizabete, de quo in articulis memoratur, vel alia quacumque. Dixit in juramento suo quod promisit, Alicia de Harpham media, quod contraheret matrimonium cum Alicia de Welewyke in presentia eiusdem Alicia de Welewyke in eventu quod cognosceret carnaliter dictam Aliciam de Welewyke et de ea prolem suscitaret, prout in depositione eiusdem Alicia probatur. Et [dicit] in juramento suo quod ipsam Aliciam de Welewyke carnaliter cognovit et de ea prolem suscitavit, ut firmiter credit, antequam contraxit matrimonium cum qua nunc stat matrimonialiter copulatus, sed de forma contractus cum dicta Alicia de Harpham vel de verbis inter eosdem tunc prolatis non recolit, ut dicit." CP, E 79–8b (1358–60).

[48] CP, E 70 (1355–56).

The litigants in the surviving fourteenth-century York marriage cases sometimes displayed a surprisingly informed knowledge of the canon law rules of marriage. Unclear replies to expressions of an intention to marry, however, such as "it pleases me to have you as my husband" or "behold my oath that I shall be at your disposal", could and did form the basis of litigation at the courts in fourteenth-century York. Through these analyses of the marriage cases, it can be seen that the cases can be more complex than has been hitherto presumed. There is evidence that the laity knew the basic canon law rules of marriage well and that these rules were used proactively to initiate, legalise and sometimes dissolve marriages among the laity. At a basic level this means that there was a clear understanding even among those members of the laity we would least expect to know canon law. The examples of the mentally retarded beggar William Bridsall (*Redyng* c. *Boton*)[49] and the servant Margaret Foxholes (*Huntington* c. *Munkton*)[50] demonstrate in different ways that they knew that words could establish a marriage without the presence of a priest. Margaret Foxholes tried to leave her mistress's daughter in "the Sandhous" in York so that she would not overhear the daughter's exchange of vows with a man to whom she knew her mistress objected. William Bridsall overheard two exchanges of vows and, before he gave evidence to the court, he eagerly informed the court that he believed that the plaintiff, Alice Redyng, had justice on her side.

At an increasing level of sophistication is the use of the courts by Maud Schipyn in *Schipyn* c. *Smith*,[51] who assembled her case in less than six weeks, and by Margaret Graystanes and Thomas Dale.[52] Margaret Graystanes argued a case that really revolved around the use of the words "placet mihi habere te", while Thomas's witnesses appear to have been aware of the illegality of the actions of the unidentified priest who presided over the solemnisation of his subsequent marriage to Emma Corry. But the most sophisticated in his understanding of the law was Robert Midelton in *Welewyk* c. *Midelton and Frothyngham* who promised to marry only if a sexual union proved to be fertile.[53] His knowledge and exposition of the law was as clear as his solution to the problem of how to make such a promise was ingenious.

---

[49] CP, E 92.
[50] CP, E 248.
[51] CP, E 70.
[52] CP, E 215.
[53] CP, E 79.

An important question of interest to both legal and social historians has been left unanswered: how representative were these cases of the average person's experience of marriage? Although the York material contains cases which were initiated by people from all areas of life and from all classes of medieval society, a systematic analysis of the social setting of the court will be undertaken later in Chapter 9. That chapter sets out to answer questions such as who the individuals who litigated at court were and which factors – geographical, economic, or cultural – influenced the decision to litigate. However, in consequence of the results of the investigation in this chapter, it is first necessary to question where the litigants and the witnesses who appeared before the archbishop's court acquired their knowledge of canon law. In the meantime, it may still be concluded that, among the people who appeared before the court of the archbishop in York in the fourteenth century, there existed some understanding of the canon law rules of marriage and a willingness to use the courts. We may also conclude that, once they had initiated contact with the courts, litigants knew how to argue and present their case in accordance with the rules of canon law to attempt to obtain a sentence which would be favourable to their case. We may also conclude that unclear promises to marry, like the one found in Chaucer's *Troilus and Criseyde*, could and did form the basis of litigation in the church courts of Chaucer's own time, and that a contemporary audience, regardless of their status, would understand the matrimonial character of such vows.

4

Lawyers in the Northern Province

It is not surprising that the members of the laity in fourteenth-century northern England should exhibit such a familiarity with the law and with legal procedure. Since the earliest years of Christianity, bishops had been charged with looking after their flock's wellbeing. Not only were they to administer the sacraments to them, they were also to teach the Gospels and were charged with settling disputes touching the spiritual health of their congregation. As one of their duties, bishops also had to educate the laity in the basic rules of Christian life, and, as time passed, marriage became a central issue in this teaching. Likewise, as the duties of the office of bishop became more numerous, the bishop's household began to develop specialised offices to take care of an increasing number of the bishop's duties and by the fourteenth century a host of officers ensured that the diocese could continue running even in the bishop's absence.

Synodal legislation provided ample opportunity for the laity to become acquainted with canon law rules of marriage and the church's teaching on the matter. Despite some of the early Church Fathers' hostility to the married state, the medieval church encouraged Christians to marry and taught that the married state was an honourable state. Although there were many written texts which dealt with the honour of marriage,[1] the laity probably received most of their knowledge of canon law from other sources, particularly through the instruction of their parish priests or from their confessors. Sermons on the wedding in Cana, which were part of the liturgical year, and *ad status* sermons (sermons preached to particular congregations of people) aimed at married people were specifically meant for the ears of the congregation. They provide some insight into the attitudes to marriage that the church wanted to encourage.[2] Such sermons, however,

---

[1] Jean Leclercq, *Monks on Marriage: A Twelfth-Century View* (New York, 1981), pp. 26–85.

[2] The study of marriage sermons is still in its early stages. See the analysis of a number of *ad status* sermons in D. L. d'Avray and M. L. Tausche, "Marriage,

concerned the state of marriage and rarely touched upon the subject of how one entered that condition, so an alternative means of instruction for would-be spouses was probably available. On the parish level the priest was required by most English medieval synods to instruct his parishioners in the creed, the seven deadly sins, and the seven sacraments of the church, one of which, of course, was marriage. This instruction was presumably seen as an efficient means of acquainting the laity with the rules for marriage. A reasonable level of knowledge of the canonical impediments to marriage among the laity was necessary if the marriage banns were to be effective in identifying obstacles to proposed marriages as these obstacles had been identified in 4 Lateran 51 (1215).[3] Though already a part – and probably a well-known part – of English synodal legislation as early as 1329,[4] the need to explain the rules of 4 Lateran 51 to the congregation in the vernacular on several solemn days was first emphasised in the diocese of York by the constitutions of Archbishop John Thoresby in 1361.[5] Without such instruction of the laity by the parish priest the church could not have expected reliable results from the publication of marriage banns. It is clear that the banns were, if not feared, then at least identified by the cause paper litigants as a potential stumbling-block to their marriage plans. Thus Robert Midelton, the defendant in *Welewyk* c. *Midelton*, offered Alice Welewyk a settlement of twelve marks to ensure her silence during the reading of the banns between

sermons in *Ad Status* Collections of the Central Middle Ages", *Archives d'histoire doctrinale et literaire du moyen âge* (1981), pp. 71–119; D. L. d'Avray, "The Gospel of the Marriage Feast of Cana and Marriage Preaching in France", in *The Bible in the Medieval World: Essays in Honour of Beryl Smalley*, edited by Katherine Walsh and Diana Wood, Studies in Church History (Oxford, 1985), pp. 207–24; Nicole Bériou and David L. d'Avray, "Henry of Provins, OP's Comparison of the Dominican and Franciscan Orders with the 'Order' of Matrimony", *Archivum Fratrum Praedicatorum*, 49 (1979), pp. 513–17 A full survey of marriage sermons on the text of John 2:1, which d'Avray and Tausche identified as possibly the most important source for the attitudes to marriage that the church wanted to communicate to the laity, still has not been undertaken.

[3] António García y García, ed, *Constitutiones concilii quarti Lateranensis una cum commentariis glossatorum*, Monumenta Iuris Canonici, Series Glossatorum, 2 (Città de Vaticano, 1981), p. 91.

[4] Council of London (1329), c. 12, in David Wilkins, *Concilia magna Britanniae et Hiberniae a synodo Verolamiensi AD CCCCXLIV ad Londinensem AD MDC*, ii (London, 1737).

[5] Michael M. Sheehan, "Marriage Theory and Practice in the Conciliar Legislation and Diocesan Statutes of Medieval England", *Mediaeval Studies*, 40 (1978), p. 439.

him and Elizabeth Frothyngham, while the reading of the banns in the case of *Hiliard* c. *Hiliard* seemed to be performed in a way that was designed to prevent any objection being raised on that occasion. Likewise, in *Greystanes* c. *Dale* the witnesses heard for the marriage of Emma Corry and Thomas Dale proudly announced that the banns were successfully published, though they were less forthcoming on the subject of when, where and by whom the marriage had been solemnised.[6]

Synodal legislation instructed the parish priest to teach their congregation the exact words that were to be used to contract marriage, both in English and in French,[7] and most of the cause papers contain exchanges in the standard canonical form. It is clear that Elizabeth Lovell and Thomas Marton knew of the canonical formula and tried to use it to establish a binding marriage.[8] Although they failed by mistakenly using the formula that created an engagement, they repeated their vows using the correct words as soon as their mistake was pointed out to them by his confessors. Agnes Huntingdon tried to establish a union with John Bristol in *Huntington* c. *Munkton* using words that were recited without hesitation, almost in defiance the rebuke she had earlier received from Margaret Foxholes. All three of the actors in the situation she outlined to the court were acutely aware of the implications of the words used. Robert Midelton and Elizabeth Frothyngham were instructed how to go about their *sponsalia* by a priest who was called especially for that purpose. Katherine and John Hiliard exchanged their vows in a church in the presence of a priest, who presumably was one of the men behind the somewhat unusual arrangements surrounding the ceremony.[9]

Another opportunity for the laity to learn the church's doctrine of marriage was provided by the act of confession. In three of the cause paper files the confessional played a major part in the progress of the case. Interestingly, two out of three involved confession to a friar rather than to a parish priest. In the case of *Lovell* c. *Marton*, Thomas Marton was informed "by his confessors, the friars", that his first exchange of vows with Elizabeth Lovell was not legally binding

---

[6] CP, E 215 (1392).

[7] Michael M. Sheehan, "Marriage and Family in English Conciliar Legislation", in *Essays in Honour of Anton Charles Pegis*, edited by J. Reginald O'Donnell (Toronto, 1974), p. 445. French was still the language preferred by the English nobility.

[8] *Lovell* c. *Marton*. CP, E 18 (1327). See below, p. 115

[9] See below, p. 166 - 169

without further actions. Thomas's confessor chose to instruct him in the correct words to create a fully binding marriage, rather than telling him that subsequent intercourse created a *matrimonium presumptum*, which, though it carried the full legal implications of a marriage in this world, did not create a full canonical marriage in the eyes of God.[10] In *Redyng c. Boton*, the witness Thomas Fouler was instructed by his confessor that he could not remain a member of the church if he did not testify to the church court about his knowledge of the existence of a marriage between Alice Redyng and John Boton.[11] The final case is a little more complex: in *Paynell c. Cantilupe*, Katherine Paynell was instructed by her father's chaplain that she would have to wait before she could bring her case of impotence to the court in Lincoln.[12] The decision to proceed with the case was made in her internal forum (her *foro conscientie*), which may have meant that *she* made up her own mind to proceed, but which can also be taken to mean that she was instructed to do so by her (unnamed) confessor.

A final source of knowledge of the canon law rules of marriage among the laity was the courts themselves. In some cases the litigants received their knowledge from previous encounters with the courts. This is certainly the case in all the *sub poena nubendi* cases – cases where habitual fornicators were required to swear an oath that the next time they had intercourse they would be *ipso facto* married. In these cases the imposition of a sentence of abjuration *sub poena nubendi* simply would not make sense unless the parties were instructed in the significance of the oath they were required to swear before the court. There could be some doubt as to the correct understanding of the oath, as is demonstrated by the fact that, in the case *Stry c. Rowth* (1372), the court in York allowed at least one litigant to use, as the basis of his appeal, the argument that his oath was not an oath that he would be married if he subsequently had intercourse but an agreement to be whipped around the church and market in Beverley.[13] Hugh Stry's understanding of the oath was eventually shown to be wrong, but only after a transcript of the acts of the court

---

[10] James A. Brundage, *Law, Sex, and Christian Society in Medieval Europe* (Chicago, 1987), pp. 299, 354, 412–13, 436, 502, 515–16; Sheehan, "Marriage Theory and Practice in Conciliar Legislation", pp. 429–30.

[11] CP, E 92 (1366) .

[12] CP, E 259 (1368).

[13] CP, E 114. See below p. .

in Beverley showed that he had in fact sworn the standard abjuration *sub poena nubendi*. It says something for his legal training (or his legal advice) that he immediately switched his defence and won the appeal on a defence of pre-contract. Alice Partrik, the plaintiff in *Partrik* c. *Marriot*, had also understood the implications of her abjuration, but her ruse to force her lover to marry her was ineffective when he refused to have intercourse with her in circumstances where she could produce witnesses to their union.[14] He had presumably also understood the implications of the sentence passed against him in his previous court appearance.

A further suggestion made below is somewhat controversial. The case of *Palmer* c. *de Brunne and Southbrunne* seems to indicate that the courts might instruct individual members of the laity on how to obtain an annulment when their marriages were clearly beyond repair.[15] Such action by the courts was strictly uncanonical and contrary to the law. But a strong impression is created by the facts of this and other cases in the cause paper material that individual members of the court would turn a blind eye to fraudulent claims.[16] However intriguing such activities may be, the cause paper files do not allow us to confirm that they actually did take place: the essence of a fraudulent claim is that it must be presented to the court in such a way that it looks like a real claim.

The litigants thus appear to have been well aware of the possibilities that the law opened for them. They must also have had some reason to believe that their cases would receive a sympathetic treatment in the courts. This reason, it may be suggested, was the quality of the personnel of the courts, who were well trained in law and procedure and familiar with the intricacies of the law. Although the laity sought the arbitration of the bishop, by the fourteenth century most cases were not heard by the bishop in person. Instead, in step with the increasing responsibilities of the episcopate, his *familia* had developed a number of independent offices. For the performance of mass in the

---

[14] CP, E 211 (1394). See below, p. .

[15] CP E 25 (1333). See below p. .

[16] See *Garthe and Newton* c. *Waghen* in which Agnes Waghen, the daughter of William Cawood (one of the proctors of the court of York) was claimed in marriage by two men: that case took less than a month from beginning to end and involved three witnesses who testified that one of the men exchanged the bare minimum of words necessary to create the marriage bond with Agnes and testified to the exchange of a ring. The other man does not seem to have produced any witnesses. CP, E 245 (1391).

bishop's absence there was the cathedral chapter and for the administration of the diocese in the bishop's absence there were auxiliary, or
suffragan, bishops. The chapter also elected a new incumbent when a
bishop died. The chapter was therefore particularly active *sede vacante*
when it took over the daily running of the diocese until the new
incumbent had received his *pallium*. Whether the bishop was in
residence or not, the chapter usually kept very good records, as they
had to answer to him for their administration, but only one fragment
of the fourteenth-century York chapter act books survives to this day.
Among the bishop's other officers were the archdeacons, who looked
after various aspects of his duties during the bishop's pleasure.
Deacons did not have a specified remit in all dioceses in Europe.
Instead, their letters of appointment listed their duties. In England
archdeacons were often found in the bishop's central administration or
administrating large geographical areas for the bishop. The bishop's
chancellor was another office developed in the high middle ages. He
was the secretary of the bishop and the keeper of his seal. The
chancellor also often presided over the bishop's special court of
audience. The bishop also had a vicar general, his vicar "in a general
way". He was given his powers by the authority of the bishop, who
also determined the extent of these powers. There was a tendency to
appoint the vicar general for a long period of time by the fourteenth
century.

By the fourteenth century the offices of the ecclesiastical courts had
been fixed and bishops' households across Europe contained more or
less the same officers. In York, Archbishop Greenfield issued a series of
statutes for the *Curia Eboracensis* in 1311 which put an upper limit to
the number of officers of the court and fixed the cost of litigation.
With regard to the personnel of the consistory court, Archbishop
Greenfield decreed that there should be two examiners,[17] twelve
advocates, eight proctors, six notaries and one registrar.[18] Added to

---

[17] One of these was to be the official's commissary general, the other was an unspecified *clericus ad registrum curiae conservandum*. The wording of this section of the
statutes allows the interpretation that the examiner general was identical to the
registrar. There is no firm evidence that the two offices were separated until the
middle of the fifteenth century. K. F. Burns, "The Medieval Courts", vol. 1 of
"The Administrative System of the Ecclesiastical Courts in the Diocese and
Province of York", unpublished manuscript, Leverhulme Research Scheme (York,
1962), p. 101.

[18] There is no distinction made between duties of the proctors and the notaries
public. They are simply mentioned together in the same sentence: "In eodem

these was an unspecified number of clerks to write up documents and depositions.

One of the examiners was always the official's commissary general while the other – the examiner general – was appointed among the members of the court. The two examiners conducted interrogations of witnesses in court or out of court in the witnesses' home parish. Normally, they were not to be paid more than 12d. per witness examined, but if the litigants had handed in articles of excessive length, the examiners were allowed to charge 1d. for every twelve lines of deposition taken down. The charge for copies of these or other documents was 1d. for every twenty-four lines.[19] The examiners' fee was to be waived if the litigant for whom they performed the examination was a pauper or a "miserable person".[20] The examiners often served a double function as examiners of witnesses and as judges – although the examiner general served as a judge less frequently than the commissary general. Since the examiner general's commission did not include judicial powers he needed to receive a special mandate to deputise for the official or commissary general in a specific case, or a general mandate to hear cases during their absence or during their pleasure.[21] The office of the examiner general fell into disuse in the 1430s, perhaps due to the falling volume of court business in that century. But during the fourteenth century the examiner general and the commissary general for the most part divided the work of the court between them so that the examiner general conducted the examination of witnesses while the commissary general gave the judgment.

The office of the bishop's official had developed rather slowly, but by the thirteenth century the institution had taken its final form. The office of the official developed because the canon law became increasingly complex in the twelfth and thirteenth centuries. The official's role was defined in his letters of appointment. His main function was to help the bishop avoid hearing "quarrels". Such minor disputes were

autem consistorio octo procuratores, et sex notarios duntaxat esse volumus, juxta praesedentis arbitrium assumendos", Wilkins, *Concilia magna*, ii, p. 410. The duties of the proctors are outlined later in the statutes, but the notaries are not mentioned again.

[19] Each line was to be written in a clear legible hand, ten inches long and with adequate spacing between the lines, ibid.

[20] Ibid. Compare Brian Tierney, *Medieval Poor Law: A Sketch of Canonical Theory and Application in England* (Berkeley and Los Angeles, 1959), pp. 15–19.

[21] Burns, "The Medieval Courts", pp. 129–30.

heard by the official, who was appointed for a number of years or indefinitely. In order to ensure his impartiality, his salary was paid from the bishop's income.

The official's office included many general duties. Therefore his office in turn developed its own personnel: the official's commissary and the assessor (*vice-gerens*) advised on judgments to be passed; advocates of his court advised on legal matters, but could not sit in judgment; the sealer (*sigiler* or *sigilifer*) sealed the documents issued by the commissary's court and oversaw the work of the scribes; the receiver of acts was in charge of copying letters for the court; the registrar kept records of the court's business, functioned as the court's archivist and collected fees; the *promotor*, who appeared relatively late in the fourteenth and fifteenth centuries, was a functionary of the court who protected the interests of the common good. Finally there was the apparitor, also known as the beadle or the summoner, who was a sort of court warden, who cited people, led them into, and kept order in the court.

In contrast to the examiner general, the office of the commissary general flourished right through the fourteenth and fifteenth centuries. Greenfield's statutes name him as one of the two permanent judges of the *Curia Eboracensis*. The other judge was the official himself. The two officers were required to take the same oath of office and were to be shown the same obedience by the members of the court. But this did not mean that the court of the official and the court of the commissary general were interchangeable. Like the official, who was a deputy of the archbishop specially commissioned to be his *locum* in judicial and administrative matters, the commissary general was a deputy of the official whose commission was to hear and determine civil cases that were referred to the court. In practical terms, this meant that the commissary general's decision could be appealed to the official, whose decision could only be appealed to Rome.[22]

A judge of the *Curia Eboracensis* was assigned to a case in one of two ways. He was either the judge by virtue of his appointment as the archbishop's official or to the office of the official's commissary general, which gave him the right to judge cases appearing before the court, or he might have received a commission from a judge of the court to act as his deputy, or special commissary, to hear and determine a specific case. Archbishop Thomas Corbridge, who appointed

---

[22] Burns, ibid., pp. 128 and 197.

John Nassington to be his official in May 1300, was the first archbishop of York to specify the official's duties. Nassington was appointed to act as the archbishop's deputy in all cases, suits and other matters whose cognizance belonged to the archbishop, whether these cases belonged to him directly, on appeal or *ex officio*. Nassington was also commissioned to hear cases that were transmitted to the court in York on appeal from the archbishop's suffragans or their officials or from any other of the archbishop's subjects. [23] Finally, Nassington was charged with inquiring into and correcting offences *ex officio*.

Nassington was a competent administrator well suited to such an office and his career shows the high calibre of the personnel of the court. Although his early career is obscure, it is known that he served as an official of the court of York for a period of some fifteen years between 1296 and 1325, filling the office under archbishops Thomas Corbridge and William Greenfield. Originally he appears to have been a canon of the parish of Nassington in the diocese of Lincoln who arrived in York to serve under Archbishop Romeyn. He served as official of the dean and chapter *sede vacante* in 1296–98 and again in 1299 after the death of Archbishop Henry Newark.[24] After his last period as official for the dean and chapter, Archbishop Thomas Corbridge kept him on as his official until Corbridge's own death in 1304.[25] Nassington then continued to look after the duties of the official as dean and chapter official *sede vacante* until 1306 when he was confirmed in the office as the archbishop's official almost immediately upon Archbishop William Greenfield's accession. He held other offices and incomes as a canon of Beverley (from 1304) and York (from 1309) and he also served as the king's clerk. He also found time to serve in a number of other capacities during the period when he was the official of York *sede plena*, among other things as vicar general for two months during Archbishop Greenfield's absence at parliament in 1310.[26]

---

[23] William Brown, *The Register of Thomas of Corbridge, Lord Archbishop of York, 1300–1304,* i, Surtees Society, 138 (Durham, 1925), p. 1; Burns, "The Medieval Courts", p. 99.

[24] The office as the archbishop's official was held by its incumbent during the pleasure of the archbishop. Upon the death of the archbishop the official's commission expired and his duties devolved on the dean and chapter official, Burns, "The Medieval Courts", p. 94.

[25] Brown, *Register of Thomas Corbridge*, i, pp. 1–2.

[26] John Nassington's career is sketched in Burns, "The Medieval Courts", pp. 93–94.

Although we know little about Nassington's legal training he was in good company among the judges of the York court. Among the other judges who practised in the fourteenth century we find at least one doctor of canon law (Walter Skirlaw 1374–?), four doctors of civil law (Denis Avenel 1319–?, Thomas Samson 1331–?, Richard Conyngton, 1381–1408, and John Newton 1397–?) and two graduates *in utroque jure* (John Aton, 1335–?, and William Cawod, 1398–?).[27]

The official and his commissary general were appointed to act as judges by virtue of their commission. But both of them could delegate their authority to another member of the court in specific cases. Most commonly they appointed the examiner general or one of the rural deans in the West Riding (most frequently the dean of the Christianity of York) who already served as a judge in his own jurisdiction.[28]

As has been shown, the judges of the *Curia Eboracensis* – whether they served as such by virtue of their office or as special deputies – met the requirements of a judge in the ecclesiastical forum. They had a degree in law and they were thoroughly familiar with the procedure and practice of the court. No act books survive from the fourteenth century but, on the basis of the surviving fifteenth- and sixteenth-century act books, figures showing how often the courts met under the presidency of the official, the commissary general, the examiner general or under other special commissaries can be computed. These act books cover between a quarter and one-third of the days on which

At present little is known about the Nassington family but its members appear to have made up a virtual dynasty of lawyers serving in ecclesiastical courts across the country. Two members of the family – Master Henry Nassington and Master Robert – served in various capacities in the thirteenth-century courts in Canterbury, Lincoln and the court of Arches in London. See the notes on the following pages of Norma Adams and Charles Donahue, "Introduction", in *Select Cases from the Ecclesiastical Courts of the Province of Canterbury, c. 1200–1301*, Selden Society, 95 (London, 1981), pp. 449, 454, 467, 470, 575, 634, 635.

[27] Burns, "The Medieval Courts", pp. 89, 138. Some other examples of the careers of (mainly fifteenth-century) episcopal officers can be found in R. L. Storey, *Diocesan Administration in Fifteenth-Century England*, Borthwick Papers, 16 (2nd edn, York, 1972), pp. 13–18.

[28] Burns, "The Medieval Courts", pp. 130–33, suggests that the reason for the popularity of using the examiner general in the early fifteenth century was due to the extraordinary effectiveness of the two examiners general in office at the time – Master Richard Burgh and Master Robert Alne – rather than to a tradition in York for appointing the examiner general deputy judge. The surviving fourteenth-century cause papers support this contention: the examiner general rarely functioned as a judge.

the court sat in session.[29] The commissary general was by far the most common president of the court, sitting at least twice as often as his nearest associate and three to six times as often as the official. During the first half of the fifteenth century the examiner general presided over almost one quarter of the court's sessions, but sometime after the break in the act books in 1425 he was no longer used in this capacity. The use of special commissaries stayed at the constant low level of between one and seven days a year.[30]

The registrar of the court was charged with keeping the books of the court. It was his job to keep a record of the court's daily business, to take down the names of those subjects who had incurred the punishment of the court for non-appearance or for refusing to respond to citations. He kept a list of excommunicates and in general looked after the archives of the court. He was responsible for sending the necessary letters concerning ecclesiastical judgments to the local deans. He also issued copies of depositions to the litigants at court, for which service he was allowed by the statutes to charge a fee of 6d. per witness – except in the case of paupers who were to receive the transcripts free of charge.[31] To help him in his day-to-day business he had a staff of scribes to copy and transcribe the documents of the court.

The registrars of York were required to hold a university degree and to be notaries public, but their main qualification was probably that they had a good sense of order and were good administrators. The office consisted "in practica pocius quam speculativa", to use the phrase Archbishop Thoresby used to reprimand his official for appointing the precentor of Beverley, who did not have the necessary qualifications to be registrar in York.[32] As remarked before, the registrar may have been identical to the examiner general and as such have discharged more duties than listed above. He was usually present in

---

[29] Burns, "The Medieval Courts", p. 131. There is no reason to think that Burns's fifteenth-century figures varied substantially from the situation in the fourteenth century.

[30] Ibid., pp. 132–34, surmises that changes in notarial practice during the period for which no act books survive (1430–84) may have caused this startling change, and suggests that the days when the examiner presided over the court may have been noted under the examiner general's name, but without noting his office. For this argument to work the proportion of days presided over by special commissaries would have had to show an increase. They do not.

[31] Wilkins, Concilia magna, ii, p. 410.

[32] Burns, "The Medieval Courts", p. 143.

the court: during the entire period 1417 to 1430 – the only sustained period for which act books survive – the registrar is recorded as absent for only twelve days.[33]

Advocates and proctors needed the same personal qualifications: they had to be twenty-five years old and legally competent. For this reason excommunicates, women and the insane could not be constituted proctors or advocates.[34] The two differed in the level of their expertise. Among advocates this level was high: the officials mentioned below had almost all served as advocates in the *Curia Eboracensis* before their preferment: the three advocates appointed to defend the countess of Surrey – John Nassington Jr, William Stanes and Philip Nassington – all served as advocates before their promotions. John Nassington and William Stanes went on to become officials in 1315 and 1328, respectively, and both served as the auditor of cases for the York dean and chapter. Philip Nassington served as the archbishop's appointed commissary general *sede vacante* in the archdeaconry of Richmond.[35]

The Nassington brothers were from a family of lawyers: they share the surname of two other Nassingtons who served as lawyers in the southern province. Henry Nassington was the dean of Arches in London at the end of the thirteenth century,[36] while Robert Nassington served as a deputy examiner in the consistory court in Lincoln.[37]

Advocates and proctors were to be present in court when it was in session, and they were not allowed to leave it without permission from the president of the court. The salary of advocates was to be no more than 50s. per case per year, while proctors could only charge 10s. per case per year. If they overcharged they were to be suspended from exercising their office during the official's pleasure and they were to pay back to their client the excess they had charged. Members of the court were to behave in a proper fashion and not create a disturbance. If they disturbed the peace of the court persistently they could be denied a hearing of their case and be suspended from the court during the pleasure of the president. They were also to discharge their cases

---

[33] Burns, "The Medieval Courts", p. 145.

[34] This rule is largely academic. In practice it was rarely invoked since no challenges to proctorial mandates have been found in the cause papers.

[35] Burns, "The Medieval Courts", pp. 140–42.

[36] H.P.F. King, J.M. Horn and B. Jones, eds, *John Le Neve: Fasti Ecclesiae Anglicanae* (1962–67), iii, p. 55.

[37] Norma Adams and Charles Donahue, *Select Cases*, p. 454.

without delay and not to enter false quarrels or unjustified appeals under pain of the same penalty.[38]

The advocates are not very much in evidence in the cause papers themselves. According to the remaining *acta* in the cause papers, written documents and oral presentations were delivered in court by the proctors. However, Greenfield's statutes required the proctors to consult with an advocate of the court before presenting any written document and stipulated fines for those proctors who did not comply with this requirement.[39] Although advocates' careers are thus not easy to trace, they appear to have been well educated. In accordance with canon law they had to be graduates in law, canon or civil: a number of the advocates practising in the consistory court in York during the fourteenth century had graduated in both.[40] Whereas Archbishop Greenfield's statutes decreed that their number should be twelve, the surviving fifteenth-century act books show that only between five and eight advocates practised in York in any of the years for which act books survive. The fact that Greenfield assigned three advocates to defend the countess of Surrey in a divorce case brought by her husband suggests that at least twice that number practised in the court in York in 1314 but there is not enough surviving litigation to estimate their numbers during the rest of the fourteenth century.

Analysing the fourteenth-century documents it is impossible to estimate the number of advocates practising in the consistory courts. In the fifteenth-century act books surviving from between 1417 and 1430, however, only four or five advocates are named. Likewise, in the documents that record the admission of new members to the court in 1420 and 1427 – when one would expect a full turnout – the tally of advocates is only four and three respectively.[41]

The advocates of the courts were expected to have at least three years of university training and practical experience of varying lengths (depending on the statutes of the court). It goes almost without saying that women, serfs, and excommunicates could not be advocates of the

---

[38] Wilkins, *Concilia magna*, ii, p. 411.

[39] Ibid.

[40] Burns, "The Medieval Courts", p. 138, maintains that a degree was not a requirement. York was not the only northern European diocese that did not insist on a degree: a number of Danish dioceses, among them Viborg, Ribe and Roskilde, had presiding judges with no formal degree. Troels Dahlerup, *Viborg stifts officialer* (Copenhagen, 1964); Troels Dahlerup, *Studier i Dansk senmiddelalderlig kirkeorganisation* (Copenhagen, 1963)

[41] Burns, "The Medieval Courts", p. 136.

court. Priests could function as advocates but were urged to not function as such, except for the poor and in matters pertaining to their own church. An advocate almost always pleaded orally before the court and therefore the advocate is a shadowy figure, because it is difficult to ascertain their contribution to the documents of the court cases left to us: they drew up the libels, exceptions and other documents in court and in consultation with the parties' proctors. Advocates pleaded orally in a large summary of the case, just before the passing of sentence. There was a kind of legal aid in the middle ages, under which *miserabiles persones* would be assigned an advocate by the bishop who also paid the advocate's fee.

The proctors of the consistory court are the most clearly visible members of the court in the cause papers. Their office was derived from Roman law. They had become common in European church courts by the thirteenth century and are mentioned by the second council of Lyon. A proctor could be employed by a legally competent person: someone not barred from prosecuting a case. Proctors did not have to be professionals and lay people could, and did, function as proctors. Women could not be proctors. A proctor was a person named as the representative of one of the parties and had to be appointed either before the judge in person or by letter. After the *litis contestatio* a proctor could appoint a substitute or a helper for himself if the case was large. Proctors could also represent a professional body, such as a guild or a monastery. Proctors eventually began to organise in guilds themselves towards the end of the middle ages. Keeping within the limits set by Greenfield's statutes, six to eight proctors practised in any one given year in the court. Their job was to represent their clients in court – quite literally to be their stand-ins, responding to the questions of the judge, presenting the documents of the case, in short, functioning as the intermediary between the court and the litigants. They were required to consult with the advocates before every step of the case and could not enter documents in the case on their own authority. Proctors who neglected their duty to have documents ready in time for the sessions of the court could be fined half a mark for the fabric of the church and risked suspension from their office.[42]

A proctor had to be admitted to practise in the court and, like an

---

[42] Wilkins, *Concilia magna*, ii, p. 411.

advocate, he took an oath of office every year. There are no known formal demands about a proctor's education but we must presume that they acquired a familiarity with the rules of the court during the year they attended the court before they were admitted to practice. Although a litigant was not obliged to make use of a proctor, most litigants did. Among the matrimonial cause papers there are no cases heard entirely without the aid of a proctor. A number of litigants tried to conduct their cases without their aid in the early stages of their cases, but they all hired a proctor to appear for them during the later stages.[43]

There is no way to ascertain the workload of individual proctors in the fourteenth century, but from the remaining fifteenth century act books it is apparent that work was not distributed evenly among them. Instead, a fair amount of competition existed among the proctors. In most years one or two proctors conducted up to half of the court business assigned to proctors, leaving the rest to the four to six other proctors allowed to practise in the court. It is probable that their workload was a reflection of their reputation as reliable officers of the court. Inexperienced proctors sometimes had to wait a long time for their first commissions: John Morland was admitted as a proctor to the court in December 1427 but did not receive his first commission until June 1429.[44] This did not mean that the less successful proctors were idle. Many aspects of court administration were open to them by virtue of their general mandate to work in the court. John Morland, mentioned above, was probably not the only notary public who continued to function in this role after his admission to the court.[45]

Proctors were commonly chosen as mediators in cases which went to arbitration by the mutual assent of the parties; they could be appointed substitute proctors in the event that the main proctor in a case was absent at a meeting of the court; and they could serve as substitute registrars when the registrar general was absent, or even acquire the post as registrar for one of the other courts in York, for instance in the court of the dean of the Christianity of York or for the dean and chapter.

All members of the consistory court were appointed by the archbishop's official, who was charged with maintaining a full contin-

---

[43] See e.g. *Chapelayn* c. *Cragger* (CP E 1) and *Huntington* c. *Munkton* (CP, E 248).

[44] Burns, "The Medieval Courts", p. 148.

[45] Compare CP, F 141, where he authenticated a document in his function as notary public.

gent of officers of the court. Advocates and proctors were required to spend at least a year studying the practice of the court before they were admitted to practise there. This year allowed them to understand and then continue the court's legal practice themselves. New advocates were admitted to the court in the first consistory meeting of the court after Michaelmas,[46] when all members – new as well as old – were required to recite the oath of office.

This oath set high ethical standards for the exercise of their office. It required them to do everything within their power to ensure that *justice* was done rather than to try to win a case which they knew to be wrong. The oath bound them to give up those cases that they did not believe in, even if it only became clear to them that their client's claim was unjust after they had initiated their case at court.[47] The annual recitation of the oath of office was a tradition that had been observed since the reign of Archbishop Wickwane (1279–85) who, within three weeks of receiving the *pallium* in 1279, had instructed his official – himself only appointed the day before – to make sure that canon 19 of the second council of Lyons (1274), which required the annual oath of office, was adhered to in the court.[48]

The archbishop's court of audience could intervene in cases heard

---

[46] 29 September.

[47] The full wording of the oath is as follows: "Ego N. juro ad haec sancta dei evangelia, quod in omnibus causis, quarum patronus sum et ero in hoc consistorio, vel coram Domino Archiepiscopo, vel ipsius specialibus commissariis, fidele patrocinium praestabo; quodque omni opera ac diligentia id, quod justum et verum aestimavero, meis clientibus in suis causis et negotiis procurabo, et circa hoc, quatenus est mihi possibile fideliter laborabo; nec aliquid dicam, proponam vel faciam, seu per alium dici, proponi vel fieri, quantum in me est, scienter et malitiose permittam, ad partis alterius justitiam auferendam, vel etiam indebite differendam; nec etiam contra Eboracensis Ecclesiae jurisdictionem, aut Eboracensis Curie consuetudines vel statuta; ita quod si in quacumque parte judicii mihi innotuerit clientulos meos malam seu injustam causam fovere, seu defendere, quae mihi visa fuerit desperata, amplius non patrocinabor eidem, nec in eadem praestabo consilium, vel auxilium clam vel palam: sic me Deus adjuvet, et haec sancta Dei evangelia." Wilkins, *Concilia magna*, ii, pp. 410–11.

The punishment for trying to prosecute a case knowing that it was wrong was substantial: the statutes demand that the culprit be suspended from office in perpetuity. For a general study of the requirements of the personnel of the English courts in the middle ages see R. H. Helmholz, "Ethical Standard for Advocates and Proctors in Theory and Practice", in *Canon Law and the Law of England* (London, 1987), pp. 41–58.

[48] William Brown, *The Register of William Wickwane, Lord Archbishop of York, 1279–1285*, Surtees Society, 114 (Durham, 1907), pp. 208–9.

by the consistory court and the court of the archbishop's exchequer. Although in theory it was possible to appeal a decision from any of the lower courts to this court at any time in the proceedings – or even to bring it before the archbishop in the first instance – this court is rarely seen to be active in the cause papers.[49] Only one case – a divorce case which began as a plea for the restoration of marital rights (*Huntington c. Munkton*, 1345–46) – has left substantial papers from the archbishop's court of audience. As we have seen even this case was eventually referred to the consistory court after a period of six months.

In general the archbishop's court of audience seems to have heard cases on the grounds of the importance of the issues involved or cases arising out of contempt of court in the archbishop's other courts. The court of audience also dealt with spiritual offences, such as heresy or apostasy, and criminal cases. It could sometimes function as a court of first instance if one of the archbishop's subjects felt that to be appropriate. In contrast to the consistory court, which was held in a fixed place in the *locum consistorii* in York Minster, the archbishop's court of audience was held wherever the archbishop happened to be in the diocese. During his absence, the court of audience was presided over by the archbishop's vicar general.[50]

Since few acts survive from the archbishop's court of audience, it is difficult to trace more than the outline of its history. The first identifiable auditors of the court were Master Hugh Corebrigg and Master Gilbert Sancto Leofardo who appear in Archbishop Giffard's register in 1267.[51] In this year – sitting in tribunal in the porch of the archbishop's chapel at Cawood – they heard a complex suit among other things about a pension due to the rector of Rempstone.[52]

The next indication of the activities of this court are found in the year 1308, when Master Peter Dene and Master William Beverley interrogated the rector of Skerne against whom a charge of immorality

---

[49] Burns, "The Medieval Courts", p. 201.

[50] Burns, "The Medieval Courts", pp. 216–17.

[51] Gilbert Sancto Leofardo served as the archbishop's official in York before becoming the treasurer of Chichester and official in Canterbury. He was the dean of Arches sometime before 1288 in which year he became bishop of Chichester, Robert Brentano, *York Metropolitan Jurisdiction and Papal Judges Delegate, 1279–1296* (Berkeley, 1959), pp. 23, 73, 184). See also Adams and Donahue, "Select Canterbury Cases", pp. 29, 31.

[52] Burns, "The Medieval Courts", p. 217.

had been made during the archbishop's visitation. Peter Dene appears again, this time with Master Roger Pickering, as the archbishop's auditor in a case of annulment of a marriage "for certain impediments not admitting dispensation". This case was not heard to the end, but remitted to the consistory court at the request of the sheriff of York.[53]

By the middle of the fourteenth century the position of auditor of cases for the archbishop became a permanent appointment. In 1335 Archbishop Melton appointed a certain Master Hamo Ceszay to be auditor of cases to deal with all cases, disputes and complaints, whether by instance or *ex officio*. He was also charged to inquire into the crimes, failings and sins of all the archbishop's subjects and to correct and punish their transgressions. Later on in the fifteenth and sixteenth century the office of the auditor gradually merged with the office of the vicar general until by 1539 we find the same person – Master William Clyff – presiding over the court of audience specifically in his capacity as vicar general.[54]

There is thus good reason to maintain that the laity of the northern province was well provided for in terms of access to justice. Its members learned the rules of law not only when they were summoned before the courts but were also made aware of the church and its rules about marriage, its courts and their legal tradition through the systematic teaching of the church in sermons and in confession. Not only did the liturgical year leave ample opportunity for the transmission of the church's teaching, but there is no doubt that the impact of such teaching was strengthened by more informal means, such as attendance at court cases or by informal networks of friends and benefactors that have left only shadowy traces in the sources. Cases certainly show a good basic grasp of the principles of the law and in some cases, such as *Huntington* and *Munkton*, the litigants demonstrate what can only be described as a virtuoso knowledge of the procedure of the court. Whether this knowledge was learned before the litigants appeared before the courts or if it was instilled in them by their legal advisers cannot be established on the basis of the cause papers.

It is also clear that the system of courts in the northern province was well developed and well staffed in the fourteenth century. Almost

---

[53] William Brown and A. Hamilton Thompson, *The Register of William Greenfield, Lord Archbishop of York, 1306–15*, i, Surtees Society, 149 (Durham, 1934), pp. 146 and 168.

[54] Burns, "The Medieval Courts", pp. 220–21.

from the beginning of the surviving records the jurisdiction of the *curia Eboracensis* was well defined. Archbishop Greenfields's 1311 statutes for the court and the earliest surviving records combine to give the impression of a smoothly operating administration of justice. The court, which could consist of up to two examiners, twelve advocates, eight proctors, six notaries and one registrar in charge of a scriptorium for the production of procedural documents and depositions, was set up to despense justice at reasonable cost to the litigants. Although the outline above shows maximum numbers, the decreasing number of court sessions in the fifteenth century demonstrate that the court did meet the demands for justice from the laity and from the church itself at least during the fourteenth century. Not only was the court charged with making the archbishop's justice available to all for a reasonable fee, it also consisted of well educated and well trained members of the courts, being rarely challenged on procedure. Both the judges of the court and the advocates that practised there were university graduates in law, usually both in canon law and in civil law. Proctors were not admitted to practise in the court unless they had serve a one year internship and had become thoroughly familiar with the courts way of working. Furthermore, the president of the court had the authority to maintain the courts high standard by means of disciplinary measures vested in him by Archbishop Greenfield's statutes. The courts therefore served a useful funtion in fourteenth-century York and were a integrated part of the regulation of people's lives. By extension the courts became the final arbiters of whether a marriage should be considered legitimate or a scandal to the local community.

5

The Laity and the Church Courts

In a recent essay Barbara Hanawalt has argued that, by the end of the fourteenth century, the laity in London had developed a substantial system of tribunals and courts for dealing with conflicts outside the royal system of justice.[1] In the course of her essay Hanawalt demonstrates that such courts even claimed jurisdiction in preference to the ordinary legal system and that, on the whole, this local administration of justice worked efficiently. Her work prompts the question of whether a similar institutional framework can be said to have existed when the laity was supposed to deal with that other great monolith of judicial power – the church – and, in particular, with its jurisdiction over marriage, or if the church had managed to have its claim to exclusive jurisdiction over marriage accepted by the fourteenth century. There is evidence for such an extra-curial system of justice in York and it seems sensible to attempt to answer the question of whether the laity developed out-of-court institutions like the ones identified by Hanawalt. This chapter will give some examples of the forms that these tribunals took, but the tribunals documented in the York material never developed standardised forms, rituals and powers like the lay courts identified in Hanawalt's article. Therefore it can be argued that these tribunals were never a part of the formal legal system and that – on the contrary – the fact that the York tribunals were so disparate in form indicates that the laity never seriously challenged the jurisdiction of the church in marriage cases.

Although Maitland's characterisation of the medieval canon law on marriage as a "seducer's charter" overstates the case,[2] medieval canon law did offer many opportunities for people to contract marriage

---

[1] Barbara A. Hanawalt, "The Power of Word and Symbol: Conflict Resolution in Late Medieval London", in *Of Good and Ill Repute: Gender and Social Control in Medieval England* (Oxford 1998), pp. 35–52.

[2] Frederick Pollock and Frederic William Maitland, *The History of English Law before the Time of Edward I*, i, revised by S. F. C Milsom (2nd edn, Cambridge 1968).

under informal circumstances. The surviving court records are filled with instances of marriages contracted under the most unusual circumstances: in beds, taverns, fields, cowsheds and outhouses or private rooms, with or without witnesses. The ease of contracting marriage and the ample scope for unintended marriages to be created by parties using the wrong formulae made it desirable for the parties to ensure that some sort of semi-legal circumstance surrounded the exchange of vows. One common way of safeguarding a marriage was to make sure that someone representing the church was present to supervise the exchange of vows. But even the presence of clerics or notaries public could not ensure that a contract did not become the subject of an investigation by the courts. The presence of clerics in these sorts of cases, however, moved the marriage negotiations towards a more formal performance of a legal act. Tribunals with undefined legal powers also appear in the marriage cases with some regularity. Usually such tribunals assembled to investigate whether there was a case to answer before an ecclesiastical court and in most cases they included some people with legal training. Although the authority of these tribunals was never questioned and rarely, if ever, defined, they were clearly assembled *ad hoc* and never settled or became fixed in their composition. Sometimes they consisted of lay people, sometimes of clerics and sometimes of a mixture of the two. In most cases these tribunals did a good job, but it is clear that they were open to manipulation.

The case of *Brathewell* c. *Dowson* has already been mentioned, as has another example of negotiations found in *Greystanes* c. *Dale* (1394). During the hearing of the latter case at the York court the witness John Helcott, a forty-year-old parishioner of Staindrop, elaborated on the circumstances of the negotiations. He explained that he and many others had been present with the bride and groom, the father of the bride, three of her uncles, the rector of a local church and Adam Alwent, a chaplain and kinsman of the groom on 20 March 1392 in a place called "Lonefield" where marriage negotiations had taken place. It was agreed that the bride should bring a dowry of twenty marks and in return the groom, swore that he had not contracted marriage with any other woman and that he did not want any other woman in marriage. Later, at an unspecified date, banns were read and the two married *in facie ecclesie*. After the negotiations had been concluded, the parties called for another priest to prompt the exchange of marriage vows *verba de futuro*. The priest prompted the parties and a marriage was celebrated some weeks later. Neither this impressive turnout nor the publicity surrounding the event prevented the marriage, however, from becoming the subject of litigation when the groom's jilted girlfriend won a case of enforcement of marriage vows in Durham, a decision which was then challenged in York. The eventual outcome in York was that the marriage between Thomas Dale and Emma Corry was upheld, in part because of the presence of the clerics at the occasion of the exchange of vows.

A more detailed impression of the function of a single cleric attending marriage negotiations can be gleaned from *Lyremouth and Holm* c. *Stokton* (1381) in which Master Geoffrey Cave, a twenty-eight year-old notary public in York, attended the exchange of vows between William Stokton, a servant of Roger Moreton, a citizen and merchant of St Saviourgate parish in York, and Isabel Holm of York and later participated in a tribunal to establish the legality of the vows.[3] The vows were a fairly standard *verba de presenti* exchanged around Palm Sunday a year earlier.[4] However, the attendant circumstances of the case proved to be less than straightforward. For William Stokton had contracted with another woman, Elena Lyremouth, three years earlier. At that time, he could not take up cohabitation with her because of the terms of his apprenticeship. However, William's master, Roger Moreton, wanted William to marry Isabel Holm and by some means he managed to get William to agree to this marriage. Not surprisingly this caused some consternation in Elena's house. In Elena's presence, the witness Cecilia Hessay asked William about his wedding plans with Isabel some time before the ceremony took place, and, swearing on a scroll, he confirmed that he was going to marry someone else. Cecilia added that she often heard William swear that he would rather have married Elena than Isabel at the end of his apprenticeship. About two years after his exchange of vows with Elena, however, the ceremony between Isabel and William took place in the room of Geoffrey Hebston in Roger Moreton's house in St Saviourgate in the presence of Geoffrey Hebston and Geoffrey Cave. The presence of a notary at the marriage negotiations proved a wise precaution, for around Christmas 1381 Roger Moreton assembled a tribunal in his house, "Le Somerhall", consisting of himself, another of his servants called John Flayreburgh, Geoffrey Cave and Master Thomas Rednesse, a chaplain, who interrogated William to find out more about his marriage to Isabel. On this

---

[3] *Lyremouth and Holm* c. *Stokton*. CP, E 126 (1382).
[4] CP, E 126-5 (Galfridus Cave).

occasion, William swore that he had married Isabel and that he had no right to any other woman.[5] This tribunal came to the conclusion that there was a case to be answered and the case was heard by the court in York.

William Stokton was thus exposed to two tribunals, one very informal, the other convened under the auspices of his master. We know that he swore on a scroll in the informal meeting in Elena's house, which indicates a certain degree of formality in the proceedings, but the meeting in "Le Somerhall" was a more elaborate attempt at arriving at the legality of the second marriage.

It therefore appears that it was common for the intending parties to allow an investigation into their previous affairs in response to objections to their current marriage arrangement. The exchange of vows was often attended by what may be characterised as expert witnesses, in most cases clerics who could be expected to have a more detailed understanding of the canon law rules of marriage formation. In desperate circumstances, however, such as the case of Agnes Huntington, whose marriage to Simon Munkton was analysed above in Chapter 2, the meeting of a formal tribunal to establish the validity of vows called for immediate action by the litigants who therefore did not take the precautions outlined above. Furthermore, the case underlines that these tribunals were open to manipulation, not only by the intending parties but also from their parents. In *Huntington* c. *Munkton* the tribunal was manipulated both by Agnes, who wanted her marriage to John Bristol upheld, and by her mother, who emphatically did not. Agnes claimed to have already married John Bristol, but her stepfather and mother disliked John, and they alerted the dean of the Christianity of York to the fact that there might be fornication or a possible clandestine marriage between John and Agnes. In preparation to the court meeting proper, the dean's court assembled a tribunal consisting of three clerics – Gilbert Pocklington, David Ledes and John Couthorp (the last being a kinsman of the Huntington family) – who assembled in Agnes's parents' house on the morning of 7 February 1340 to discuss the matter with Agnes's parents, her uncle William Huntington and John Bristol's parents. Agnes's mother wanted the tribunal to find that there was no marriage, while John and Agnes tried to persuade Agnes's parents to consent to their marriage. John stated his willingness to marry Agnes, even if it meant losing the inheritance left to her

[5] Johannes Flayreburgh heard that him swear to the marriage and "quod nullam jus habuit ad habendum aliquam aliam in uxorem". CP, E 126-5.

by Richard Huntington. He even offered the money to Agnes's stepfather, Hamo Hessay, if only he would agree to the union. But Agnes's mother was adamantly opposed to the marriage. Gilbert Pocklington, one of the three clerks of the dean's court present at the meeting said that:

> He heard the said Agnes's mother say threateningly that she [Agnes] would draw a maternal curse upon herself if she swore to any [marriage] contract unless it be a conditional one, namely [on condition that] her parents agreed.[6]

After the preliminary meeting in Mulberry Hall, John Couthorp, a clerk of the court of the dean of the Christianity and a kinsman of Agnes, continued to investigate the case and found out that John and Agnes *had* exchanged unconditional marriage vows on several occasions. Both John, Agnes and Margaret Foxholes confessed this privately to him and John Couthorp decided to confront Agnes's mother with this information. Her reaction was prompt: if John Couthorp did not stop associating with John of Bristol, Agnes's mother would have his legs broken.[7] Thus, by a mixture of intimidation and persuasion, Agnes's mother and Hamo Hessay managed to keep evidence of an unconditional contract out of the court of the dean of the Christianity when it met a week later. They even went so far as to threaten one of the officers of the court.

The meeting was an official affair. It was convened by the authority of the dean of the Christianity in York and presided over by three representatives of that court. The parties' parents were also present, as was the uncle of Agnes Huntington, who was later to prove a staunch friend to her. The purpose of the meeting was also well defined: it was the intention to establish whether there was a case to answer before a fully convened meeting of the dean's court. As it happened, Agnes tried to produce evidence for her marriage to John Bristol, even going so far as to almost forcing a household servant to witness an exchange of vows against her will.

---

[6] "Dicit etiam idem juratus quod audivit matrem eiusdem Agnete sibi dicere comminandem quod inferret sibi maledictionem maternam si aliquem contractum faceretur nisi conditionale, videlicet si parentes dicte Agnete consentirent." CP, E 248-23d.

[7] "Audivit etiam idem juratus matrem dicte Agnete cominare eidem jurato quod dimitteret societatem dicti Johannis vel frangi faceret crura eiusdem jurati." CP E 248-23d, John de Couthorp.

The tribunal in the case of *Huntington* c. *Munkton* was convened as part of the ordinary work of the court of the dean of the Christianity in York. In another, earlier case, a tribunal met under what appears to be secular authority. The case was brought before the *Curia Eboracensis* by Elizabeth Lovell, the daughter of Sir Simon Lovell, against Thomas Marton, the son of Robert Marton. In her depositions Elizabeth claimed that she had conducted marriage negotiations with Thomas,[8] that they had contracted a legitimate marriage by exchanging vows *verba de presenti* and that Thomas had sworn to the existence of a marriage at a meeting held in the church of Hovingham which brought together "many people worthy of trust", in particular Elizabeth's and Thomas's families. On the surface the case was fairly straightforward. The court needed to determine whether Elizabeth and Thomas had exchanged valid marriage vows. But additional complications soon arose. Since this exchange of vows Thomas had solemnised his wedding to Elena, daughter of Jordan of Aneport from the diocese of Lichfield.[9] But this solemnisation was not argued as an impediment to his marriage to Elizabeth: we only know about it from a memorandum published by the court granting Thomas the right to live separately from Elena until the case had been determined in York. Furthermore, in his responses in York, Thomas did not deny that he had exchanged marriage vows with Elizabeth, but he emphasised that he had made it clear at the meeting in the parish church of Hovingham that the vows had been conditional upon the consent of his friends.

Elizabeth brought nine witnesses who testified that she had contracted marriage with Thomas on two separate occasions. Two of these witnesses had been present at an exchange of vows on the Sunday before the Purification of the Virgin just past (2 February 1326). The exchange had taken place in Thomas's father's brewing house in Drokom in Rydale, where Thomas had said to Elizabeth, "behold my oath that I will take no one as my wife except you" and

---

[8] "Tractatus habebatur inter eosdem de matrimonio inter eosdem ineundo." *Lovell* c. *Marton*. CP E 18-5 (1327–28).

[9] "[Thomas Marton] confessus fuit . . . se solemnizasse matrimonium cum quadem Elena, filia Jordani de Aneport commorantis apud Ryngoy in episcopatu Cestr' pendente lite super matrimonio inter Elizabath' filiam domini Simonis Lovell' militis pendente indecisa; asseruit tamen se precontraxisse cum prefata Elena antel litem inchoatam." CP, E 18–7, Printed in R. H. Helmholz, *Marriage Litigation in Medieval England*, Cambridge Studies in English Legal History (Cambridge, 1974), p. 195.

The diocese of Chester was not created until 1542. The phrase *in episcopatu Cestr'* therefore must refer to the diocese of Lichfield.

she replied, "behold my oath that never will I have anyone as my husband except you".[10] In token of their marriage they held hands and kissed each other in the presence of Elizabeth's sister, Agnes, and a certain John Bartholomew.

Though Elizabeth and Thomas doubtless intended to contract marriage on this occasion, they had in fact only contracted a marriage *verba de futuro* by their words, and this flaw was pointed out to Thomas by his confessors, the Dominican friars. In the morning of 16 April 1326 Thomas – lying naked in his bed – and Elizabeth discussed the validity of their contract in the presence of Agnes and Euphemia, another of Elizabeth's sisters, who had come to visit Thomas in his father's manor:

> The said Thomas said then that it had been said to him by the friars, his confessors, that the previous contract was not valid; but that both [he and Elizabeth] could contract marriage with another wherever they wanted. And then by the free will of both of them they uttered the words written below, with the said Thomas first speaking and holding the said Elizabeth by the right hand: "here I take you Elizabeth as my faithfully joined wife to have and to hold until the end of my life and I give you my word for this". To which the Elizabeth replied: "here I take you, Thomas, as my pledged husband, to have and to hold until the end of my life and I give you my word on this". And immediately following this contract they kissed.[11]

This contract was witnessed by Agnes, Euphemia and Richard Hyman, Thomas's servant. Thomas and Elizabeth contracted their marriage without the knowledge and consent of their parents.

On 7 November 1326, a meeting took place in the parish church of Hovingham some twenty miles outside of York. By whose authority it

---

[10] "'Ecce fides mea quod non ducam aliquam in uxorem nisi te.' Et ipsa statim respondebat: 'Ecce fides mea quod nullo tempore habebo aliquem in virum nisi te habeam'." CP, E 18-5.

[11] "Et dictus Thomas tunc dicebat quod a fratribus confessoribus suis eidem fuerat dictum quod prior contractus non valuit; quin licuit utrique cum alio contrahere matrimonium ubi vellet. Et tunc ad voluntatem utriusque verba infrascripta adinvicem protulerunt, dicto Thoma primo dicente et ipsam Elizabet per manum dexteram tenente: 'hic accipio te Elizabet in uxorem meam fidelem conjugatam, tenendam et habendam usque ad finem vite mee et ad hoc do tibi fidem meam'. Cui dicta Elizabet respondebat: 'Et hic accipio te Thomam in fidelem virum meum desponsatum, tenendum et habendum usque ad finem vite mee et ad hoc do tibi fidem.' Et post ipsum contractum adinvicem osculabantur." CP, E 18-5, printed in Helmholz, *Marriage Litigation*, pp. 203–4.

was convened is unknown, but we know that it was presided over by
Sir Simon Lovell, Elizabeth's father. Among those present in
Hovingham were Elizabeth's father, her aunt and Thomas's parents.
Also present were Edmund Stanley, William Easingby and two men –
William Appleton and William Thornton – whose role in the proceedings, as we shall see, remains ambiguous.[12] What is certain about the
meeting in Hovingham is that those present met to discuss the
evidence for or against the existence of a marriage between Elizabeth
and Thomas. The evidence put forward is outlined above, but when
Thomas had finished his evidence, something unusual happened. In his
deposition, Thomas had confirmed every detail of Elizabeth's story,
which should have been the end of the story. But when he had told his
version of events and returned to the small group consisting of Elizabeth, William Appleton and William Thornton, the four of them
started whispering among themselves. Within a short while, Thomas
returned to add detail to his story: he might have consented to the
marriage, he said, but in his mind he had expressed a reservation – he
had not wanted to marry Elizabeth unless his *amici* consented to the
marriage.[13] Legally, this was a poor excuse, and it would hardly have
had any impact in a normal trial. What possessed Thomas to express
these reservations before the tribunal can only be guessed at, but it
may be speculated that it was not unrelated to his parents' attempts to
marry him off to Elena Aneport outside the diocese. Thomas's statement may have been designed to sow just enough doubt about the
validity of his marriage to Elizabeth to force the informal (and presumably, family-based) tribunal to send the case to be heard by another,

---

[12] The documentation for this period of the court's existence is sparse, but a certain
William Appleby was a proctor of the court some thirteen years later. Since the
suffix -ton is the English version of the Scandinavian suffix -by it may be suggested
that William Appleton could have been a member of the court in York at this time.
William Appleton certainly seems to have been there to advise Thomas and
Elizabeth on the canon law of marriage.

[13] "Et postmodum, dictus Thomas, post huiusmodi confessionem dicte Elizabet,
parum deliberavit cum Willelmo de Thornton et Willelmo de Appilton. Et statim
rediens ad dictum Simonem et alios superius nominatos, fatebatur se talia verba
matrimonialia in forma per ipsam Elizabetem recitata eidem Elizabeti dixisse et
protulisse. Adiecit tamen idem Thomas quod tempore quo talia verba matrimonialia fecit et protulit dicte Elizabete, in mente et voluntate cogitavit quod dictum
contractum non adimpleret nisi adesset voluntas amicorum suorum. Et tunc dicta
Elizabet eidem respondebat quod de cogitatione nescit, sed ille contractus fuerat
simplex, sine conditione aliquali. Cui asssertioni dictus Thomas nichil in
contrarium respondebat." CP, E 18-5.

professional, tribunal consisting of trained lawyers who would settle once and for all in a public forum whether a marriage existed between Thomas and Elizabeth. It may also have been part of his considerations that a professional tribunal would have the power to prevent his marriage to Elena Aneport, as indeed it did. Whatever Thomas's motives were, in his mind and in the estimation of his advisers his admission of mental reservations posed a threat to the legality of the vows between him and Elizabeth. Thomas's objections were disregarded by the court in York and a sentence for Elizabeth and for upholding the marriage was passed on 27 October 1328.

The exact nature of the meeting in Hovingham church is unclear. Richard Helmholz called it "a meeting of the important men of the community in the parish church",[14] but it seems rather to have been a meeting of the parties concerned and their families, presided over by Sir Simon Lovell. The meeting was probably called to investigate whether there was a case to answer before the court in York. The case might have ended with this meeting, but, if it had, Thomas and Elizabeth's marriage could have been challenged at a later date. Thomas Marton's defence may deliberately have been just strong enough to sow doubt about the validity of the marriage, but not strong enough to prove that it existed precisely in order to force a decision by the court in York. The venue and the way in which two of the people present – William Appleton and William Thornton – acted as legal counsel to Thomas and Elizabeth make it clear that Thomas knew what he was doing and that he did so after consultations with his apparent opponent, Elizabeth.

This case appears among the cause papers as an instance case. In other words, Elizabeth Lovell appears to have sued to have the court enforce her marriage to a reluctant Thomas Marton. However, a closer examination suggests that neither Elizabeth nor Thomas were averse to the marriage. Instead, it seems that Thomas's father, Robert Marton – who in sharp contrast to Elizabeth's father, Sir Simon Lovell, was not referred to by title by the court scribe – had other plans for Thomas. Just how marrying Thomas to Elena Aneport during the hearing of the case in York fitted into his plans is impossible to say. One would have thought that Thomas Marton's father would have been happy to have Elizabeth, a member of the aristocracy, as a member of his family. Whatever his reasons, Robert Marton's actions

---

[14] Helmholz, *Marriage Litigation*, p. 191.

were an unambiguous attempt to circumvent the court in York. The marriage to Elena Aneport took place in a diocese outside the jurisdiction of the northern province where the reading of the banns was unlikely to attract attention and it took place after the beginning of the case in York. It was only claimed for York because a case had already been initiated there. However, despite initial appearances, the case is not simply a case of a teenager who spoke too soon and later regretted it, but can be seen as a manifestation of teenage insistence on marrying against the wishes of their parents. It has already been argued above that the laity had a good grasp of the basic church rules of marriage, but Thomas's surprising action at the meeting in Hovingham suggests two other things: that the laity had developed means, including pre-court hearings like the one above, to determine whether a case should be heard by a proper legal tribunal, and that people like Thomas Marton and Elizabeth Lovell were willing to use these hearings to force a decision in their cases.

The meeting in Hovingham carries a number of hallmarks of a legal occasion. It took place outside the parties' family homes, it included the parties and their advisers, and the parties' families were present. The parties also took advice and formally deposited their statements before the tribunal. The formality of the occasion contrasts to the meeting attested to in *Foston* c. *Lawless* (1393).[15] In this case we find a informal grouping of people gathered together in the room of a Sister Margaret Ely, a nun in St Clement's monastery in Clementhorpe, who enquired under informal circumstances into an exchange of vows. The case proper was heard by the church courts from October 1393 to July 1394. The matter of the suit was the legality of the vows exchanged between Alice Foston, the widow of Thomas Walshe, jeweller of York, who had moved to Ireland, and Robert Lofthouse, a draper of York, with whom she had two children. Present at the meeting in Margaret Ely's room in the monastery of St Clement were the parties, Margaret Ely, Alice Foston's son William (who is the source of the information that follows), and Sister Beatrice Benyngton. William told the court in York that he had not been specifically called to be present on a certain day between the feast of the purification of the Virgin and Easter 1392, but that he happened to overhear an exchange of words between the three while he was in the room. Margaret Ely asked Robert Lofthouse:

---

[15] CP, E 198 (1393).

"why did you refuse to swear with Alice who is present here" and he responded "the troth that I pledged there I shall keep and I shall make her as good a woman as I am a man and I want to have her as my wife". And the said Alice responded "I hold myself content and I always held myself well content and you promised me this a long before this".[16]

This meeting was informal, and shows few of the characteristics of the Hovingham meeting. William Foston was only present because his mother was there and the occasion was not surrounded by any of the paraphernalia of a legal occasion. The parties did not have representation and they did not consult with advisers. Nor did they formally deposit their testimony. In fact, the only other witness to the occasion, Sister Beatrice Benyngton, said that she had to move closer to Alice and Thomas to hear what they were saying. Nevertheless, the occasion also seems to carry some special importance, due to the presence of the two nuns. Though it is doubtful whether it can be characterised as a tribunal, properly speaking, it did manage to fulfil the same function, namely to establish whether there was a case to be answered before a more formal court under the auspices of the *Curia Eboracensis*.

The previous cases have illustrated that it was common for the litigants in York to explore the issues of their cases before they came before the court proper. These investigations took several forms, from the informal meeting in Sister Margaret Ely's chamber in Clementhorpe to what appears to be a very formalised meeting at the parish church of Hovingham in the case of *Lovell* c. *Marton*. Mostly these meetings were convened, but the informal meeting in Clementhorpe seems more casual. What these meetings had in common, however, was that they explored the issues at hand and established whether there was a case to answer before a larger ecclesiastical tribunal.

Not all tribunals met solely to establish the facts of a case before submitting it to the church courts. They served an additional function in the impotence case *Lambhird* c. *Sanderson*.[17] The defendant in this case, John Sanderson of Wele, was cited before the court in York in

---

[16] "Dicta Margareta quesivit a dicto Roberto Lofthous, tunc presente, quomodo nitebat fateri cum Alicia de Foston, predicta ibidem presente. Et ipse respondebat: 'Fidem quam ipsam promisi, servabo et faciam eam bonam mulierem sicut ego sum vir et volo habere eam in uxorem meam'. Et dicta Alicia respondebat: 'Teneo me bene contenta et semper tenui me bene contenta, et ista promisistis mihi longe ante istud tempus'." CP, E 198-1, William Foston.

[17] CP, E 105 (1370).

June 1370 by his wife Tedia Lambhird, who petitioned to have their marriage dissolved alleging his impotence. They had previously cohabited for four years, after which time Tedia moved away from John. The couple was then summoned before the dean of Holderness, Thomas of St Martin, who ordered them to resume their cohabitation. They did so for an unspecified length of time, but in the six months preceding the hearings in York they had lived in separate households. John Sanderson was exposed to two tribunals with two different aims: one was an informal attempt by his family to discover if his impotence could be cured; the other was a formal physical examination by the court in York.

The first tribunal, if it can be called this, met in a barn in the grounds of John Sanderson senior's house. The witness Thomas, son of Stephen, from Wele had seen Tedia and John:

> in a barn in Wele belonging to John Sanderson, the father of John, the defendant, on a certain day around the feast of the Ascension of Our Lord three years ago, before the hour of nones of that day, trying to perform intercourse with due diligence for that work. And he says by his oath that he then saw the member of said John laying low and in no way rising or becoming erect. And at that time he saw the brother of said John stroke the said member of John. And he says that he often saw the said John and Tedia, concerned in this case, both before and after that time lying together in one bed, but he did not see them trying to perform intercourse.[18]

It is impossible to tell from the evidence whether this attempt at intercourse occurred before or after Tedia's and John's first encounter with the legal system of the church in the shape of the court of the dean of Holderness. The incident appears very informal and is certainly not the kind of activity that one not would expect the church to condone. Regardless of its good intentions, the attempt was to no avail, for the

---

[18] "In orreo Johannis Sanderson, patris carnalis Johannis, de quo agitur, apud Wele quodam die circa festum ascensionis domini, tribus annis elapsis, ut credit, ante horam nonam ipsius diei, carnali copule operam adhibentes cum diligentia debita in hac parte. Et dicit in juramento suo quod tunc vidit virgam ipsius Johannis submissam et nullo modo se erigentem vel erectam. Et tunc vidit fratrem carnalem ipsius Johannis, de quo agitur, palpare ibidem virgam Johannis predictam. Et dicit quod sepius tam post quam ante dictum tempus vidit ipsos Johannem et Tediam, de quibus agitur, uno lecto simul nudos jacentes, sed non vidit eos carnali copule operam adhibentes." CP, E 105 (1370).

neighbourhood rumour was that John and Tedia never consummated the marriage.

Considering the evidence contained in the results of the second tribunal, it can be said with certainty that there was a good physical explanation as to why John and Tedia did not have intercourse. When the case was heard in York, the court decided to have John examined *per aspectum corporis*. This kind of investigation was performed by a group of women appointed by the court to attempt to arouse sexually the man in a case of alleged impotence.[19] The description of John's penis given by the three women who investigated him leaves no doubt that his impotence had a physical explanation:

And she says that the member of said John is like an empty intestine of dead skin not having any flesh in it, nor veins in the skin, and the middle of its front is totally black. And said witness stroked said member with her hands and put it in semen and having thus been stroked and deposited it neither expanded nor grew.[20] Asked if he has a scrotum with testicles she

---

[19] James A. Brundage, *Law, Sex and Christian Society in Medieval Europe* (Chicago 1987), pp. 163–64, 290–92 and 376–78, describes the canon law stance on impotence. This rather surprising way of establishing the fact of a man's impotence seems to have been unique to England, Helmholz, *Marriage Litigation*, pp. 87-90. For a history of this kind of tribunal, see the two articles by Jacqueline Murray, "Trial by Congress", *Lawyers Weekly*, 6, no. 44, 20 March, 1987, pp. 20–21. 31; "On the Origins and Role of 'Wise Women' in Causes for Annulment on the Grounds of Male Impotence", *Journal of Medieval History*, 16, (1990), pp. 235–49. *Women in England, c. 1275-1525: Documentary Sources*, ed. P. J. P. Goldberg, Manchester Medieval Sources (Manchester, 1995), pp. 219–22 contains a translation of an impotence case (CP, F 111, *Russel* c. *Skathelok*) from 1432. By placing this transcript in the section on prostitution, Goldberg implies that the women who appears such tribunals were prostitutes. This seems unlikely given that the women were always married and described as of good standing in the community.

[20] This appears to be the only known instance of this nexus of words being used in English sources. My decision to translate it as "semen" is based on the following reasoning: Charlton T. Lewis, *A Latin Dictionary Founded on Andrews' Edition of Freund's Latin Dictionary Revised, Enlarged, and in Great Part Rewritten* (Oxford, 1987), *flos*: has the translation "the best part of something" or "the highest part, the top, crown, head of a thing, froth of wine"; R.E. Latham (ed.), *Revised Medieval Latin Word-List from British and Irish Sources* (London, 1965), s.v. "flos", has "menstruation". *Flos* thus refers to some sort of distillation or effluent. Its conjuction with the masculine *fratris* makes it impossible for it to refer to an effluent from the female body, such as menstrual blood, and it therefore refers to an effluent from the male body. (I would like to express my gratitude to the neo-Latin discussion group on the Internet whose comments about the meaning of the phrase are condensed in this note.)

says that there is in that place the skin of a scrotum, but the testicles do not hang in the scrotum but are connected with the skin in their extremities as is the case among young infants.[21]

Judging from this description of John's penis which the tribunal of "good and honest women" gave to the court, John suffered from a relatively common malformation of his penis called hypospadias and the court annulled the marriage, an unsurprising outcome given the evidence.

The cause paper evidence in York thus suggests that the church monopoly on the settlement of matrimonial disputes was never seriously challenged. It also suggests that this monopoly was wholeheartedly accepted by the laity. It is also clear, however, that the laity sometimes attempted to settle their disputes over marriage without the involvement of the court proper. The preceding analysis shows that such dispute settlement was always performed on an *ad hoc* basis, as evidenced by the fact that informal attempts at dispute settlement took on a plethora of forms and never settled into one specific form or procedure. The existence of such a consensus about the dispensation of justice in marriage cases is the only way to explain the various levels of formality and the multitude of structures that surrounded these tribunals that assembled to hear and determine whether individual cases should be heard by the church courts. Indeed, although they existed and were very active, lay tribunals were not there to replace a meeting of a church court. Instead they supplemented the church courts and weeded out those cases that the church tribunals did not need to hear. They were, in other words, intended to supplement rather than replace the church courts.

[21] "Et dicit quod virga dicti Johannis est quasi quedam intestina vacua de mortua pelli, non habens carnem interius nec venas in cute et est medietas anterior eiusdem nigra totaliter. Et ista testis palpavit dictam virgam cum manibus suis et posuit eam in flore fratris et sic palpata et deposita nec dilatabat se nec crescebat. Interrogata si habet bursam cum testiculis dicit quod est ibi pellis bursalis sed testiculi non pendent in bursa sed sunt contigui cum carne in unguibus sicut est in juvenibus infantibus." CP, E 105 (1370).

6

Courts and Communities

Litigants in the York cause papers had good reason to use the legal system, either in the court proper or by using informal ways of investigating marriage disputes. In court, their cases were judged on their merits,[1] the court's personnel was well trained and the cause papers show that they usually gave good advice to their clients. The laity also trusted the courts and their personnel, even though their previous association with the court may not have been to their liking. It was often the case that a former witness or litigant either bequeathed money and goods to named members of the courts years after their contact with the courts or that they appointed members of the courts to be executors of their wills. For example, despite his good reason to be disenchanted with the court's treatment of the marriage of his son to Agnes Huntington, John Bristol, senior, trusted the court with appointing executors for his bequests on his death.

Despite the willingness of most litigants to seek the decision of the court, there were some instances in York where the cases were brought to the court as a last resort, either because a local tribunal had failed to find a satisfactory solution or because of difficulties in assembling such tribunals. Although many marriage disputes were doubtless settled in the local community, the courts sometimes had to step in. The cases presented in this chapter are unusual either because the litigants come from isolated rural areas where there was no local community or because they dealt with matters that one of the litigants would rather not have broadcast locally, such as a noble woman's inability to defend herself,[2] or a nobleman's case of annulment for impotence.[3] The cases also suggest that the absence of a local community may have made it more likely that a conflict deteriorated into violence, though the absence of reliable population figures for these

---

[1] Only one litigant ever saw fit to challenge a decision of the court on procedural grounds.

[2] *Carnoby c. Monceaux.* CP, E 179 (1390). See below, p. .

[3] *Paynell c. Cantilupe.* CP, E 259 (1368). See below p. .

areas make it impossible to say for certain. A proportion of the cases that came before the court were therefore cases that included the improper use of force to persuade one litigant to conform with another litigant's wishes, whether they be that he or she marry or remain silent about sexual impotence. The cases investigated in this chapter will show why it was an advantage for the laity to seek the adjudication of the courts: although the violence alleged often brought about a solution, this solution was often short-lived and lasted only for so long as one party was able to maintain their superior force. The solution backed by the church was of a more permanent character. One of the parties in a violent case may have seen the violence as the quick solution to the problem of establishing or maintaining a marriage, but the person on whom the violence was performed always had the possibility of challenging the marriage at almost any time, at least as long as the couple remained faithful. It may thus be said that these cases illustrate the difficulty the laity ran into when trying to regulate their marriages without the proper rule of law.

The voluntary consent of the parties was essential for the validity of a marriage contract. The defence that a marriage had been contracted under undue pressure was often heard by the courts in York,[4] as canon law allowed marriage only if it had been contracted voluntarily. The force had to be severe, however, before the court allowed a marriage contracted by *verba de presenti* to be dissolved. The phrase that came to be used as a measure for the legality of the force applied was that it caused *metus qui cadere potest in constantem virum/mulierem* (the fear that can fall upon a constant man/woman).[5] Among the parties who claimed to have been exposed to force there seems to have been an uncertainty as to what extent of force was admissible as an impediment to marriage. The alleged force ranged from unspecified pressure to consummate marriage (*Aungier* c. *Malcake*),[6] to threats by family

---

[4] Five cause papers alleged that marriage had been contracted under duress: CP, E 23, 26, 33, 62, 85.

[5] The phrase is used in C. 22 q. 4 c. 22; X 4.14.14–15; X 4.2.9; and X 5.16.1. Compare James A. Brundage, *Law, Sex and Christian Society in Medieval Europe* (Chicago, 1987), pp. 335, 345, 454; Charles Donahue, Jr, "The Policy of Alexander the Third's Consent Theory of Marriage", in *Proceedings of the Fourth International Conference of Medieval Canon Law*, Stephan Kuttner (ed.) Monumenta Iuris Canonici, 5 (Città del Vaticano, 1976), p. 272; R. H. Helmholz, *Marriage Litigation in Medieval England*, Cambridge Studies in English Legal History (Cambridge, 1974), pp. 90–94 (with sample cases pp. 220–28) .

[6] CP, E 76 (1357).

members to cut off the plaintiff's ear (*Crane* c. *Draycote*);[7] to virtual raids on the house of the defendant, incapacitating her household servants and forcing her to marry (*Carnoby* c. *Monceaux*).[8] In those surviving cases which preserve a sentence, we can see that the court insisted that weapons had to be drawn before passing a sentence annulling a marriage for force and fear.

The duress argued in the York cases had to be severe to stand up as an objection to marriage in the court. Among the threats disallowed by the court was those alleged in *Crane* c. *Draycote,* where the plaintiff's aunt threatened to cut off his ear if he did not consent to a marriage. The unspecified force argued in *Acclum* c. *Carthorp* is incidental to a claim of previous intercourse with a kinswoman of the defendant.[9] The violence in *Hopton* c. *Brome* consisted of force of an unspecified kind being applied to persuade a young widow to marry her guardian's seven-year-old son, while the claims in *Marrays* c. *Rowcliff* were of threats of being thrown into a well and of not receiving a dowry.[10] Only the widowed *pars rea* in *Hopton* c. *Brome*, Constancia, daughter of Walter Brome from Skelmanthorp, was successful in her plea, but she also argued that she had later contracted a valid marriage to a certain John Bosewell, and that her union to William the son of Adam Hopton was consanguineous.[11]

Although force was used in a number of cases, a successful plea based only on the existence of force is rare. Each instance of violence in the cause papers will be treated in turn below, but it is informative to begin with the only successful case among the fourteenth-century cause papers based solely on a defence of force and fear. This is *Penysthorp* c. *Waldegrave* in which John Penysthorp petitioned the *Curia Eboracensis* to have his marriage to Elizabeth Waldegrave dissolved.[12]

---

[7] CP, E 23 (1332–33).

[8] CP, E 179 (1390).

[9] CP, E 33 (1337). See below, p. .

[10] *Hopton* c. *Brome* and *Marrays* c. *Roucliff.* CP, E 62 (1365–1366), and 89 (1348). See below p. and p. .

[11] See below p. .

[12] *Penysthorp* c. *Waltegreve.* CP, E 26 (1334). Some depositions from this case are printed in Helmholz, *Marriage Litigation*, pp. 221–23. Compare Donahue, "Policy", p. 264. Although William Aungier, the fourteen-year-old plaintiff in *Aungier* c. *Malcake*, claimed to have been exposed to force and was successful in his plea to have his marriage dissolved, I find it more likely that he won his case because of nonage at the time of the alleged contract. Force is only one of several

On 25 May 1334 Thomas Laysing from the village of Penysthorp was interrogated by the consistory court in York. He told the court that John Penysthorp had disappeared from his father's house on the first day of August the previous year and that John's father had ordered Thomas and his fellow witness William, son of Thomas, to go and find him. Thomas and William believed that John had gone to see Elizabeth Waldegrave in the village of Wynsted, and therefore, at dusk Thomas and William followed him. They entered the garden by her father's house, where they hid in the dark.

> By the light of the stars and from behind a haystack, they heard and saw five or six men wielding swords, knives and other weapons enter the baking house where John was waiting for Elizabeth. Soon after, Elizabeth came to the house and Thomas heard her brother, Richard, threaten John that he must contract marriage with his sister: if he did not Richard would kill him. Thomas Laysing heard John Penysthorp respond that he would rather comply with Richard Waldegrave's command than die, whereupon he took Elizabeth's hand and said "Here I give you my oath to have you as my wife, if Holy Church permits this". Elizabeth answered at once "Here I give you my pledge to do the same". Asked whether John was threatened with force that could sway a constant man and whether John had protested sufficiently, the witness answered "Yes", because – he believed – if John had not complied he would barely have escaped with his life.[13]

He added that John had run away from Elizabeth that same night and

---

impediments argued in *Brome* c. *Hopton*. The defendant, Constantia Brome, also argued that she had contracted a valid marriage with another man. The existence of force is alleged but is not argued as an impediment to marriage in *Carnoby* c. *Monceaux*.

[13] "ac viderunt et perceperunt per lucem stellarum quinque vel sex ingredi pistrinam infra gardinum predictum gladiis cultellis extractis et aliis generibus armorum in qua erat tunc dictus Johannes expectans adventum dicte Elizabeht. Et modicum post audivit Ricardum fratrem eiusdem Elizabeht dicere et cominari eundem Johannem quod dictam Elizabeht per manum caperet et matrimonium cum ea contraheret. Alioquin ipsum interficeret. Et audivit prefatum Johannem sibi respondere quod hoc faceret antequam moreretur. Audivit prefatum Johannem dicere eidem Elizabeht: 'hic do tibi fidem meam habere te in uxorem meam, si sancta ecclesia hoc permitteret'. Dicta Elizabeht respondit statim: 'Hoc do tibi fidem meam ad idem faciendum' ... Dicit quod bene novit quod idem Johannes fuerat qui minas passus est et contraxit ac Ricardus et Elizabeht supradictos quia voces eorumdem diu ante bene notas habebat. Requisitus an idem Johannes per vim et metum qui cadere poterant in constantem virum extitit compulsus ad matrimonium contrahendum ut premittitur dicit quod sic, quia in juramento suo verisi-

had lived in a different county since he returned with Thomas and William to his father's house in Penysthorp.

The court also interrogated Elizabeth's brother, Richard Waldegrave, the man who was behind the violence. Richard explained that he had expected John to come to Elizabeth's father's house on that night because he had learned that he had common access to his sister. Richard agreed with Thomas Laysing in most details, although he did not specify how many people were present at the incident. In answer to the crucial question of why he had drawn his sword, Richard explained that he had drawn to prevent John from leaving the baking house. Indeed, Richard Waldegrave confirmed to the court that he believed that John would not have contracted marriage with Elizabeth unless Richard had been present and had acted as he did. Whether his threat had been enough to sway a constant man he could not say.[14]

In all, four witnesses were interrogated before the commissary general in York, and all confirmed that the marriage had been contracted with weapons drawn. Based on these depositions the court annulled the marriage, declaring that it was invalid and had never legally existed because John had not freely consented to it. Despite the fact that Richard Waldegrave maintained to the last that he did not consider the threat of violence to be of such a nature that it invalidated his sister's wedding, his heavy-handed threats were held to be the kind that would make a constant man change his mind.

The case of *Penysthorp* c. *Waldegreve* demonstrates the limitations of self-regulation. It seems that Richard Waldegreve's actions and his insistence on a quick regularisation of the liaison indicate that he was outraged by their irregular affair. He also acted without the presence – and, one presumes, knowledge – of his father, who was almost certainly still alive.[15] The disadvantage to his course of action would

---

    militer credit idem juratus quod nisi Johannes contraxisset matrimonium cum eadem Elizabeht ... idem Johannes magnum malum in corpore suo habuisset et vix cum vita evasisset. Idemque Johannes quatenus potuit et audebat huius contractum contradixit et reclamavit reputatione ipsius jurati." CP, E 26 (1334).

[14] "Et credit verisimiliter quod idem Johannes predicto modo non contraxisset nisi ipse juratus fuit et modo quo premittitur fecisse. Sed an idem metus potuisset in constantem virum cadere qui ut dicitur eidem Johanni fuerat per eundem Ricardum illatus nescit." CP, E 26 (1334).

    Richard Waldegrave's deposition is published in full in Helmholz, *Marriage Litigation*, pp. 221–22.

[15] It is unlikely that the witnesses would refer to Elizabeth's *father's* house if he was not alive at the time of the alleged contract.

soon have become apparent to Richard Waldegreve: his solution depended entirely on his own ability to enforce it. He could have reported John Penysthorp and his sister to the local church court for fornication, had he so wished. He chose to settle the matter himself without the help of the local community or the church courts. John Penysthorp, on the other hand, had the opportunity of taking the case before the courts to obtain an ecclesiastically sanctioned solution to his problem.

Litigants naturally had to make a strategic decision about how to argue their cases before the court, but incidental information sometimes makes it clear that one of the litigants had been exposed to a threat of violence which could have invalidated the contract itself. In at least two cases the legal argument of the case could have been strengthened by an inclusion of some of the circumstances under which the vows were pronounced. In one case (*Carnoby* c. *Monceaux*, 1390–91), the plaintiff John Carnoby, who had forced the lady of Barmston Manor, Johanna Monceaux, to contract marriage, may have settled the case out of court.[16] In another case (*Aungier* c. *Malcake*, 1357–58) the court allowed the fact that the plaintiff appeared not to have been fully grown because of illness in his infancy, and possibly the fact that he had grown up as a member of the household of the uncle of his fiancée, as evidence that he could not have made an entirely unforced vow. But this leniency was not a general feature of the practice of the court, as is seen in *Crane* c. *Draycote* (1332–23) and *Marrays* c. *Rowcliff* (1365–66).

On 3 October 1390 John Carnoby brought a suit against Johanna Monceaux, lady of Barmston in Holderness. John claimed to have contracted marriage with Johanna on the Wednesday before the Purification of the Virgin by words of present consent, and that the exchange of vows was followed by intercourse. Two weeks later, however, he submitted another set of positions which were identical to the previous set except for the fact that he no longer claimed to have had intercourse with Johanna. John's three witnesses confirmed that an exchange of vows of present consent took place in front of a cupboard in the living room of the manor of Barmston.[17] One of the

---

[16] Raine, *Testamenta Eboracensia*, i, p. 398.

[17] "Audivit prefatum Johannem et Johannam matrimonium inter se contrahere sub hac forma, ipso Johanne primo sic dicente, 'hic accipio te Johannam in uxorem meam et ad hoc do tibi fidem meam'. Eadem Johanna statim respondente, 'hic

witnesses added that Johanna on separate occasions had sworn to the marriage in front of other witnesses.[18]

Johanna countered with the claim that John was below her social class in the prestige of his name and in income, implying that therefore she could not have consented to him as her husband. She brought five witnesses to testify to her wealth. All five confirmed that not only was Johanna a wealthy *domina* with an annual income from rent of 300 marks but she was also of royal blood. In addition, they claimed that John's witnesses were his servants and therefore not to be trusted.

Johanna Monceaux's proctor did not argue what may have been her best defence: she had clearly been forced to contract with weapons drawn. This circumstance of the contract only became clear during the questioning of Johanna's twenty-one-year-old son William Monceaux, who was her third witness. William explained to the court that he knew that John's witnesses were his household servants who lived and rode with him in his retinue. Asked how he knew this, William answered that he had heard John say so in the hall of Barmston Manor. William also explained that he had seen the four of them there:

> while John was speaking to the said Johanna, with various weapons drawn – as this witness saw – and they prevented the other servants of Lady Johanna and the witness from doing the duty of their office in that house.[19]

Other witnesses heard for Johanna confirmed William's story that the marriage was contracted under the threat of violence. It seems almost as if Johanna did not fear that John's plea would be successful. The case was not followed through after the hearing of Johanna's witnesses, and the case was dismissed on the 15 February 1391 after

accipio vos Johannem in virum meum et ad hoc do vobis fidem meam' ... Interrogatus an stando vel sedendo sic contraxerunt dicit quod stando juxta unum *copborde* in aula predicta." CP, E 179.

[18] "Super secundo articulo requisitus dicit quod diversis vicibus de quibus non recolit audivit dictam Johannam fateri hunc contractum in presentia eiusdem Johannis, istius jurati, et aliorum de quorum nominibus non recolit a tempore citra quo huius contractus habitus fuit, ut prefertur." CP, E 179.

[19] "[dum] Johannes Carnoby loquebatur cum domina Johanna predicta, et cum diversis armis extractis – prout iste juratus vidit – et impediverunt alios servitores eiusdem domine Johanne et istum juratum debita officia sua facere et eadem exercere in domo predicta." CP, E 179.

John Carnoby's third consecutive non-appearance.[20] One can only guess at the reasons for John abandoning the case: he may have realised that he had already lost the case or have been detained by someone. One piece of information, however, indicates that the case may have been settled out of court and ended in the marriage of Johanna Monceaux to John Carnoby. In her will, which was proven in 1420, Johanna asked to be buried next to her husband, John, in the parish church in the village of Carnoby.[21] Her marriage to John Carnoby must, however, remain speculation: the cause paper file itself does not give us any indication why John abandoned his case.

Johanna Monceaux presented a particular version of the events of her marriage to John Carnoby to the court of York. Instead of making the embarrassing admission that she had been taken unawares by John – and that her household was unable to protect her in her own manor – Johanna Monceaux chose to present a strong case that she had never agreed to marriage with him. She probably felt that the obvious difference in estate spoke for itself. Her proctor – who would be familiar with the practice of the court – would know that Johanna stood a better chance of avoiding marriage entering the defence that she had never consented to marriage – and thus that a marriage never existed – rather than having to argue that the attendant circumstances made it invalid – and thus have an existing marriage annulled.

Another reason why Johanna Monceaux did not argue that she had been coerced into marriage may have been that the court in York rarely dissolved marriages because of force and fear. This was particularly true in cases where one or both parties were not yet of marriageable age. Although the law allowed people to contract marriage from the age of seven, they could either dissent or consent to the marriage when they reached the age of puberty. The dissent had to be made before an ecclesiastical court and in public. Many litigants waited too long before they sought the judgment of the court. This was especially the case for those litigants who were in their teens when they contracted marriage. Here two such cases, *Crane* c. *Draycote* and

---

[20] "XV die mensis februarii predicto parte actrice ut supra comparente nullo modo. Ideo contumatus reputatur et in pena contumatie sue conclusum est causa." CP, E 179.

[21] Johanna Monceaux's will suggests that she eventually married John Carnoby. In it she asks to be buried beside her husband John in the parish church of Carnoby. Borthwick Institute of Historical Research, probate register, vol. 2, fol. 495. Extracts of the will are printed in J. Raine (ed.), *Testamenta Eboracensia: or Wills Illustrative of the History, Manners, Language, Statistics, &c. of the Province of York from the Year MDCCC Downwards*. Surtees Society, 4 (Durham, 1836), p. 398.

Marrays c. *Rowcliff*, the former of which was appealed to York from the court of the archdeacon of Nottingham, will be presented.

Crane c. *Draycote* dealt with the validity of an exchange of vows that had taken place eight years earlier while the couple were in their early teens.[22] The marriage had clearly been an arranged affair: according to the witnesses heard for the plaintiff, Alice daughter of Richard Draycote, the vows were exchanged before an assembled group, consisting of Henry Kykton and his wife, Felicia; one of her kinsmen, John Draycote;[23] one of the servants of the household, Adelina, daughter of Robert Crophill; and the wife of another servant, Elizabeth Crane.[24] These witnesses claimed that the parties had contracted by *verba de presenti* eight years earlier and that they had just been old enough to contract marriage: both of them had turned fourteen years of age at the time of the contract.[25]

William Crane contested this version of events. In his exceptions to the witnesses, he claimed that he had been only thirteen years of age at the time of the contract, not the required fourteen. As a further objection he claimed that he had been forced to marry by Elizabeth Crane's threats. His witnesses explained that she had threatened to cut off William's ear if he did not marry Alice.

That the threat scared William to obey seems clear. But he and Alice never consummated the marriage, and the witnesses heard for William all agree that there had been no cohabitation and that the couple had no children. The witness Hugo Wodecok, who was heard on 27 September 1333, explained that:

from the time of the said contract he often heard said William protesting

---

[22] CP, E 23 1332–33.

[23] He described himself as *unus de familia* [*partis actricis*].

[24] An extract of the libel, four witness accounts (one for the plaintiff, three for the defendant) and the sentence passed by the archdeacon in Nottingham are printed in Helmholz, *Marriage Litigation*, pp. 210–14. A short précis of the case is printed in Donahue, "Policy", p. 264.

[25] "audivit ubi Willelmus accepit dictam Aliciam per manum sic dicendo: 'Hic accipio te Aliciam sicut in uxorem meam legitimam habendam et tenendam usque ad finem vite mee si sancta ecclesia hoc permittat, et ad hoc do tibi fidem meam,' muliere statim respondente: 'Willelme, hic accipio te in virum meum legitimum habendum et tenendum usque ad finem vite mee si sancta ecclesia hoc permittat et ad hoc do tibi fidem meam' ... Vir erat tunc temporis tresdecim annorum et amplius, mulier erat fere quatuordecim annorum." CP, E 23.

and denying and he saw him avoid the company of that woman in all those places where he saw them.[26]

But the case was not brought to court until Alice demanded a judgment in the case eight years after William should have indicated his lack of consent. A sentence from the court in York does not survive. Even though there had been no cohabitation, the fact that he had not brought the case to court immediately had been taken by the court in Nottingham to indicate William's consent to the marriage.

The court in Nottingham passed a sentence upholding the marriage, but it seems that the judge was somewhat uncertain about whether he had reached the right decision. A transcript of the case was sent to the consistory court in York after two meetings of the court of the archdeacon of Nottingham had been taken up with unspecified *deliberationes* between the judge and the proctors of the court, and the case was allowed to proceed to York almost immediately. There are no further papers and no sentence from York. Whether the *Curia Eboracensis* agreed with the sentence and saw no reason to proceed with its own investigation, the case was settled out of court after its transmission from Nottingham, or the papers of the court in York have not survived, the case seems to have been settled to the parties' satisfaction.

Another case of teenage marriage, *Marrays* c. *Rowcliff*, is comparable to *Crane* c. *Draycote*. Alice was abducted by Lord Brian of Rawcliff eighteen months after she solemnised her marriage to John Marrays and she may have brought the case at Lord Brian's instigation. Like William Crane, the defendant Alice Marrays claimed that she was under age at the time of the contract (and indeed she appeared in court under the tutelage of her proctor). She also claimed that she was coerced to contract with John Marrays. According to witnesses, her uncle had threatened that if she did not comply with the marriage she would never receive a dowry, and her brother had threatened that if she refused the marriage he would throw her into the nearest well. Like William Aungier, the plaintiff in *Aungier* c. *Malcake*, she had lived with her future spouse's family before the marriage took place. These factors, which no doubt persuaded the court to pass sentence against William Aungier's marriage to Johanna Malcake, were disallowed by the court in this case. The court decided in favour of

---

[26] "dicit etiam quod a dicto tempore contractus citra semper audivit reclamantem ipsum Willelmum et renitentem, et vidit ipsum consortium illius mulieris in omnibus locis fugientem in quibus ipsos videbat". CP, E 23.

marriage between Alice and John Marrays, because the court heard evidence that Alice had not only expressed a wish to marry John Marrays on several occasions but had also confessed to her desire to have him treat her as his wife.

The case started sometime before 27 September 1365 when the court in York appointed Edward Cornwall, one of the court's proctors, as a guardian for Alice, the teenage daughter of Gervase of Roucliff.[27] This was most likely done in response to an oral libel entered by John Marrays, who claimed to be Alice's legal husband. John also appointed a proctor on 4 October 1365. He chose to be represented by John Stanton, another experienced proctor of the court in York.[28] The issue was joined in a written libel on 14 October. In his libel John claimed that he had married Alice in the presence of her parents and family and that he had married her with their express consent by the help of words of present consent. He further claimed that she had been of a legal age when she later consented several times to the union in front of several people worthy of trust.[29] The case was thus a fairly simple case of nonage. But in spite of its fairly straight-forward legal argument, the witnesses in the case provide a fascinating insight into the early development of a young girl's sexuality.

John's witnesses were interrogated at the same time as Alice's. His first twenty-three witnesses were interrogated from 16 November to mid December 1365.[30] Their function was to establish the facts as John's side saw it: that John and Alice had celebrated marriage in front of witnesses around Christmas 1364; that they had spent a night together in the nuptial bed; that they behaved like a married couple; and that Alice had been of sufficient age to contract marriage. John's witnesses told the following story: John's sister, Annabile, the wife of Stephen Wastelyn, told the court that John had introduced Alice, a physically mature twelve-year-old, into her household three weeks before Christmas the previous year and that two weeks later Alice had married John.[31] The ceremony had taken place in a room called "the Steward's chamber" in the monastery of St Mary in York and had

---

[27] CP, E 89–13 (1365–66).

[28] CP, E 89–28.

[29] CP, E 89–25.

[30] The last recorded date for the interrogation of these witnesses is 8 December, but a further four witnesses were heard before January 1366.

[31] "Item dicit quod dicta Alicia toto tempore quo stetit in comitiva istius jurata ... per aspectum corporis apparet quod sit etatis quattouordecim annorum." CP, E 89–27.

been witnessed by a number of people. Most important among these was Richard Bernard, in whose room the exchange took place, but also Master Adam Thornton (a notary public), Elena, the widow of Gervase Roucliff (who was also Alice's mother), and Robert Roucliff.[32] Richard Bernard presided over the exchange and prompted the parties with the words to be used. He could therefore confidently assert that the marriage had been contracted by *verba de presenti*.

The issue of whether Alice had been forced to contract against her will received special attention. Richard Bernard informed the court that Alice had not been forced and had contracted freely and with a happy face.[33] Katherine, the wife of Robert Roucliff, had been specially concerned about whether Alice understood the implications of being married to John. Alice stayed with her on the night preceding the ceremony in St Mary's and Katherine had repeatedly asserted that she was happy with the arrangement. In fact, Katherine said:

> this witness then asked the same Alice if she was in good will to go to Karthorp to her mother and she responded that "yes" because she wanted, as she said, to go to any place where John wanted to send her.[34]

As an affirmation of the contract the couple lay together in the same bed for at least one entire night on the night of the feast of the Apostle Thomas (21 December 1364) to ratify the marriage.[35] After the contract, Alice stayed in Annabile's household from Christmas to the feast of St James (25 July 1365), when she was abducted by Lord

---

[32] At least a further two people were present: William Pottel, the estate carpenter, and Adam Porter, the janitor of the monastery of St Mary in York, accompanied Alice home after the ceremony. See below.

[33] "fuerunt presentes in camera dicti jurati infra scepta monasterii beate Marie Eboracensis Johannes Marras, Alicia dudum filia Gervasii de Roucliff, dominus Adam de Thornton, Elena, mater carnalis dicte Alicie, Robertus de Roucliff et iste juratus, ubi et quum Johannes et Alicia matrimonium adinvicem per verba de presenti contraxerunt ... Et dicit in juramento suo quod dicta Alicia voluntarie et cum bona vultu ac nullius vi vel metu ducta contraxit ut supra deposuit." CP, E 89–27, Richard Bernard.

[34] "Et ipsa jurata interrogavit tunc eandem Aliciam an fuit in bona voluntate eundi apud Karthorp ad matre sua et illa respondit quod sic quia voluit ut dicit ire ad quemcumque locum ubi dictus Johannes voluit eam mitere." CP, E 87–27.

[35] CP, E 89–27, Annabile Wastelyn. The abbot of St Mary's monastery in York, William Marrays, told the court that this event took place on the night of the feast of the Apostle Thomas (21 December 1364).

Brian Roucliff's men.[36] During her stay at the Wastelyn estate she was clearly regarded as John's wife and she continued to accept gifts from John "as if she was his wife".[37]

Following this public display, the couple had attempted to have sexual relations under more private circumstances, according to at least two other witnesses. But their attempt met with rather less success than the parties (and their parents) may have hoped. The abbot of St Mary's monastery in York, William Marrays (despite his absence from the exchange of vows, obviously a kinsman of John), explained to the court that he had been told by Alice's bedfellow, Joanna Rolleston (who was John's cousin),[38] and by John and Alice, that the couple had intercourse at least two or three times in the countryside of Grimston during the following Easter. Joanna also told William Marrays that "she heard noises between them as if they were having intercourse and how Alice two or three times moaned quietly as if she had been hurt by the activity of the said John".[39]

The attempt clearly was painful to Alice, but according to John's sister, Alice had been actively seeking the consummation of the marriage. Annabile Wastelyn explained that Alice had come to her, around the feast of the Epiphany,[40] and had explained to her that she and John had spent the night together, from bedtime to the next morning in Annabile's house in Knarsthorp. For this reason, she requested that Annabile let the marriage be solemnised, because "I am

---

[36] She was abducted by force and with weapons (*vi et armis*) according to CP, E 89–27, Stephen Wastelyn.

[37] The exact legal force of this exchange is, of course, what is at issue in this part of the case. There can be little doubt that the people at the Wastelyn estate regarded her as John's wife, but how *they* regarded her exact legal status is somewhat unclear. Although the union created in the monastery of St Mary was a legally binding one (if we are to believe John's witnesses), it is as if the inhabitants of the estate were aware that she could not have full sexual relations with John and they therefore searched out visible demonstrations of her consent to the union. Accepting his gifts (which were mundane) is clearly one such indicator. See below.

[38] A certain *Alice* Rollston, the daughter of Annabile and more than fourteen years of age, gave evidence to the court on 16 November. Although the scribe who took down William Marrays' deposition may have confused the name Johanna for Alice, William Marrays' informant would appear not to be the same, especially since Annabile Wastelyn also refers to her daughter *Johanna*.

[39] "audivit inter eosdem strepitum ad modum se adinvicem carnaliter cognoscentum et qualiter dicta Alicia bina vel trina vices reconquerabatur tacite propter opus dicti Johannis ac si fuisset tunc ex huius opere lesa". CP, E 89–27, William Marrays.

[40] Actually described as a fortnight after the Saturday before Christmas. CP, E 89–27.

of sufficient age to be his wife, but not to be his lover".[41] Instead of allowing Alice to continue speaking, Annabile asked her to wait and to repeat her statement to John when he returned home. Hence, later in the day, she repeated the request to John but added:

> Master, I will not lie with you in bed any more until marriage is solemnised between us because I am sufficiently old that I might be your wife and not your lover.[42]

John stopped Alice at this point. He pointed out that he had entered into a contract with her parents and kin according to which he would marry her at a specific date.[43] He also emphasised that he would have to pay a fine of one hundred marks or pounds to the family if he did not keep to his side of the bargain.[44] The matter seems to have rested after this, although Alice clearly was dissatisfied and wished that the question of the legality of the marriage be settled once and for all.[45] However, according to John's witnesses, Alice did not protest and continued to accept gifts from John as if she was his wife.[46]

In fact, John's witnesses present a confusing picture of how Alice thought about her sexuality in marriage. We have already seen how John's sister, Annabile, claimed that Alice actively sought her out and demanded that the marriage be consummated after the ceremony in the monastery of St Mary in York. We have also seen that John's uncle claimed to have been told by Alice's *socia in lecto* that John and Alice had attempted to consummate the marriage, but that the attempt probably was unsuccessful. Despite this attempt, it seems that Alice

---

[41] "Ego sum in sufficiente etate constituta et satis senex ad essendum uxor sed non amica sua, anglice *lemman*." CP, E 89–27, Annabile Wastelyn.

[42] "Domine, ego nolo amplius jacere vobiscum in lecto antequam matrimonium sit inter nos solempnizatum quia satis sum senex ut sim uxor vestra et non amica, anglice *lemman*." CP, E 89–27. Alice used the formal *vos* to address John.

[43] This statement flatly contradicts John's witnesses Adam Thornton and Richard Barnard who were at pains to point out that the marriage was contracted by *verba de presenti*.

[44] "Cui dictus Johannes respondit, dicens 'non dicas sic amplius. Tu scis conventionem inter matrem tuam et alios amicos tuos et me quod ego desponsabo te ad diem futuram ad quem ego servabo conventionem quia ego nolo perdere centum marcas vel centum libras.'" CP, E 89–27, Annabile Wastelyn.

[45] The court is only interested in whether this incident can illuminate whether there existed a binding marriage between John and Alice. Therefore the court does not register Alice's reaction to John's statement.

[46] For example CP, E 89–27, Annabile Wastelyn, William Marrays.

still wanted to be married as late as around Whitsun 1365, when her stepbrother, John Fische, shared her room on a visit in Stephen Waste-lyn's house. During the night he jokingly asked her:

> if she never wanted to be married to the said John or lie thus alone. And he says on his oath, that said Alice answered this witness that she would sooner be found to be married to the said John than to lie thus alone.[47]

Perhaps the more relaxed circumstances of her brother's visit brought this admission about, for she was much more curt with John's servants. William Pottel, the carpenter on the Wastelyn estate, made the bed in which Alice and John were put after the ceremony in St Mary's. He related to the court how he became acquainted with Alice's sharp tongue, when he met her some time later. He asked her how she liked her new master. She replied that she was well satisfied:

> and then this witness said to the said Alice: "May you grow well so he can do to you what is fitting". And she said, responding to him: "I am fully sufficient to be his wife, but not to be his whore!"

It is impossible to say what finally brought matters to a head, but it is clear that Lord Brian Roucliff, an otherwise unknown local noble, came to hear of the case. Although he never appeared before the court, he had clearly developed an interest in the fate of Alice. On 25 July 1365 his men rode to the Wastelyn estate and forcibly abducted Alice. As in the case of Agnes Huntington, the timing of the abduction seems to have been calculated to give Alice the longest possible breathing space away from John and his family. It coincided almost perfectly with the York court's summer recess and, as we have seen, the case did not begin in earnest until the court convened again in September 1365.

Canon law allowed a legal separation of the spouses to take place if one of three conditions applied: adultery,[48] "spiritual fornication"

---

[47] "iste juratus et ipsa Alicia jacuerunt in una camera per totam dictam noctem. Et burdando iste juratus petivit a dicta alicia, sorore sua, nuncquid mallet esse conjugata cum dicto Johanne vel jacere sic sola. Et dicit in juramento suo quod dicta Alicia respondit isti jurato quod citius mallet esse conjugata invenda cum dicto Johanne quam jacere sic sola." CP, E 89–27.
[48] X 4.19.4 and X 4.19.5.

(apostasy, heresy),[49] and attempted murder of the spouse.[50] By the fourteenth century the practice of granting a divorce to spouses for adultery had died out, and pleas for separation for adultery are rare in the surviving English marriage cases.[51] The separation for spiritual fornication does not appear in the York cause papers at all. A fourth condition grew out of the interpretation of the third condition in the practice of the courts: cruelty (*sevitia*). Reconciliation between the parties after an act of cruelty denied the possibility of a divorce *a mensa et thoro* to the parties, at least until another instance of cruelty occurred.[52]

There are only two cases that plead for a divorce *a mensa et thoro* in the fourteenth-century cause papers,[53] but at least two matrimonial and divorce cases arose out of severe disagreement in marriage. The violence and maltreatment alleged in the two divorce cases was severe: Margery Nesfeld, the plaintiff in *Nesfield* c. *Nesfield* (1394), claimed that her husband had attacked her with a stick, beaten her with it, stabbed her in the arm with his dagger and broken her "spelbon". His anger was so great that:

> he would surely have killed her, as it appeared to this witness, if he had not been pulled off her by this witness, Johanna White, her fellow witness, and John Semer, the servant of said Thomas.[54]

Margery Nesfeld left her husband as soon as she was well enough to walk (which took a fortnight). However, the case was not a straightforward case of unprovoked wife-beating. Against Margery's two witnesses to the above attack, her husband Thomas brought three

---

[49] X 4.19.7.

[50] X 4.19.1.

[51] Brundage, *Law, Sex and Christian Society*, pp. 455–56; Helmholz, *Marriage Litigation*, pp. 100–7.

[52] *Argumentum quod religiosi* to c. 27 q. 2 in Pembroke 101 fol. 60r: "Ar. quod per reconciliationem coniugii redditur fornicanti potestas in corpore alterius, ut c. scripsit [c. 27 q. 2 c. 26]. Alioquin Teberga sine uoluntate Lotharii converti posset." (quoted in Brundage, *Law, Sex and Christian Society*, p. 373.

[53] *Devoine* c. *Scot* (1348) and *Nesfield* c. *Nesfield* (1396). To these two cases of simple divorce *a mensa et thoro* must be added three others which deal with the payment of alimony to a separated wife: *Colville* c. *Darrell* (CP, E 14), *Maynwaring* c. *Tofte* (CP, E 15) and *Sub Monte* c. *Le Roser* (CP, E 241v).

[54] "et ipsam tunc voluit, ut videbatur isti jurate, occidisse nisi impeditus fuisset per istam juratam, Johannam White, contestem suam, et Johannem Semer, servientem eiusdem Thome". CP, E 211.

witnesses who testified to several instances when Margery had threatened to kill him. In at least one instance Margery had provoked the attack in such a way that it would appear to the neighbours that Thomas set upon her for no apparent reason. Thomas's servant, John Semer explained the situation:

> [The witness] says that on a certain day which he does not remember around the feast of St John the Baptist four years ago (23 June 1390), he was present in the said house where he heard the said Margaret threaten and say to the said Thomas, her husband, that she could kill him in his bed some night if she wanted to. Moved by anger, that same Thomas wanted to strike her with a blow. She escaped outside the door shouting, bellowing and crying and publicly saying that Thomas, her husband, wanted to kill her.[55]

Two instances of the court held against Margery and upheld the marriage but required Thomas to give surety that he would not maltreat Margery in the future. She tried to appeal the case to the Holy See but the official refused to defer to the appeal.[56]

In this instance the courts in York were unwilling to intervene in the marriage. The violence, or the threat of violence, was mutual and therefore not of the kind that gave the court the mandate to grant permission to the litigants to live apart. An example of a plea which could have allowed the court to grant such a separation is *Devoine* c. *Scot* (1348). The outcome of the case is uncertain since the file consists of only one document, the depositions, and even that is in a poor state of preservation. Although the depositions are difficult to read, it is possible to reconstruct the main lines in this case. It concerns severe cruelty by Richard Scot to his wife Margaret Devoine. Some years earlier, when Richard was called before the official of the archdeacon of Northumbria, Hugh Tisdale, and Master Ralph

---

[55] "Dicit etiam iste juratus quod presens fuit quodam die de quo non recolit circa festum nativitatis sancti Johannis Baptiste huic [sic] ad quatuor annos elapsos in domo predicta ubi audivit dictam Margeriam minari et dicere eidem Thome marito suo quod ipsum potuit si voluit in lecto in noctibus occidere, qui quidem Thomas, iracundia motus, voluit ipsam cum pugno percussisse, ipsa statim fugit extra ostium in altum vicum clamando, ululando et plorando et publice dicendo quod Thomas maritus eius voluit ipsam occidisse." CP, E 221.

[56] When a judge refused to defer to an appeal against his judgment, a memorandum to that effect was added to the document containing the sentence, either on its dorse or on a free area on the original face of the document. The judges in York never stated the reasons for their decision in these memoranda.

Blaykeston, the official of the dean of Newcastle, for his adultery with five other women, he was said to have admitted to it and to a number of illegitimate children, all of whom were looked after by Margaret. He appears to have had a rather exaggerated idea of the rights he had over these women, for he explained to the court that he had a right to beat his women.[57]

According to several witnesses, on a day some time before the witnesses were heard, Richard had attacked Margaret and beat her so badly with a stick that her eye had fallen out of its socket.[58] A doctor who was called to look after her immediately requested she be moved to the hospital. Richard threw him out of the house, but she managed to get to the hospital herself. She refused to leave the hospital for fear of her life and appears to have brought the case from the relative safety of the hospital in Newcastle and with the support of at least one cleric there, John Halghton, who appeared as a witness in her case.

The court had to determine two things in this case: whether there was sufficient violence to grant a divorce *a mensa et thoro* and whether the spouses been reconciled after the incident. There seems to have been sufficient evidence that there was cruelty involved in the marriage and that in general it did not work out. There is also no evidence that Richard and Margaret even spoke to each other after the incident. The case does not preserve a sentence; but on the strength of the evidence it seems safe to assume the court would have dissolved the marriage between Margaret and Richard.

The official's court in York was directed by its statutes to maintain local traditions, but in most marriage cases it appears not to have implemented any local canons to supplement Gratian's *Decretum*, the *Decretalists* and the *Decretals*. There were some deviations in cases of marriage contracted *sub poena nubendi* and in annulment for impotence cases. The court held strictly to the rules that the parties who contracted marriage had to be free to marry and have made an informed decision to marry, but the court allowed some latitude in determining whether the parties were old enough to contract marriage: women and men who could be presumed to be able to have children were considered old enough to marry.

The cause papers contain almost equal numbers of cases pleading

---

[57] "Dixerit se licentiam habere verberandi uxorem suam et alias mulieres de quibus in articulo fuit mentio." CP, E 257.

[58] "Vidit dictum Ricardum prefatam Margaretam verberare cum uno bacculo tam in humeris quam in caput eiusdem et [sic Ricardus occulum] extraxit." CP, E 257.

for the enforcement of a contract as they contain cases which plead for a dissolution of marriage. A third group, *causae matrimoniales et divortii*, plead for the dissolution of one marriage and the enforcement of another. A broad presumption in favour of marriage and a preference for upholding the *status quo* runs through the cases preserved in the cause papers. This is especially the case in cases of marriage contracted *verba de presenti*. Only two plaintiffs who alleged *verba de presenti* were unsuccessful in their plea. It was more rare to win a case of marriage *verba de futuro*. All the *verba de futuro* cases that were successful in the cause papers claimed and proved subsequent intercourse. A similar tendency can be demonstrated in multi-party litigation: where there was a conflict between two marriages, the court preferred the ongoing marriage to the claimed one: the court was reluctant to dissolve those marriages in which the parties already lived together.

Canon law allowed objections to the witnesses brought by either party to a case. More than a third of the cases contain exceptions to the witnesses, usually alleging their unreliability for such reasons as poverty or a general lying disposition. None of the exceptions filed in York can be shown to have been successful. Only a few cases alleged significant exceptions to the witnesses: mental deficiency, subornation or excommunicate status at the time of the deposition. These claims, however, were neither substantiated or disproved by the evidence of witnesses when they came to be heard by the court.

Annulment and divorce cases were also heard by the court. Two annulments were granted for male impotence, and at least one annulment was granted on the grounds of forced marriage. Perhaps most surprising, however, given the criticism that canon law has received from modern historians, is the fact that according to the cause papers no marriages were annulled because of consanguinity. One marriage was dissolved because of the litigant's minority.[59] The impediment of a marriage vow given while a previous spouse was still alive is alleged in three cases, none of which appear to have been successful. Two separation cases are preserved among the cause papers. Their outcome is uncertain but they showed severe violence in the marriages in question.

The practice of the court in all these cases can best be characterised

[59] *Aungier* c. *Malcake* will be analysed in chapter , p. .

as pragmatic: unless convincing proof was brought before the court it would pass sentence in favour of the *status quo*, maintaining those marriages that were *de facto* at the time the cases were first heard by the court.

7

Uses and Abuses

In general, the legal system served the people well in York, but there are a number of surviving cases that raise the question of whether the courts were not only used but also sometimes abused by the laity. The question is not whether the laity tried to manipulate the legal tribunals for their own ends but rather to what extent they did. It is the nature of a successful fraud that it is not discovered, but some surviving cases must ring alarm bells with the modern observer. Inconsistencies in depositions such as those found in the depositions of John Marschall and Emma Munkton in *Huntington* c. *Munkton*, contradictions between witnesses produced on behalf of the plaintiff and the defendant in cases where the defendant claimed *alibi*, and, sometimes, outright confessions of fraudulent activity make it clear that the medieval courts were as open to abuse as modern day courts. The modern observer must tread a narrow path between outright rejection of all evidence produced in the courts and a blanket acceptance of the veracity of the depositions and procedural documents presented in the courts and by the application of common sense hope to arrive at what is a close approximation of the truth. This has been the method applied so far. But there are a number of cases where the courts appear to have been stretched to the limits of legality. This chapter investigates six such cases in which the legal proces was either demonstrably abused or where attempts were made to break the spirit of the law by members of the laity who had a good knowledge of the law or, indeed, by clerics whose judgment appears to have been clouded either by a sympathy for one of the parties or by a too strong conviction about the facts of a case.

It has already been pointed out that, in the case of Agnes Huntington and Simon Munkton, the parties silently recast their argument in terms that allowed the courts to arbitrate between them. Their dispute originated in a disagreement over the Agnes's dower which Simon wanted her to consent to sell. The case as it stands is a mess: like the great east window in the York Minster, whose individual panels are a marvel but whose overall design is a disaster, the various permutations of the truth that were presented to the court in the case make sense when considered individually but clash and contradict when they are seen as a whole. Furthermore, the legal arguments presented to the court seem to bear little or no relation to the real dispute in the case. It is only through a close reading of the documents that the real reason – the dispute over Agnes's dower – becomes clear. As we know, canon law was not designed for the protection of the wife's marital property, but in the final analysis this case was a virtuoso attempt at using canon law for that particular purpose. However, the *Huntington* c. *Munkton* case is not the only one where the legal process was used to purposes other than that for which it was designed.

In a libel from 1333, Alice Palmer, the plaintiff in *Palmer* c. *Brunne and Southburn*, a *causa matrimonialis et divortii*, demonstrated to the court's satisfaction that she knew the law of marriage and had used it to gain her own ends by confessing to the York court that, with the help of perjured witnesses, she had procured a divorce in the court of the archdeacon of the East Riding from Geoffrey Brunne, her real husband, seven years earlier.[1] Alice brought new witnesses that she had obtained this annulment by paying witnesses to perjure themselves before the court of the archdeacon. The idea to use perjured witnesses to end an unhappy and conflict-ridden marriage came to Alice after she had appeared before that court to answer questions about her constant quarrelling with Geoffrey and about their public threats to do each other harm. The history of the marriage between Geoffrey and Alice, as it was presented to the court in York in 1333, was the story of a rapidly deteriorating marriage that had descended into unaccep-table violence. Given the vehemence of feeling between the two marriage partners, it is not surprising that Geoffrey contested Alice's claim. If successful, it would mean that he would have had to resume cohabitation with her. Geoffrey had married again and appeared before the court as the co-defendant with his de facto wife, Johanna Southbrunne.

Alice and Geoffrey had married some years earlier in the village of Folkton, but almost immediately disagreement had sprung up between them. Two witnesses testified that Geoffrey often beat Alice badly,[2] but Geoffrey was not the only party prone to violent outbursts:

---

[1] CP, E 25 (1333).

[2] The witnesses were Hawisia, daughter of Alfred Flixton, and Alice, the widow of Robert Flixton. CP, E 25–9.

William, the vicar of Scalby, who had been present at their marriage ceremony, reported that the violence was not always committed by Geoffrey. According to his testimony, Alice had tried to kill Geoffrey by poisoning him with arsenic.[3] The volatile tempers of the two parties clearly made a solution by traditional means difficult, if not impossible. William of Scalby then proceeded to tell the court in York about the solution that was employed to solve the problem. Alice, he said, sought the advice of her father, who suggested that they find someone to pass as her husband in an earlier marriage. She hired Ralph Fouler to impersonate her husband of an alleged earlier marriage. For this she paid him 5s.: he, in his turn, provided the canonical minimum number of two witnesses who would secure the annulment by testifying to the truth of Alice's case; the four of them convinced the court of the official of the dean of the East Riding – who may already have been in on the plan to annul the marriage – that a previous marriage had been contracted.[4] After the annulment had been granted, Geoffrey married Johanna Southbrunne, and William, the vicar of Scalby, was present to bless their nuptial bed. William was careful to point out that he was not present at the solemnisation of the marriage between Geoffrey and Johanna.[5] Had he been

---

[3] "Dicit insuper quod publicum fuit et est in parochia de Scalby quod d[icta Alicia i]ntoxicavit eundem et venenum eidem dedit ad bibendum, videlicet resalgar, quam intoxicationem et venenis potationem eadem A[licia] coram officiali Estriding' decano et Stephano Deancole clerico in capitulo Estriding' fatebatur, prout idem juratus ab eisdem referri audivit." CP, E 25–9.

[4] "Et, ut publice dicebatur, prefata Alicia una cum Gilberto Palmer, patre suo, convenerunt cum Radolfo Fouler quod ipsi darent sibi quinque solidos argenti ad hoc quod ipse veni[ret] coram officiali Estriding' et peteret matrimonium divortiari inter prefatos Galfridum et Aliciam contractum et sibi eandem in uxorem adjudicari, ratione precontractus initi inter ipsum Radolfum et eandem Aliciam ante omnem contractum matrimonialem et solempnizationem eiusdem inter Galfridum et Aliciam antedictos. Idemque juratus vidit postmodum predictum Radolfum duas mulieres in testimonium producere in causa ipsa divorciali coram dicto domino officiali Estriding' in capitulo suo." CP, E 25–9.

Strictly speaking, the marriage could have been proved by the testimony of one person, *plus* unspecified additional evidence, but the most common way to prove a point in a church court was to provide two eye witnesses.

[5] "Requisitus si scit [aliquid dicere de contractu ma]trimoniali inter predictum Galfridum et Johannam de Souhtbrune' [sic] quam tenet in uxorem dicit quod presens non interfuit aliter contrac[to solempnizato in]ter eosdem sed publicum est et notum in parochia de Brunne et parochia de Scalby quod idem Galfridus et Johanna matrimonium contraxherunt et [solempnizarun]t circiter festum Advincula beati Petri nunc proximo preterito fuerunt duo anni elapsi. Et lectum eorumdem

found to have been present, and knowing about a possible impediment to the marriage, he faced a penalty of suspension from office for three years.

The sources do not allow us to show that William of Scalby told Alice how to proceed, but there are indications that someone with a good knowledge of canon law had advised her. The economy of her measures must lead a modern observer to question whether she was advised by the court. It is clear that she either did not know how to or did not wish to have her marriage annulled before her encounter with the law. But soon after her appearance in court Alice knew how to go about obtaining her annulment with the minimum amount of fuss. It is known that the official and his assistant, Stephen Deancole, subsequently approached William Scalby as the local priest after Alice's first appearance and told him about the case. William Scalby's evidence then deviated from the evidence of the two other witnesses: he claimed that Alice's father had put her up to procuring an annulment, while carefully making sure that he could not be indicted himself for not objecting to the subsequent marriage of Geoffrey and Johanna Southbrunne. Finally, Alice's father appears, rather conveniently, to have died in the intervening years: he certainly did not give evidence to Alice's perjury as one would have expected. There are, of course, good reasons why one should expect to find no concrete evidence for direct clerical interference. The aiding and abetting of a miscarriage of justice by a cleric, then as now, carried a heavy penalty. Gilbert Scalby may well have been covering his tracks when he claimed that Alice's father had put her up to procuring an annulment. Furthermore, by telling the court in York that he did not solemnise Geoffrey and Johanna's marriage, he was also carefully making sure that he could not be accused of not objecting to the subsequent marriage. Regardless of such speculation, Alice's abuse of the legal system demonstrates that she knew how to go about obtaining her annulment. Like many other litigants in the cause papers, Alice demonstrated an intimate and surprisingly detailed knowledge of the canon law of marriage; but, unlike the majority of litigants, she also admitted to have manipulated the legal process to her own ends.

The involvement of the court in Alice Palmer's case must remain

---

Galfridi et Johanne conjugum cum venerant apud Scaby' [sic] idem juratus benedixit." CP, E 25–9.

guesswork. In the case of *Merton* c. *Midelton* the interference of the court was blatantly obvious.[6] Despite the conspicuous interference of the judge in the case, Master Ralph Waleys, however, it cannot be said that he was willing to go as far as to employ the kind of illegal strategies suggested before. Marjorie Merton's case in York was a standard *sub poena nubendi* case, but the case file contains a number of depositions about how the original sentence had come about and these statements suggest a strong bias on the part of the judge in favour of Marjorie.[7] In particular, witnesses were interrogated about the impartiality of Master Ralph who – together with Thomas Raventhorp, the summoner of the court – was alleged to have interfered in the case by goading and guiding the plaintiff when the case was first heard in Beverley on 2 October 1363.

The main argument in the Beverley case was about the exact words used when Marjory's partner, Thomas Midelton, proposed marriage. According to Master Ralph's subsequent deposition in York, Thomas claimed that he had asked Marjorie to marry him conditionally "if she behaved well and honestly", and then had sex with her.[8] These actions would, of course, have created the presumption of a marriage in the eyes of the church, but the impression of an easy confession given by this statement is contradicted by several other witnesses. In the words of master John Hatfield, a cleric who was also present at the Beverley meeting, Marjorie had initially denied that there was any contract between her and Thomas Midelton:

> and afterwards Master Ralph Waleys said to said Marjorie: "Woman, you know better: I have heard that it ought to be different" and Thomas Raventhorp, then whispering, said to said Marjorie (and this witness heard this because he inclined his ear) "say that he betrothed you". And afterwards (for the first time and not before) the said Marjorie at the instigation of the said Master Ralph and Thomas Raventhorp pursued that marriage case.[9]

---

[6] CP, E 102 (1365–67)

[7] See below , p. , for a detailed discussion of *sub poena nubendi* cases.

[8] "'Ego promisi predicte Margerie quod ducerem ipsam in uxorem si bene et honeste se gereret' dicta Margeria dicente 'Ego me bene geram per dei gratiam'." CP, E 102.

[9] "Et postea magister Radulphus Waleys dixit dicte Margerie 'Mulier, habeas de

Both master John Spynk, and the lay people (Richard Stryngham and John de Terthum) confirmed the interference of Ralph Waleys, adding that he had advised her that "you will never marry: you litigate poorly in your own case".[10] All four witnesses agreed that Marjorie initiated her case with strong support and inspiration from the two officers of the court. What inspired Master Ralph and Thomas Raventhorp to their heavy-handed interference in the case can only be guessed at. As in the previous case, however, seen from the perspective of a court eager to impose their interpretation of Christian marriage on the laity and to attract business, there was good reason to interfere to regularise the union between Thomas Midelton and Marjorie Merton, especially since they were well known to be lovers in their community. Marjorie was the single mother of Thomas Midelton's child, if we are to believe an item in her articles mentioning their six-year-old son. Although Thomas was an itinerant chapman, it is clear from other witnesses that Thomas considered their union to be serious: their property was held in common and the litigation expenses – which halfway through the case amounted to 55s. – were paid out of their joint purse.[11] A number of witnesses also commented on the fact that Thomas and Marjorie quarrelled a lot. Clearly their disagreement had not reached the level of vehemence found in the case of *Palmer* v. *Brunne* but their discord was sufficient to make at least one witness wish to see them live somewhere else. Marjorie Merton was told by two officers of the court to change her story and present her case to the court in such a way that she might increase her chances of having the alleged marriage upheld.[12]

A knowledge of the canon law rules for marriage permeated every level of society from the highest to the low. William Bridsall, the

---

melius: audivi quod aliter deberet esse.' Et Thomas de Raventhorp tunc auriculando dixit dicte Margerie (et hoc audivit iste juratus quia posuit aurem): 'dicas quod affidavit te' et extunc (primo et non ante) dicta Margeria ad instigationem dicti magistri Radolpho et dicti Thome de Ravensthorp prosequebatur causam matrimonialem." CP, E 102.

[10] "Tu nuncquam iugebis! Tu male litigas in causa tua propria." CP, E 102.

[11] "Et tunc idem Thomas interrogavit dictam Margeriam quantum expendiderat in prosecutione dicte litis. Que dixit quod quinqueginta quinque solidi. Et tunc ipse dixit 'de hoc satisfacam te et habe hic xx solidos in partem'." CP, E 102.

[12] For a detailed discussion of this case and for my reasons for thinking that the case was an attempt by Agnes to make sure that she kept control of her property, see Chapter 2 above.

mentally retarded beggar in *Redyng c. Boton*, understood the rules.[13] At the other end of the social scale we find Katherine Paynell, a noble woman from Lincolnshire who knew about these rules from her personal confessor. Her opponent, Nicholas Cantilupe, who was the grandson of the fourteenth-century judge of the same name at the King's Bench, probably knew the canon law rules of marriage from members of his family.

Given Nicholas's family background, it is perhaps surprising that he is one of a small number of litigants who tried to keep their disputes out of the courtroom by extra-judicial force. Katherine, the daughter of Sir Ralph Paynell, had initiated the case in the court in Lincoln in the first instance. There she pleaded to have her marriage with Nicholas dissolved because of his impotence. One of her witnesses explained that Katherine had often tried to find Nicholas's genitals with her hands when he was asleep, but "she could neither touch not find anything there and ... the place in which his genitals ought to be was flat like the hand of a man".[14] Nicholas presumably feared the embarrassment of an investigation into this matter for two reasons: one reason was the indignity of having to be stripped naked and having his manhood ascertained by a committee of "honest women", as outlined in the Sanderson case; the other was that the charge was probably true.[15] Not only did Nicholas try to delay the case at every

---

[13] CP, E 92. See above, p.

[14] "Et dicit quod audivit dictam Katarinam referre quod sepius temptavit manibus suis cum jacuit in lecto cum dicto Nicholao et ipse dormiebat locum genitalium dicti Nicholai et quod nulla palpare nec invenire potuit ibidem et quod locus in quo genitalia sua deberent esse est ita planus sicut manus hominis." CP, E 259–16.

[15] See above, p. Like John Sanderson, the defendant in *Sanderson c. Wele* (1370), which is the only other impotence case in the cause paper E series, Nicholas seems to have suffered from one of a series of relatively common conditions which today would be classified as "ambiguous gender". The condition from which Nicholas Cantilupe suffered affects one in six thousand male babies, while John Sanderson's conditions is seen in one in two hundred male babies. Nicholas's condition "male pseudo-hermaphroditism", has four primary characteristics: insufficiently developed sexual organs, excessive height and a deep voice, the inability to procreate and a short life expectancy, since it adversely affects the individual's immune system. Nicholas met three of these criteria: according to the inquisitions post mortem, Nicholas died without offspring at Avignon on the Friday before St Peter in Cathedra, 45 Edward III (21 February 1371). If he gave his correct age to the court in York (it differs by two years from the age given in the inquisition post mortem after his father's death), he would have been only twenty-nine or thirty years of age when he died. *Calendar of Inquisitions Post Mortem and Other Analogous Documents Preserved in the Public Record Office Prepared under the*

stage (he was threatened with excommunication for non-appearance at three consecutive meetings of the court before the case eventually started in earnest in York), but, in an attempt to make Katherine abandon the case, he abducted her and a group of her servants to one of his castles, Greasley in Nottinghamshire, which bordered on the Paynell estate. There he forced her to swear not to proceed.[16] His embarrassment over the substance of the case was clear. Robert Bekeby, a chaplain in Katherine's father's household was one of the group of people who were abducted by Nicholas's men. He explained to the court that they were met at the castle gate by Nicholas who spoke,

> saying with a grim expression: "Woman, you are cursed among all women". And he led her and this witness and the other aforementioned fellow witnesses into a certain chapel situated within that castle, and there he spoke to said Katherine in these words: "You know well that I am suffi-ciently potent to copulate with you having genitals that are good enough for married life". And she answered: "Yes". The said Nicholas added: "I demand that you swear that I am able to have intercourse, having sufficient natural instruments, as has been said, and that you henceforth do not leave my company without my special permission and that you do not reveal this

Superintendence of the Deputy Keeper of the Records, 13, 44–47 *Edward III* (London, 1954).

I am grateful to Professor I.A. Hughes of Addenbrooke's Hospital, Cambridge, for discussing the medical aspects of these two cases with me and to Dr Richard Mackenzie of Clare Hall, Cambridge, who first suggested that it might be possible to arrive at a diagnosis. However, I am solely responsible for any errors in the diagnoses in these two cases.

[16] The deposition of Katherine's father's priest Thomas Waus, a former official of the archdeacon of Stow, reads in part: "discordia suscitata occassione impotentie coeundi dicti Nicholai, sed ea non obstante, dicta Katarina die jovis proximo post festum purificationis Beate Marie Virginis ultimo preterito fuerunt duo anni elapsi traducta fuit in domum dicti Nicholai, in castrum videlicet de Cryselay. Et idem Nicholaus dictam Katarinam statim, ut premittitur, traductam ad Sancta Dei Evangelia juramentum prestare compulit corporale quod ipsa consilium suum in omnibus concelaret et nullatenus revelaret. Interrogatus qualiter compulsa fuerat ad jurandum dicit quod dictus Nicholaus dixit isti jurato quod nuncquam cum eo moraretur nisi tunc prestaret huiusmodi juramentum. Et nicholominus iste juratus vidit locum ad modum carceris ordinatum quem dictus Nicholaus sibi ostendit pro mora et inclusione dicte Katherine nisi juramentum huiusmodi prestitisset. Et postquam dicta Katherina dictum prestiterat juramentum audivit iste juratus ipsam dicere dicto Nicholao: 'Quicquid vos dicitis ego volo fateri vobiscum et in omnibus concordare'." CP, E 259–11.

counsel in any way". To which said Katherine answered: "I will swear to whatever was said by you".[17]

The witnesses do not say how Katherine and her fellows escaped from Nicholas, but it is clear that they were concerned to preempt any attempt by Nicholas to prove that she had said in public that he and she had intercourse. When the commissary general decided that the marriage should be annulled, Nicholas appealed to the Apostolic See. He died two and a half years later, on 21 February 1371, in Avignon while prosecuting the case.

Katherine Paynell did not do badly out of Nicholas's early death. When he died, he was in possession of six manors in Buckinghamshire and Lincolnshire. He was also enfeoffed by the archbishop of York with Greasley Castle in Nottinghamshire. The inquisition post mortem mentions that his wife, Katherine, was in possession of his manors Withcall, Kynthorp and Lavington in Lincolnshire. The case, which was originally initiated before the bishop of Lincoln, was probably transferred to the York court because Nicholas held Greasley Castle in fee from the archbishop of York. [18]

Having tried to keep the case out of court by the help of violence, Nicholas Cantilupe had to accept that the way he must conduct his case was not through intimidation but by working within the law. When he finally embraced the law he worked within it with vigour. His earlier behaviour is all the more surprising since he can be shown to have been familiar with the law. His grandfather, Nicholas Cantilupe, was often appointed on commissions of *oyer et terminer* in the north of England before his death in 1355. When he signed a petition to the pope asking him to determine the English right to the French

---

[17] "Aloquens torvo vultu 'Maledicta es mulier inter omnes mulieres.' Ipsamque statim una cum isto jurato et aliis contestibus proximo prenotatis in quodam oratorium situatum in eodem castro introduxit, ibique dictam Katerinam alloquitam fuerat sub his verbis: 'Tu scis bene quod ego sum sufficienter potens tecum carnaliter comiscere habens instrumenta ad coeundum satis apta'. Que respondit: 'Sic'. Dicit insuper dictus Nicholaus: 'Volo quod tu jures quod ego sum potens ad coeundum habens instrumenta naturalia, ut premittitur, et quod tu de cetero non recedas a comitiva mea sine licentia mea speciali, et quod consilium meum nullatenus reveles'. Ad que dicta Katerina respondit: 'Volo jurare quecumque vobis fuerunt prolata'." CP, E 259–11.

[18] There is no known surviving record in the Vatican Archives that shows that Nicholas continued to pursue the case. However, the conclusion is drawn from the facts presented in his inquisition post mortem above, *Inquisitions Post Mortem, 44–47 Edward III*, pp. 76–78.

crown together with the barons of the realm in 1354 he signed himself as "Nicholaus de Canti Lupo, Dominus de Grisley" – the castle to which his grandson abducted his wife.[19]

It is difficult on the basis of the two surviving fourteenth-century impotence cases to say whether a social stigma such as the one in France under the Ancien Régime was attached to impotence in fourteenth-century England.[20] John Sanderson and his family were certainly not secretive about it, but Nicholas Cantilupe reacted very strongly to the possibility of a court case and had Katherine Paynell abducted to his castle in Lincolnshire when she opened the case against him.

Among the many kinds of cases heard by the court in York, abjuration *sub poena nubendi* ("under the penalty of marrying") cases deserve particular attention, as they presented ample opportunity for the litigants to subsequently manipulate the legal process.[21] An abjuration *sub poena nubendi* was imposed by the church courts when they found that a couple had habitually fornicated. The parties were required to swear before the court that if they ever had sexual intercourse again they were married. The form of the oath was something along the lines of "I, N., swear that I here take you as my lawful spouse if I know you carnally from this time forward". For this kind of sentence to work as a deterrent from fornication it was imperative that the courts who imposed these sentences explained the consequences of subsequent intercourse to the litigants when sentence was passed or when the oath was required. Nevertheless, some confusion over the consequences of an abjuration *sub poena nubendi* is evident among the litigants and this "draconian form of contract" was clearly open to abuse.[22] All the surviving cases of this kind were brought by women

---

[19] Thomas Rymer, *Foedera, conventiones, littera et ejusconque generis acta publica, inter reges anglae et alios quosvis imperatores, reges, pontifices, principes, vel communitates: ab ingressu Gulielmi I in anglicam, AD 1066 ad nostra usque tempora habita aut tractata* (London, 1827).

[20] Described in Pierre Darmon, *Trial by Impotence: Virility and Marriage in Pre-Revolutionary France*, trans. Paul Kegan (London, 1985).

[21] For a discussion of the legal aspects of these kinds of cases, see R. H. Helmholz, "Abjuration *Sub Poena Nubendi* in the Church Courts of Medieval England", in *Canon Law and the Law of England* (London, 1987), pp. 145–56; first published in *The Jurist*, 32 (1972), pp. 80–90. See the later discussion of the same subject in R. H. Helmholz, *Marriage Litigation in Medieval England*, Cambridge Studies in English Legal History (Cambridge, 1974), pp. 172–81 and 208–12.

[22] Michael M. Sheehan, "The Formation and Stability of Marriage in Fourteenth-Century England: Evidence of an Ely Register", *Mediaeval Studies*, 33 (1971), p. 255.

who had already been in contact with an ecclesiastical court that had imposed such a sentence on them and their partner, so their understanding of the law can be expected to be somewhat more sophisticated than the understanding evinced by litigants who had no previous experience of the court.

In one case – *Rowth c. Stry* (1372–73) – the party making the appeal, the *pars appellans*, Hugh Stry, initially argued that he had not sworn in front of the official of the dean of Beverley that he would marry Cecilia Rowth if they had intercourse: the vow to which he had agreed was that he would be lashed around the church and the market in Beverley on six separate days as a penance for his transgression "unless he could obtain a better grace".[23] Hugh Stry's defence was probably not taken seriously by the York court, particularly after the court in Beverley sent a notarised copy of the sentence. He may have entered it simply to gain time to assemble a better defence and in order to prevent his being forced to take up cohabitation with Cecilia before appearing before the court of York. In the end, he did win his case on another defence. He presented witnesses to the court to testify that he had been absent from Beverley on the day when intercourse was alleged to have taken place.

The institution of abjuration *sub poena nubendi* was clearly open to abuse by a scrupulous litigant who was willing to trap the partner they abjured: in the case *Partrik c. Mariot*, Alice Partrik from Thirsk actively pursued such an aim by trying to set a trap for her partner, John Mariot, shortly after their abjuration in 1394.[24] When she appeared before the court in York she asked it to enforce her marriage to John Mariot from Sowerby, which she claimed had been contracted by abjuration *sub poena nubendi* and subsequent intercourse. Alice and John had abjured each other before the dean of Bulmer in the morning of the feast of the Purification of the Virgin that year (2 February 1394) in the standard form.[25] Their previous relationship must have lasted for a considerable time, for she claimed that she had several children by him. The abjuration may have made John more determined to end the relationship: he certainly lived in a house alone.

---

[23] "Si dictus Hugo ipsam Ceciliam extunc carnaliter cognoverit per sex dies circa ecclesiam predictam et sex dies circa forum Beverlacensis fustigaretur nisi meliorem gratiam potuerit optinere." CP, E 114–13.

[24] CP, E 211 (1394–95).

[25] This date comes from a transcript of the act book of the dean of Bulmer, which he sent at the request of the commissary general. Alice Partrik's witnesses were surprisingly vague about the date.

After the abjuration Alice set a trap for John. Knowing what she needed to do, she called William Stabyll and Richard Lambe, a parish clerk, to her. She explained that she was going to go and have sex with John that evening and asked them to make sure that they could testify to her actions. That evening, approximately half an hour after the two witnesses had seen John open his door and let Alice in, they went to his door and demanded that he come out. John did so, but contrary to what Alice clearly hoped he would do, he had not had sex with her.[26] An added complication in this case was that the two witnesses were more than usually vague about the time of the abjuration: Richard Lambe put it "sometime between the feasts of St Michael [29 September] and Christmas last", while William Stabyll put it "on a certain day", but did not even remember the time of year.[27] A memorandum from the dean of Bulmer's court, which was eventually asked for a precise date, eventually placed the abjuration on 2 February 1394. The York court decided against the existence of a marriage, but as usual it did not give its reasons. There is, however, little doubt that, despite her avowed intention and her determined method of pursuing her aim, Cecilia presented a weak case to the York court.

The confusion over the appropriateness of a sentence *sub poena nubendi* even stretched into the ranks of those passing sentences themselves. In *Forester* c. *Staynford* a judge who passed a sentence of abjuration *sub poena nubendi* seems to have been perhaps a little too keen to force fornicators to marry.[28] In 1329 John Staynford was compelled by Ralph Cournebourgh, the archdeacon of York, to solemnise a wedding with Alice, daughter of Thomas Cissour, with whom he had an adulterous affair. This sentence was imposed despite the

---

[26] "Quodam die jovis proximo post vicesimum diem natalis domini ultimo preterito dicta Alicia retulit isti jurato et Ricardo, contesti suo, quod ipsa convenit eadem nocte venire ad lectum dicti Johannis. Et infra noctis tenebras eiusdem diei, ipsa Alicia pulsante ad fenestram camere dicti Johannis, idem Johannes aperuit ostium camere sue eidem Alicie et permisit eam intrare, videntibus isto jurato et Ricardo conteste suo qui fuerunt prope cameram ipsius Johannis ad explorandum eos. Et infra dimidiam horam postea dictus Johannes fatebatur isti jurato et Ricardo, contesti suo, dictam Aliciam esse ibidem in camera cum eo, asserens tamen se ipsam nolle carnaliter cognoscere." CP, E 211–8, William Stabyll.

[27] "Quodam die de quo non recolit inter festa Sancti Michaelis et ... natalis domini ultimo preterito"; "quodam die, de quo non recolit, nec quo tempore anni, nec quando ..."

Both quotes are from CP, E 211–8.

[28] CP, E 37 (1337).

fact that John was already married. We know this because he appeared before the court eight years later as the defendant in a matrimonial and divorce case in which his *de facto* wife pleaded to have their prior marriage enforced and his marriage to Alice Cissour, which had been solemnised as a result of the previous conviction for fornication, annulled. The court granted the annulment. During the course of the case John's witnesses claimed that John contracted the second marriage out of fear of the archbishop's official, Ralph Cournebourgh, who had threatened to put him in gaol if he did not do so. It is unclear why John did not defend himself in the first case by claiming his prior marriage. Perhaps he feared an even worse penalty for admitting to adultery.

In these *sub poena nubendi* cases the litigants were clearly attempting to bend the rules of the law to fit their own ends: Hugh Stry tried to convince the court that a technical flaw in his oath to the court in Beverley made it invalid. He was probably also aware that the argument he put forward was not likely to be taken seriously by the court; he therefore presented a defence of *alibi* when the case was heard in York, and this argument won him the case. Alice Partrik, the plaintiff in *Partrik* c. *Mariot*, tried set a trap for the defendant, John Mariot, but the obviousness of her attempt to seduce him and her witnesses' vagueness about the date of the events made it easy for the court to find in favour of John Mariot. It is clear, nevertheless, from these abjuration *sub poena nubendi* cases that the litigants understood at least the outlines of the consequences of their previous meeting with the court and that in some cases they actively sought to create situations that would make it possible for them to prosecute at the court in York.

The church courts in York were clearly both being used and abused by the laity. Sometimes the laity showed considerable skill in creating acceptable narratives or creative solutions to legal problems which the canon law of marriage was not intended to solve. At other times they seem to have received some help from the courts that increased their chances of a favourable outcome. In this chapter it has been argued that the court interfered directly in two cases. In the case of Alice Palmer the evidence is circumstantial, in contrast to the clear intervention by Master Ralph Waleys in Marjorie Merton's case against Thomas Midelton. In the other cases, the litigants themselves metamorphosed their quarrel.

Despite its intricate nature, the canon law of marriage was a successful body of legislation. It penetrated to every corner of Europe in a remarkably short time. It determined the legality of a married couple's offspring, and, once its form had been finalised, it set the parameters of marital behaviour for a period of over 300 years. The imposition of the rules of the canon law of marriage may have been so successful because the courts and the laity found themselves in agreement about the goals of the courts and because the courts were willing to turn a blind eye to legal irregularities. Despite these irregularities, in the final analysis the situation as it appears in the fourteenth-century York cause paper material shows a situation from which both the church and the laity benefited. Not only were the courts successfully regularising the unions of the laity, thereby reducing the possibilities of disputes over inheritance, but spouses found a way of gaining a legal sanction against a number of abuses from their partners.

8

Marital Affection

In the spring of 1357 William Aungier, a fourteen-year-old man, sought the help of the archbishop's court in York to have his marriage to Johanna Malcake, a sixteen-year-old woman, annulled. William's father, Thomas Aungier, had died in the first onslaught of the plague when William was less than six months old. His mother had married again almost immediately, but within the year both she and her new husband also succumbed to the plague. After this disaster the guardianship of William passed to his uncle, Thomas Bekyngham, who looked after William for just over a year. At the end of the year Thomas Bekyngham was given an offer to sell his guardianship over William to Thomas Malcake – the steward of a local noblewoman – for ten marks. Thomas Malcake had a niece two years older than William, called Johanna. Thomas Malcake and Thomas Bekyngham persuaded William to exchange marriage vows with her.[1] The marriage was celebrated in the chapel of the manor of Fenwick where Thomas Malcake lived, and William, who was eight years old, and Johanna, who was ten, were put in the nuptial bed together the following night.[2] This marriage was not yet legally binding and according to

---

[1] A witness describing himself as a neighbour of Thomas Malcake for the past twenty years whose name has been lost says: "Et bene novit quod dictus Willelmus de Malcake, frater dicti Thome et patrinus ipsius Johanne, emit maritagium Willelmi, de quo agitur, de Thoma de Bekyngham pro decem [marcas] argenti et ipsam Johannam eidem Willelmo copulavit in matrimonio eidem Johanne [sic], et ipsos matrimonium adinvicem compulit, induxit et excitavit contrahere quod sic contraxerunt et verba matrimonalia inter se protulerunt." CP E 76–12, name unknown.

[2] "Et presens fuit [Johannes Forester de Kilburn], ut dicit, in capella manerii de Fenwyk quodam die ... ubi et quum vidit et audivit dictos Willelmum et Johannam matrimonium adinvicem contrahere in hec verba, 'ego accipio [te,] Johannam, in uxorem meam, habendam et tenendam usque ad finem vita mee', et econtra illa dicente, 'ego accipio te, Willelmum, in virum meum tenendum et habendum usque ad finem vite mee.' Et eodem die vidit matrimonium solempnizatum inter eosdem in capella predicta [in presentia] plurium amicorum utriusque partis, ... Et eadem nocte uter[que] simul jacuerunt in lecto, nudus cum nuda, solus cum sola, sed bene

canon law it needed to be ratified when William came of age. Only his and Johanna's consent to the marriage at an age when they were old enough to make an informed decision would make the marriage binding. As a member of the *familia* of William Malcake, Thomas Malcake's brother, William Aungier was sent to attend school in the parish of Elsing in Norfolk.[3] He lived with William Malcake for six years until he was supposed to ratify the marriage contract. Johanna stayed with her father in Fenwick and at the estate of the duchess of Hastings.

During this time, William saw little of Johanna: he spent a week with his future parents-in-law *causa recreationis* in the years between 1355 and 1357;[4] and Johanna spent a week with William in Lincolnshire at the manor of William Malcake. Both these meetings were arranged to see if they could get along with each other.[5] But some weeks before William Aungier's fourteenth birthday, William Malcake heard the disturbing news that Johanna was no longer a virgin and that she was pregnant. While William Aungier had lived with Johanna's uncle she had had sex with several men whose names neither Johanna's uncle nor she herself knew.[6] This made him decide to send William Aungier to Fenwick as soon as possible.[7] William stayed in Johanna's house for a week, steadfastly refusing to consummate the marriage. Towards the end of the week, acting upon the unspecified

---

scit quod carnaliter adinvicem non commiscerunt, eo quod dictus Willelmus [fuit] tunc novem annorum plene ac dicta Johanna xii annos non compleverat." CP, E 76–11.

[3] "Misit dictum Willelmum statim post matrimonium, ut prefertur, solempnizatum ad partes australes, videlicet ad scolas ad ecclesiam suam de Elsyn in Northfolk causa addiscendi." CP, E 76–12.

[4] William appears to have suffered some effects of the plague which made him somewhat stunted in growth: "ipse est unus miserabilis persona modica statura ... valde parva et ut apparet ad oculum extranei qui non haberet notitiam sui ipse apparet per aspectum corporis sui nondum esse etatis ix vel decem annorum ad plus." CP, E 76–12, Johannes filius Jacobus de Redness.

[5] "Ad explorandum an ipsi inter se mutuo poterunt diligere et an vellent ratificare matrimonium inter eos". CP, E 76–12, Johannes filius Jacobi de Redness.

[6] It is of course perfectly possible that she and her uncle were simply covering for the men, but the court did not enquire into this in detail.

[7] "Quo tempore dictus dominus Willelmus Malcake, audito quod dicta Johanna passa fuit et carnaliter cognosci a pluribus [nesciens tamen quot, sed credit quattuor] vel quinque hominibus prout fama publica laboravit, misit ipsum Willelmum ab illis partibus australibus et remotis ad villam de [Swyne]flet, [ubi] dicta Johanna tunc morabatur." CP, E 76–11, name unknown.

incitements of Johanna's neighbours, William spent one night with Johanna in her bed *solus cum sola, nudus cum nuda.*[8]

William was not happy about this and he discussed his predicament with his own friends. William Raynald, a witness for William Aungier, reported to the court that William Aungier had said to him that:

> It displeases me that I knew her once for she does not prize an affection that is upheld. And therefore, for sure, I intend never to consent to her that she be my wife, nor to cohabit with her.[9]

At the end of the week he followed his friends' advice and moved away to live alone before he initiated his case at the court of the commissary general in York.

William Aungier had explained to William Raynald that he wanted to base his marriage on "an affection that is upheld", but he is the only litigant in the surviving fourteenth-century marriage cases from the archbishop's court in York who explained that he expected marriage to be based on affection. His case is unique because the choice of words reported in his statements make it clear that he had an notion of marriage which included fidelity and a lasting emotional involvement with his partner. The York cause paper cases illustrate the ambiguity of the Latin phrase *affectio maritalis* or *affectio conjugalis* as it was used by witnesses in the fourteenth-century York marriage cases and demonstrate the range of its application. While the witnesses seem aware of the idea of marital affection as "a loving state of mind",[10] the two phrases maintain an element of the early Roman law idea of marital affection as a quality of will necessary both for the establishment of a legally valid marriage and for the transfer of property.

---

[8] "Et ibidem cohabitavit cum dicta Johanna per unam septimanam et hoc coactus per amicos dicte Johanne, sed de qua vi vel metu vel qui eum astrinxerunt nescit deponere. Dicit etiam interrogatus quod una nocte ... ingressus fuit lecto dicte Johanne ad excitationem quorundam vicinorum dicte ville et sic jacuit in uno lecto cum dicta Johanna, solus cum sola et nudus cum nuda." CP, E 76–11, William Raynald.

The phrase *solus cum sola et nudus cum nuda* in other surviving cases implies strongly that the witness believes that the parties had sex. This is clearly not the case here.

[9] "Displicet michi quod uncquam novi dictam Johannam, eo quod non diliget affectionem qua tenetur. Et ideo pro certo nuncquam intendo consentire in eam quod sit uxorem meam nec cum ea coha[bi]tare." CP, E 76–11.

[10] John T. Noonan, "Marital Affection in the Canonists", *Studia Gratiana,* 12 (1967), p. 509.

The term *affectio maritalis* has a long history in law but was never given a clear definition. It was first used in Roman law to mean "intent to marry". The concept was used in three contexts: to establish the existence of a marriage; to distinguish marriage from concubinage; and to establish the right of offspring to inherit. When Justinian used the phrase in a new law, a so-called *novella*, in 538 he did so in order to introduce the requirement of a public registration of marriages among the upper classes in Roman society.[11] His purpose was twofold: public registration would help enforce a prohibition on gifts between spouses and would also help distinguish legitimate from illegitimate offspring when their parents died and inheritance was distributed.[12] Although *affectio maritalis* was necessary for a legal marriage to come into being, and although Justinian did not allow divorce, Roman law did not require marital affection to be maintained forever between the spouses. *Affectio maritalis* indicated the will of the spouses to have each other in marriage but the law was unconcerned with the duration of their *affectio* beyond the moment when the marriage was registered.

The meaning of *affectio* was virtually synonymous with *affectu*, indicating the will of both parties to transfer ownership of lands and goods. As such, the word was most often used to emphasise that a spouse had displayed a willingness to allow the legal effects of marriage to come into effect and thus to indicate the quality of will needed to enter into marriage.[13] The lack of emotional content in the phrase was emphasised by the much earlier Roman jurist Ulpian, who wrote sometime in the period AD 150–250 about the legal abilities of wards and madmen: in one instance he says that members of these groups "cannot begin to possess because they do not have the will (*adfectionem*) of possession",[14] in another he excepted the madman and the ward from the restitution of property acquired by fraud because "they lack the will (*adfectu*)" to possess things.[15] In later Roman jurisprudence, however, the phrase acquired connotations of

---

[11] *Novella*, 74. 4. 2.

[12] Noonan, "Marital Affection", p. 482.

[13] Ibid., pp. 486–87.

[14] "Furiosus et pupillus non possunt incipere possidere quia adfectionem tenendi non habent." *Digesta* 5, 16, 60, quoted in Charlton T. Lewis, *A Latin Dictionary Founded on Andrews' Edition of Freund's Latin Dictionary Revised, Enlarged and in Great Part Rewritten* (Oxford, 1987), p. 65.

[15] "Hoc edicto neque pupillum, neque furiosum teneri constat quia adfectu carent." *Digesta* 43, 4, 1, quoted in Lewis, *Lewis and Short*, p. 66.

ties of affection and dependence. It was commonly used to signify the
nature of fathers' ties with their children and the brotherly love of
soldiers. By this later use the phrase acquired, in Noonan's phrase,
"not simply a legal will but an emotion-coloured intent not far from
love".[16]

Justinian's *novella* of 538 required the written registration of
marriage partners' *affectio maritalis* and this insistence on registration
of marital intent may have been the reason why the term was not
further defined until the publication of Gratian's *Decretum* around
1140.[17] Gratian emphasised the emotional content of *affectio maritalis*
and underlined its importance for the legality of marriage. He insisted
that marital affection was necessary for the creation of the marriage
bond and that once a marriage had been established with marital affection nothing short of the death of a spouse could cause a marriage to
fail. However, like his Roman predecessors, Gratian left the exact
meaning of the term unclear. In Gratian's use of the term, marital
affection was separate from marital consent. To consent was to accept
a person as a spouse, while marital affection referred to the quality of
the relationship that thus came into being.[18] Yet when it came to
defining when a marriage was enforceable in law, Gratian, like Justinian, had to fall back on external evidence which could be substantiated in court.[19] Obviously, the existence of a marriage contracted
without witnesses could not be proved or disproved by the allegations
of the plaintiff alone, but a pronouncement could be made following
the examination of witnesses who had witnessed an exchange of
vows.[20] This requirement of external proof and Gratian's insistence on
the primacy of the spoken word in the establishment of the marriage
bond once again shifted attention away from a definition of marital
affection for a further forty years. The decretals of Pope Alexander III
(1159–81) sketched out the meaning of the term in more detail,
making marital affection not only a requirement for the establishment
of marriage but also a required part of married life. Alexander III
believed that marital affection should endure during the marriage. In

[16] Noonan, "Marital Affection", p. 488.
[17] *Novella*, 74. 4. 2.
[18] Noonan, "Marital Affection", p. 490; Michael M. Sheehan, "'*Maritalis Affectio*'
    Revisited", in *The Olde Daunce: Love, Friendship, Sex and Marriage in the
    Medieval World*, Robert R. Edwards, Stephen Spector and Paul E. Szarmach (eds).
    SUNY Series in Medieval Studies, (Albany, New York, 1991), pp. 36–37.
[19] Noonan, "Marital Affection", pp. 498–99.
[20] *Dictum post* C. 30, q. 5, c. 9.

his usage, the words incorporated "an active disposition which the spouses had a duty to cultivate" which the church courts should not only encourage, but also enforce.[21] In an elaboration of Gratian's idea that marital consent differed from consent to intercourse, Alexander now taught that a spouse must be treated as more than just another bedfellow.[22]

A concise definition of marital affection still eluded canon lawyers. Although marriage partners were required to grant their spouses sexual intercourse on demand, it was clear that marital affection did not include this aspect. Had it done so, the inclusion among the *Decretals* of Alexander III's decretal *Perveniens*,[23] which exhorted lepers' spouses to administer to them "with conjugal affection" in their illness, would not have made sense, as the following decretal, *Quoniam nemini*,[24] specifically dealt with the duty of a spouse to have sexual intercourse with their leprous partner. Thus in the usage of Alexander III marital affection was separated from sexual congress and acquired the meaning of an enduring quality in the marital relations of spouses during their life together.[25] Marital affection also maintained an uneasy connection with the freedom of consent required in the church's teaching on marriage. A certain proportion of surviving medieval marriage litigation concerns the restoration of conjugal rights. Thus a wife or husband might be ordered by the church to take back their abandoned spouse and treat him or her with marital affection.[26]

In the end, canon law made no attempts to define marital affection in terms that would make it possible for a court to decide whether marital affection existed. Instead the courts focused their attention on proving the existence of marriage by other means, most importantly on proving the exchange of spoken marriage vows by the help of witnesses. The phrase thus became a construction describing an aspect of marriage, and it is in this way that it appears in the surviving

---

[21] Noonan, "Marital Affection", p. 501.

[22] Ibid., p. 502.

[23] X 4.8.1.

[24] X 4.8.2.

[25] Sheehan, "'*Maritalis Affectio*' Revisited", p. 37.

[26] Sheehan gives an example of such a command to resume cohabitation with marital affection in "'Maritalis Affectio' Revisited", p. 257; another example is found in R. H. Helmholz, *Marriage Litigation in Medieval England*. Cambridge Studies in English Legal History (Cambridge, 1974), p. 102. As will be seen from the present study, the court in York rarely commanded litigants to live with marital affection.

fourteenth-century marriage litigation in York. *Affectio maritalis*, as the phrase was employed in York, seems to have retained a large measure of its old Roman law meaning of willing the consequences of marriage and to have been employed in the same sphere of reference, implying that the spouses had consented to communal control over marital property. Except in the example of William Aungier – who strictly speaking did not talk of "marital affection" but rather of the kind of affection he expected from his wife – the term does not contain any information on the emotional content of the spouses' lives together.

Marital affection in canon law therefore has a vague quality about it which makes it difficult to define in clear terms. Although the concept was vague and its precise meaning remained unclear, the term *affectio maritalis* was nevertheless employed in surviving marriage litigation. The term was mainly used by witnesses and is rarely seen in documents intended for internal use by the courts. The phrase is mainly reported in documents that show what lay people said about marriage, the expression being employed as a part of an argument conducted within the parameters of canon law's understanding of marriage. Even though the term does indicate something about the nature of a marriage, *affectio maritalis* – as the term is used in marriage cases preserved in York – maintained a strong connection to a specific aspect of marital consent, the consent by both partners in a marriage to joint holding of property.[27] It is clear that spouses were expected to behave affectionately toward each other by witnesses and clerics alike, but an analysis of the testimony of the cause paper witnesses makes it possible to flesh out the meaning of the phrase *affectio maritalis* as it was understood by witnesses in fourteenth-century York. Such an analysis suggests that, although the term "marital affection" was known, it retained an element of the original meaning of the phrase in Roman law and did not invariably indicate an emotional state required for marriage.

The concept of marital affection remains as hazy in the York witness accounts as it is in canon law, but a detailed analysis of the statements that survive suggests a number of common features in the way the phrase was used by witnesses when asked by the courts about the

---

[27] Helmholz, *Marriage Litigation*, p. 13, gives the impression that the use of the term "marital affection" was almost universal in surviving marriage litigation. In the surviving fourteenth-century marriage cases in York the phrase is virtually never used in documents other than depositions.

nature of a marital union. Apart from the libel of *Moritz* c. *Tirington*, the positions of *Wetherby* c. *Page*, the articles of *Hopton* c. *Brome* and *Hiliard* c. *Hiliard*, and the replications by Simon Munkton in *Huntington* c. *Munkton*, "internal" court documents do not mention "marital affection".[28] Only in *Wetherby* c. *Cane* is it impossible to show that the litigation was connected to a dispute over property.[29] In general, though, the words when used by witnesses described an ongoing process in married life which followed the exchange of marriage vows, but only one witness commented on marital affection in a case that is not demonstrably about some aspect of control over property owned by the litigants.[30] The phrase thus retained a demonstrable connection with its roots in Roman law, despite the phrase being used by only eleven witnesses in six cause paper files.[31] Each case will be analysed below and the use of the phrase put in its context.

The earliest instance of witnesses using the phrase marital affection comes from *Percy* c. *Colville* (1313). Although the case aimed to establish whether the terms of a contract had been met, the question of whether a valid marriage existed between the litigants' children was of central importance to the outcome. The case was brought before the court by Sir Alexander Percy, who alleged that he had made an agreement concerning the marriage of his under-age son, John, to Elizabeth, daughter of Sir Robert Coleville seven years earlier. In accordance with the terms of their contract, Sir Alexander had immediately endowed the couple with lands in the villages of Craythorn and Berth worth twenty-five marks to be held in fee. In return, Sir Robert was to pay a dowry of 124 marks, within two years. John and Elizabeth solemnised the marriage two years before the case was heard in York but their marriage had been brief, as Elizabeth died after six months.[32]

---

[28] CP, E 95 (1367), 36 (1338), 62 (1348), 108 (1370) and 248 (1345–46).

[29] CP, E 36 (1338).

[30] The witness in question was Thomas Wans, a butcher from York. His deposition is found in *Wetherby* c. *Page*. CP, E 36–5 (1338).

[31] Four witnesses in *Hopton* c. *Brome*, two witnesses in *Percy* c. *Colvill* and *Huntington* c. *Munkton*. In the remaining three cases (*Brown* c. *Fentryce and Normaby*, *Moritz* c. *Tirington*, and *Hiliard* c. *Hiliard*), only one witness commented on marital affection. CP, E 62, 12, 248, 77, 95, 108.

[32] The witness Robert Clyveland, who was the only witness to testify about when Sir Robert should have paid the money, presumably got the details of the agreement wrong when he said the money should be paid "infra duas annos post confectionem dicte indenture". The chronology of the case makes more sense if

As a consequence of his daughter's death, Sir Robert tried to avoid the fulfilment of his promise. The case therefore came to revolve around the question of whether the two had cohabited and whether their cohabitation had been with marital intent. Ten witnesses were heard for Sir Alexander. Six of them described some kind of cohabitation in Sir Alexander's household which they believed was a valid marriage.[33] Two of these witnesses, Robert Cleveland and Thomas Rydale, went even further. While other witnesses simply described the couple as "legally married", they volunteered the information that Sir Alexander Percy's son had lived with his wife, Elizabeth, the daughter of Sir Robert Coleville, with marital affection before her death.[34] Robert Cleveland mentioned marital affection in passing,[35] while Thomas Rydale added more information: they had exchanged marriage vows "in the usual form" and had been put in a nuptial bed at the occasion of the initial contract. After this, John and Elizabeth had treated each other with marital affection and had often been seen alone in bed together:

And for three years said John and Elizabeth lay alone together in their bed and they behaved with marital affection in all ways to each other, and the witness having seen this, as the witness says, believed them to be true married people until the death of said Elizabeth. [36]

Thomas Rydale's deposition gives a number of clues as to what he

the money had been due two years after the solemnisation of the marriage. CP, E 12–1, 12–3 and 12–4 (Richard Lyth and Robert Clyveland).

[33] CP, E 12–4, Robert Clyveland, Walter le Lange, Alexander Molendarius, Adam Kyldale, Adam Fox and Thomas Rydale.

[34] CP, E 12–4.

[35] "Vidit idem juratus, ut dicit, dictos [Johannem et] Elisabet' simul morantes apud Ormesby in manerio dicti domini Alexandri per unum dimidium annum ubi se mutuo pertractarunt affectione maritali, ipso jurato hec vidente sepius per dictum tempus." CP, E 12–4.

[36] "Et vidit [iste juratus ipsos Johannem et Elisabet matrimonium contrahere] per verba consueta de quibus non recolit ad presenti [... Et post matrimonium] celebratum maritali affectione pertractare aliquotiens apud Dale, Heseltoun, Rouclyf et Beverlacum in hospitio dicti domini [Roberti et aliquotiens] apud Sueton, Ormesby et Hevedoun in hospitio dicti domini Alexandri. Ipsosque Johannes et Elisabet vidit idem juratus ... nocte sequente post dictum contractum celebratum simul in uno lecto et postquam in lecto repositi fuerant ... Et per tres annos multotiens jacuerunt dicti Johannes et Elisabet in unum lectum sole et maritali affectione in omnibus pertractarunt et jurato hec vidente, ut dicit, pro conjugibus legitimis habebantur usque ad mortem dicte Elisabet." CP, E 12–4.

believed such marital affection consisted of. First of all, marital affection followed the exchange of marriage vows. Secondly, marital affection was described in connection with, but not necessarily as an ingredient of, sharing a bed. Thirdly, the existence of marital affection was understood to be an integral part of the marriage. It is important, too, that Robert Cleveland and Thomas Rydale were not asked directly about marital affection but volunteered the information believing that the context of their evidence made their thoughts on marital affection helpful to the court.

Like the case of William Aungier, *Hopton* c. *Brome* (1348) involved the marriage of a ward to the guardian's child. Unlike William Aungier, however, Constance, daughter of William Brome, had already been married once and had two children by her first husband.[37] Constance invoked a number of impediments to her alleged marriage to William, the son of Adam Hopton: that she had married John Rotherfield some three to five years earlier and had solemnised their marriage *in facie ecclesie*; that William was under age at the time of the alleged contract; that there was an impediment of affinity between her and William Hopton since her first husband, John Rotherfield, had been William's cousin. Finally, she alleged that she had legally married one William Boswell when John Rotherfield had been murdered a year earlier and pleaded that this marriage be upheld. Both parties in the case alleged the existence of marital affection. While denying that it existed in her marriage to William Hopton, however, Constance argued that her marriage to John Rotherfield had included marital affection. The evidence produced in the case shows a messy mixture of a guardian's attempts to retain control over his ward's lands, the ward's attempts to break free of her guardian's domination, and an attempt by the guardian to regain control of his former ward's lands when the murder of her husband once again allowed him to prosecute the case at the court in York. Four witnesses in the case spoke of marital affection.[38] Three of these witnesses can be shown to have had a good knowledge of canon law. They were all

---

[37] One of the children was still alive in 1348, the other had died. CP, E 62–3, Adam Helay.

[38] Interestingly, William Helay avoided the term entirely when he was reinterrogated by the court. CP E 62–11. CP, E 62–3 (Adam Helay and Margaret, wife of John Johnson of Danby); E 62–8 (William Helay); E 62–11 (Richard Helay).

members of the same family which included two clerics, one of whom was also a notary public.[39]

The witnesses produced by Constance in the first instance to prove her marriage to John Rotherfield told the court of two exchanges of vows. Adam Helay senior, a neighbour, said he had heard of the marriage from neighbourhood rumour; Dionysia, his daughter, said the marriage had been celebrated in Adam Helay junior's room with a subsequent celebration of mass three years earlier, while two further witnesses claimed that a marriage had been celebrated in a field near Heathcliff by a stone called "Stoupandstone" five years earlier.[40] At a later meeting of the court it became clear that Adam Helay senior was being economical with the truth and that he had previously conspired with Adam Hopton to force Constance to marry William Hopton despite a warning by his son William Helay, who was a cleric in York, that no good would come from their union. After the third and final production of witnesses, which took place after the collapse of William Hopton's case, the court could piece together the events of the case. The court learned that Constance had initially exchanged vows with John Rotherfield when she was fifteen years of age at the "Stoupandstone" in Heathcliff five years previously and that the marriage had been confirmed by a ceremony in Adam Helay, junior's room two years later. At the time of the contract by the "Stoupand-stone", Constance was the ward of Adam Hopton, John Rotherfield's uncle. Adam Hopton had a son of nine years of age called William, whom he wanted her to marry so that he could maintain control over her land. Soon after the contract at Heathcliff, Adam Hopton and Adam Helay, senior, forced Constance against her will to contract marriage with William Hopton. According to the second deposition made by William Helay, who was present at the occasion, Constance had remained "silent and unresponsive" when Adam Hopton had suggested the marriage. Adam Hopton had then threatened her that he

---

[39] The witnesses were Adam Helay, senior, Richard Helay and William Helay. A fourth male member of the Helay family, Adam Helay, junior notarised the appointment of Constance's proctor in the case. This Adam Helay junior was the son of Adam Helay senior. He drew up a copy of the appointment of Constance's proctor in the case in which he described himself as "Adam de Helay, clericus Eboracensis diocesis publicus apostolici et imperiali auctoritate notarius". CP, E 62–15. In the interest of clarity, this Adam Helay will be referred to as Adam Helay, junior, his father as Adam Helay, senior.

[40] CP, E 62–3, John, son of John the son of Alice Danby; and Elisabeth, daughter of Clarissa Danby.

would break her neck:

> And thus the said Constance afterwards, for fear of the threats uttered by the said Adam Helay and fearing the loss of her land by the said Adam Hopton, her guardian having the deeds and possession of said lands, contracted with said William even though Adam Hopton, the father of the said William had previously been warned by this witness that this marriage would not come to a good end.[41]

William Hopton was not keen on the marriage either. When Adam Helay, senior, admitted that he had helped to force Constance and William to marry, he added that the parties had to be dragged to the altar "crying and resisting".[42]

Richard Helay explained to the court that Constance and John Rotherfield had contracted marriage, had had sex and had had a child. They also "lived together like man and wife with marital affection" before the alleged contract between William and Constance.[43] Margaret, wife of John Johnson of Danby, gave evidence of the marriage between Constance and John Rotherfield. For her the sequence was the same: the solemnisation of marriage preceded marital affection, the birth of children followed the marriage, and the phrase was used to describe a quality of the relationship. After the solemnisation of marriage she saw that:

> said John and Constance lived together, mixed carnally and were close with marital affection. And all these things this witness believed to be true

---

[41] "Et sic dicta Custantia postmodum, timore minarum eidem per dictum Adam de Helay ministrata et amissionis terre sue dicti Ade de Hopton curatoris eiusdem Custantie habentis dictam terram et cartas eiusdem Custantie de eadem terra, cum dicto Willelmo contraxit, prout supra deposuit, licet Adam de Hopton, pater eiusdem Willelmi, per ipsum juratum prius fuit premunitus quod illud matrimonium bonum exitum habere non posset, ut dicit." CP, E 62–11.

[42] "[Adam de Hopton] una cum ipso Adam teste consensu mutuo compulerunt et cogerunt vi et metu et minis illatio ad contrahendum matrimonium predictos Willelmum et Custantiam multum renitentes et flentes, contradicente et negante dicta Custantia in tantum quod cum Adam de Helay predictus proferret verba matrimonii dicta Custantia noluit recitare nec recte proferre ipsa verba matrimonii. Et dicit quod nullo tempore consensit dicto Willelmo nec alio modo nec cohabitante cum eo nisi quatenus dictus Adam tenuit eam invita sub cura sua." CP E 62–3, Adam Helay.

[43] "Et maritali affectione ut vir et uxor cohabitarunt ante quemcumque contractum matrimonialem habitum seu initum inter ipsam Custantiam et Willelmum." CP, E 62–11.

because she often saw them live and join together in Constance's own house.[44]

For Richard Helay and Margaret Johnson marital affection was a visible quality of marriage and they were confident they were able to recognise it. Their choices of verbs – *cohabito* and *adhaero* with marital affection – suggest that they intended to describe the quality of the cohabitation but that they are not necessarily making a point about the marriage contract. In contrast, Adam Helay, senior, Richard and William Helay's father, used the verb *contraho*, which is commonly used to mean the making of a contract or concluding of a bargain, suggesting that he realised that the union between Constance and John Rotherfield, her first husband, was intended to be a legally valid marriage with the implication of willing the transfer of property.[45]

The two depositions by Adam Helay senior's son William Helay are particularly interesting because as a cleric he was clearly familiar with the canon law rules of marriage. At his initial appearance before the court he was the first of six witnesses, all of whom were asked about the existence or absence of marital affection between William Hopton and Constance. Alone among the six witnesses, William Helay claimed that there had been marital affection.[46] Although he alleged the existence of marital affection, he almost certainly did not mean to comment on the emotional content of the marriage. He was the only witness among the six prepared to admit the existence of marital affection and his statement was true if his use of the phrase *affectio conjugalis* was taken to imply the old Roman law interpretation of the phrase, "to will the consequences of marriage". There was indeed the intent to create a marriage between William Hopton and Constance, but, as his second deposition made clear, there was no love between

---

[44] "Dicit quod dicti Johannes et Custantia cohabitarunt et carnaliter se commiscerunt adinvicem et maritali affectione sibi invicem adhererunt. Et hec omnia credit esse vera [ista jurata] quia vidit eos sepe in domo propria dicte Custantia simul habitare et comitare." CP E 62–3.

[45] "Dicit etiam quod sepissime vidit dictos Johannem et Custantiam cohabitare in mensa et lecto et se adinvicem utrique maritali affectione contractare ut virum et uxorem." CP E 62–8.

[46] "Super tertio articulo requisitus dicit quod postquam Willelmus et Custantia de quibus in articulo fit mentio dicebantur precontraxisse prout in articulo continetur vidit eosdem per medietatem unius anni simul stare et chahabitare [sic, read: cohabitare] sponte ut virum et uxorem et affectione conjugali mutuo se tractare." CP, E 62–8.

the two. William was a cleric and therefore conversant in Latin and presumably also read and corrected the deposition which survives in the cause papers. He must have been aware of the meaning of the phrases *affectio conjugalis* and *affectio maritalis* in canon law. At first glance it therefore appears significant that he is reported as using the terms *affectio conjugalis* and that the scribe carefully erased the word *maritalis* from his statement. However, this is one instance where the evidence of the deposition is misleading if taken alone. The articles (the document which contains the questions the examiners were to ask the witnesses) uses the words *affectio conjugalis*. He also skilfully avoided giving the court his own opinion as to whether the marriage of Constance and William Hopton was legally binding, preferring instead to answer that he believed that her subsequent marriage to William Boswell had been entered legally.

The amount of property under dispute in cases where a witness mentioned marital affection ranged from several villages to about one hundred shillings, the extremes being represented by *Hiliard* c. *Hiliard* (1370) and *Brown* c. *Fentryce and Normanby* (1357), each of whom had one witness commenting on marital affection.[47] The court in York was asked to examine the validity of the marriage between John and Katherine Hiliard in *Hiliard* c. *Hiliard*. Katherine Hiliard pleaded for the restoration of her dower on John's death, but her stepson, Peter Hiliard, refused to let her have control of it. The case was referred to the court in York from the King's Bench, where Peter Hiliard argued that his stepmother's marriage to his father had been within the forbidden degrees and therefore not valid. Katherine, on the other hand, claimed that control of her dower lands had passed to John during the time when they all believed that the marriage was legal. She therefore claimed the right to have her lands restored to her control. The dower in question was substantial, consisting of a third of twenty-four messuages, one mill, sixteen bulls, twenty-one bovates, five acres of meadows, pasture for 300 sheep and 8s. annually in rents, in the villages of Arnall, Dripole, Riston, Preston, Sutton, Hedon and Carton.[48]

The marriage between Katherine and John Hiliard had been celebrated under suspicious circumstances at dawn of the Monday one

---

[47] *Hiliard* c. *Hiliard* and *Brown* c. *Fentryce and Normanby*. CP, E 108 and 77.
[48] CP, E 108–1.

or two weeks before the feast of St Martin of Tours (30 October or 6 November 1363) in the chapel of Riston.[49] The ceremony took place early in the morning, but witnesses heard for Katherine all agreed that the sun was up by the time the solemnisation was celebrated. Peter claimed that the sun had not been up and that the marriage therefore was invalid because it had not been celebrated with proper publicity. Katherine's witness, Ivo Riston, who was the chaplain who celebrated the marriage, insisted that he read the banns at dawn before the ceremony,[50] and that at this occasion neither the guests nor the parties themselves had admitted to any impediments to marriage. Ivo was contradicted by Peter's brother, Thomas, who had also been present at the marriage ceremony. He said that the church had been boarded up with linen and surplices draped across the windows and that the door remained closed during the ceremony to prevent light from the candles escaping from the church thus alerting the countryside to the marriage.[51]

Soon after, some witnesses for Peter Hiliard claimed, the couple had been denounced to the archbishop by their parish priest, and the archbishop had enjoined them to live as sister and brother.[52] Katherine

---

[49] CP, E 108–6. Eleonora Barton, Katherine Hiliard's sister is the only witness to give a reasonably precise date.

[50] "In aurora ipsius diei postquam gallus ter cantavit venit iste juratus de villa de Arnal' ad capellam de Ristoun' una cum prefatis Johanne et Katerina, Emma Hiliard, Elienora de Bartoun, Margareta de Hedoun [sic] et Thoma Hiliard et in dicta capella ante ostium chori eiusdem capelle edidit iste juratus, ut dicit, banna publice inter personas superius nominata." CP, E 108–6.

[51] "Dicit quod ipsemet interfuit in capella de Rystoun'[una cum domino] Ivone Lardmand, capellano, Emma, matre carnali dicte Katerina, Elienore de Bartoun et Margareta de Hedoun quum Johannes Hildyard et Katarina predicta matrimonium adinvicem de facto contraxherunt et ipsum ibidem solempnizari fecerunt infra noctis tenebras ante auroram diei per spacium decem miliarum anglicorum, ostio ipsius capelle clauso et fenestris eiusdem capelle cum linthiaminibus et superpelliciis suspensis in eisdem obscuratis ne lumen candelarum ibidem accensarum exterius videretur. Et dicit in juramento suo quod numquam audivit dici vel referri quod aliqua banna fuerunt edita publice in aliqua ecclesia nec aliquid propositum publice in ecclesia super huiusmodi matrimonio contrahendo." CP, E 108–13.

[52] "Dicit quod postquam matrimonium inter dictos Johannem et Katerinam contractum fuit denuntiatum domino archiepiscopo Ebor' qui nunc est per dominum Johannem de Hildeston, tunc rectorem ecclesie parochialis de Routhe prout iste juratus audivit quod ipsi Johannes et Katerina fuerunt consanguinei et illegitime matrimonialiter copulati. Et bene novit iste juratus quod dicti Johannes et Katerina fuerunt vocati coram domino archiepscopo Ebor' quod comparerent coram eodem sibi super premissis et aliis articulis salutem animarum suarum

and John cohabited for almost five years after this ceremony. Katherine's stepsister, Eleonora Barton said to the court that they had lived:

> like true and legal spouses with marital affection until the death of the said John ... and they were believed and publicly reputed as true and legal spouses in the village of Riston and neighbouring areas.[53]

Another witness, John Helbyson, a witness for Peter, explained that the two had complied with the sentence by sleeping in separate bedrooms after the citation by the archbishop.[54] By doing so they complied with the archbishop's command but, although they accepted the sentence of the archbishop's court, John and Katherine tried to obtain a dispensation permitting them to live as man and wife from the pope. Their envoy, Master John Estthorp, was however unsuccessful in his attempts to procure a dispensation for them and soon after his return to England John Hiliard died, leaving Katherine with the very real problem of how to protect her lands.

No sentence survives in the case between Peter and Katherine from the consistory court. The court possibly took the separate beds, the suspicious circumstances of the marriage and the proceedings before the archbishop's court as sufficient proof of consanguinity, or the original case before the King's Bench may have been settled before the court in York reached a decision.

John and Katherine Hiliard's elaborate attempts to avoid detection when they married, their separate bedrooms, and their open attempt to gain a dispensation from Rome to marry despite their consanguinity show that they were not only aware of the canon law rules of consanguinity when they married, but were also aware of how to challenge

---

concernentibus responsurum et dicit quod una vice fuit iste iuratus cum dicto Johanne, patre suo, coram domino archiepiscopo supradicto apud Thorp' juxta Ebor' et audivit a magistro Willelmo de Hornsee quod tunc per eundem dominum archiepiscopum fuit inhibitum ipsis Johanni et Katerine ne extunc adinvicem carnaliter comiscerent sed ut frater et soror se adinvicem haberent." CP, E 108–13, John Hiliard, junior.

[53] "Dicit quod prefati Johannes et Katerina post huius matrimonium contractum et solemnizatum ut veri et legitimi conjuges affectione maritali adinvicem cohabitarunt usque ad mortem dicti Johannes ... ac pro veris et legitimis conjugibus communiter habiti fuerunt et publice reputati in villa de Riston et locis vicinis." CP, E 108–6.

[54] "Vidit dictum Johannem habere lectum suum separatum in una camera et ipsam Katerinam lectum suum separatum a lecto dicti Johannis in alia camera et ideo credit quod habuerunt se adinvicem tamquam frater et soror." CP, E 108–13.

them and how to circumvent them. John Helbyson's assertion that they slept in separate beds may have been an attempt on his part to tell the court what he believed it wanted to hear. If his description of John and Katherine's sleeping arrangements was true, however, it shows that John and Katherine had a strong desire to conform to these rules. John and Katherine's attempts to gain a dispensation from Rome for their consanguinity emphasises this desire.[55]

The coincidence of the phrase marital affection and disputes over property is found again in *Brown c. Fentryce and Normanby* (1357). In this case, however, the value of the property in dispute was not large. In all, the defendant claimed, he was worth less than one hundred shillings. This case was a matrimonial and divorce case in which Lucy Brown, formerly the wife of William Brown, alleged that she had married William Fentryce, a farmer of Tollesby. After seven years of cohabitation, Lucy left William Fentryce but returned after a couple of months to claim reinstatement into her former marital rights or at least a share of the marital home. William Fentryce, who had allowed another woman to take Lucy's place, refused Lucy anything from the house for her maintenance during the case. Although William Fentryce cannot be said to have been rich, he was by no means poor. Witnesses claimed that he owned goods worth around 100s. and one witness mentions that he owned a plough team. The witness Thomas Wagheson, who was heard in this case, saw marital affection as something that followed marriage which was the outward manifestation of the partners' emotional involvement in each other:

> He said that he knew well that William and Lucy ... contracted marriage seven years ago and made it to be solemnised between them. And afterwards they behaved towards each other with marital affection, keeping company together and cohabiting for a long time ... [56]

---

[55] A comparable case from 1313 appears in the Register of William Greenfield, when Master Robert Pickering was appointed to hear the case of a knight and a lady who had married despite certain impediments. The case was eventually handed over to the sheriff of York to be dealt with "iuris ordinarii potestate". The entries concerning this case do not specify the nature of the suit any further, nor does it explain why the case was allowed to devolve to the sheriff. William Brown and A. Hamilton Thompson, *The Register of William Greenfield, Lord Archbishop of York, 1306–15, Part 1*, Surtees Society, 145 (Durham, 1931), pp. 148, 161.

[56] "Dicit se bene scire quod Willelmus et Lucia ... contraxerunt matrimonium huius a septem annis elapsis, et illud fecerunt solempnizari inter eos. Et postmodum se invicem mutuo pertractarunt affectione conjugali simul conversantes et cohabitantes per magnum tempus." CP, E 77–8.

Seven years later, when Lucy left William during the harvest time "without his permission", he took another woman, Alice Normanby, as his mistress. Thomas Wagheson described the new union in much more prosaic terms and carefully avoided any comment on marital affection:

> He heard it commonly said by the said William's neighbours that he knew Alice carnally ... whom this witness likewise saw twice in the last month in the house of said William. And he commonly saw her in the fields performing the work of the said William and serving him. And – as the witness says – one could see the said Alice drive the said William's plough-team during the time the said William maintained her.[57]

The court rejected Lucy Brown's claims on William Fentryce, presumably because she was unable to prove that they had actually exchanged marriage vows, despite Thomas Wagheson telling the court that her cohabitation with William was characterised by marital affection and his refusal to use the same word for William Fentryce's subsequent union with Alice Normanby.

The final example of witnesses commenting on marital affection in cases involving control over property comes from *Huntington c. Munkton*, which was brought before the court in an attempt by the husband to regain control over his wife's land. One of two witnesses in this case who commented on the existence of marital affection was interrogated in connection with another attack on Agnes by Simon, who came to William Huntington's house in Petergate in York to persuade her to resume cohabitation with him as soon as the archbishop's command to her had been published. Henry Galtres, a neighbour, told the court that Agnes and Simon had not cohabited during the last six months but that they had previously lived together in Simon's father's house in York "with marital affection".[58] Simon's

---

[57] "Audivit communiter dici a vicinis dicti Willelmi quod ipse carnaliter cognovit Aliciam ... quam similiter vidit ipse testis, ut dicit, bis in domo ipsius Willelmi infra mensem proximo preterito. Et eam in campis faciente opus ipsius Willelmi et sibi deserviente vidit communiter. Et videre potest quampluries, ut dicit, ipsam Aliciam fugare carucam eiusdem Willelmi dum idem Willelmus eam tenet." CP, E 77–8.

[58] "Dicit super primo articulo requisitus quod infra dimidium annum proximo iam elapsum nescit deponere de aliqua cohabitatione inter Simonem et Agnetem in eodem articulo nominatos prout in eodem continet. Dicit tamen quod novit eosdem Simonem et Agnetem ante temporem dimidii anni, de quo superius deposuit simul cohabitare in domo patris dicti Simonis Ebor'maritali affectione se

actions when he attacked her appeared to Henry de Galtres to be fully within the accepted norm for marital behaviour:

> he heard the cry of a woman, as it appeared to him at the time. Having heard this, the witness went to the window of his house in said neighbour-hood and saw the said Agnes lying and the said Simon on top of her in that neighbourhood with the intention, in his estimation, that he might lead her as his wife to the said Simon's house without causing any trouble for her.[59]

Like most of the other witness accounts investigated in this study, Henry Galtres' deposition strongly suggests that he used the phrase "with marital affection" in the Roman law meaning of "with the intention of creating a marriage" and that marital affection occurred only when the parties were cohabiting.

Emma Munkton, the wife of Agnes's uncle William de Huntington (and not a relative of Simon Munkton) gave a more detailed account of the way in which Simon and Agnes had lived together. According to her deposition, marital affection followed marriage but was not neces-sarily the foundation on which marriage was built. To her, marital affection consisted of the inner reality of the emotion and its external expression. She described the series of events that led up to and followed the marriage of Simon and Agnes. When Agnes had moved in with Simon in his father, Roger Munkton's house:

> she heard the said Agnes say that she had confirmed the marriage made on that account and that she would rather that the said Simon had done so long before she had the twenty pounds silver [as her inheritance from her father][60] ... And this was said in the said Roger's house where the said Simon and Agnes lived before and cohabited as spouses joined in matri-

---

adinvicem pertractantes et aliter super eodem articulo deponere nescit, ut dicit." CP, E 248–54.

[59] "Audivit clamorem unius mulieris, prout sibi tunc videbatur. Quo audito idem juratus accessit ad fenestram domus sue in vico predicto et vidit dictam Agnetam jacentem et dictum Simonem super eam in eodem vico, ea intentione, reputatione sua, ut eam posset duxisse ad mansum ipsius Simonis ut uxorem suam sine aliqua molestia eidem inferenda." CP, E 248–54.

[60] Although the archbishop's probate registers do not survive prior to 1389, Agnes's father's will is preserved in the dean and chapter probate register and was proved 14 April 1333, fifteen years before the case between Simon and Agnes was heard in York and seven years before she married Simon. In it he granted twenty pounds silver to Agnes and other items to her siblings, but asked his executors to look

mony and engendered a son called Hamo. Later at the door of the church of St Michael le Belfrey in York they contracted marriage in the customary words and solemnised that marriage in said church... She also says that she saw the said Simon and Agnes several times after the said alleged *traductio* lie together in one bed, *nudus cum nuda* with marital affection in the house of the said Roger in so far as this witness could make out.[61]

Emma Munkton describes the marriage as a process consisting of a series of steps, from the initial *traductio* of the woman into the man's household, through the solemnisation of the marriage at the church in front of witnesses to the birth of their son. The information on marital affection – which she volunteered to the court without being asked – shows that she saw it as the external expression of an internal reality. Her use of the phrase "in so far as this witness could make out" makes it clear that she was aware that she could not be sure that the external signs of affection actually covered the inner reality of the emotion. In other words, in her use of the term, marital affection consisted of two parts, an inner reality and an outer expression.

The final instance of a witness using the phrase comes from *Wetherby c. Page* (1338).[62] The sequence of events reported by the witness Thomas Wans, a butcher from York, is like the sequence of events reported by Emma Munkton. Yet, the documents of the case do not mention a dispute over property between the litigants, as might have been expected from the contexts of other statements on marital affection. The libel of the case alleged that John Page, a fuller of York, and Alice Wetherby had contracted and solemnised marriage fourteen years earlier, that they had cohabited, had had intercourse and behaved with marital affection for years, and that Alice had subse-

---

after these until his children reached their age of discretion. York Minster Library, Dean and Chapter Probate Register, i, fol. 14r.

[61] "Audivit eandem Agnetam dicere quod ratam habuit traductionem in hac parte factam et quod mallet quod idem Simon sic fecisset a diu antequam ipsa [de hereditate patris sue] habuisset viginti libris argentum ... . Et hec dicta fuerunt in manso dicti Rogeri, ubi dicti Simon et Agneta moram traxerunt prius et ut coniuges matrimonialiter copulati simul cohabitarunt et unum filium nomine Hamonem inter se procrearunt. Postquam ad ostium ecclesie sancti Michaelis de Berefrido Eboracensis matrimonium adinvicem per verba consueta contraxerunt et idem matrimonium in ecclesia predicta solempnizarunt ... . Dicit etiam se vidisse dictos Simonem et Agnetam post dictam traductionem pretensam pluries simul jacere in uno lecto solus cum sola, nudus cum nuda infra mansum Rogeri predicti affectione conjugali, quatenus ipsa jurata perpendere potuit, ut dicit." CP, E 248–4.

[62] CP, E 36.

quently married William Cave. Alice Wetherby was now trying to have her marriage to William Cave annulled because of her precontract with John Page. Thomas Wans had been present when Alice and William had contracted marriage at the church of All Saints, Pavement, three years earlier. To him there was marital affection in the marriage of William Cave and Alice Wetherby:

> He saw said William and Alice live together in one house as man and wife for many years in the city of York with conjugal affection. Concerning any subsequent intercourse he does not know for certain, but he well believes that there was subsequent intercourse as is mentioned in the article.[63]

Thomas Wans, like Emma Munkton, described a progression from the marriage contract through cohabitation to conjugal affection. Thomas Wans also saw the cohabitation and marital affection as circumstantial evidence which led him to believe that William Cave and Alice Wetherby had sexual intercourse.

Marital affection is an elusive concept which has a long history in European law. The meaning of the phrase developed over the centuries, initially meaning the willing of the (property) consequences of marriage, but developing into a phrase that encompassed an internal psychological quality of marriage. The evidence in this chapter has presented all the surviving statements on marital affection from the court in York. The scarcity of evidence on marital affection in this otherwise rich mine of information on medieval marriage and the broad range of its use suggests that the courts and the witnesses found the concept difficult and confusing. Only eleven of about 580 witnesses commented on marital affection and only six cases included depositions that alleged marital affection, while one more case alleged that a husband had terminated his cohabitation, withdrawing marital affection from his spouse, but did not produce any evidence to prove the prior existence of such marital affection. Given the scarcity of statements on marital affection and the original Roman law meaning of *affectio maritalis*, with its implications of the transfer of property, the context of all but two of these instances of marital affection in the

---

[63] "Matrimonium adinvicem contraxerunt et solemnizarunt in ecclesia omnium sanctorum super pavamentum. Dicit etiam quod vidit dictos Willelmum et Aliciam simul cohabitare in una domo ut vir et uxor per multos annos in civitate Ebor'affectione conjugali. De carnali copula subsequente nescit pro certo sed bene credit carnalem copulam fuisse subsequenter prout in articulo continetur." CP E 36–5.

York cause papers suggests that the phrase continued its connection with the question of control over property.

There was a wide variation in the meaning of the phrase and no consensus among the witnesses on how to apply the term. One litigant, William Malcake, said that he was concerned that his spouse did not "choose an affection that is upheld" and terminated their relationship because she had not excluded other men from her sexual favours. The way in which witnesses like Thomas Wans and Emma Munkton referred to spouses' marital affection suggested that they were using an understanding of the emotional aspects of the marriage under investigation by the court not far removed from its meaning in the decretals of Alexander III. In their use of the phrase, marital affection was a necessary ingredient in marriage and indicated what appears to be a psychological aspect of the union of two people. Perhaps because of the rule that sexual congress following an exchange of vows created a valid marriage, the witnesses are reported as making separate comments on marital affection and sexual activity, but the separation of the two follows the use of the phrase suggested by Alexander III. In the case of Thomas Wans, marital affection was circumstantial evidence for sexual intercourse between the partners. Other witnesses, like William Helay, Thomas Rydale and Robert Cleveland, used the phrase in a way that has its origins in Roman law. For them the phrase appears to describe a special quality in a marriage, a willingness among spouses to admit the legal consequences of marriage. For the latter two witnesses the phrase indicated that a marriage had been entered into and that the spouses had lived together with the intent of being a married couple, admitting the legal consequences of their marriage. William Helay's deposition gives an even sharper definition to the phrase: in his use the spouses entered marriage with the intention of allowing the transfer of control over property, but this intention was of short duration and most certainly his use of the phrase did not admit an emotional involvement among the parties.

The ambiguity of the phrase *affectio maritalis* remains even after this analysis of its use in fourteenth-century York marriage cases. The word *affectio,* which was first used in Roman law to indicate the willingness to permit the transfer of property, in its combination with a word indicating marriage has continued to evolve in western European thought over the centuries to the point where, by some time after the fourteenth century, "affection" lost its initial meaning of "will" and became the word used to describe an internalised ongoing psychological process in the emotional involvement of one person in another. We may never know precisely how and when this change in meaning came about but the evidence of the York cause papers suggests that the meaning of the phrase was as elusive to the ordinary litigant as it was to the academic commentator. It also suggests that the connection between marital affection and property found in Roman law was subtly continued in the practice of the court in York.

9

Demography and the Courts

The previous chapters have given an impression of the richness of the sources found in the diocesan archives in York. It has been argued that the laity understood and accepted the jurisdiction of the church over marriage and that, although occasional deviations from the law can be found, in general the litigants that appeared in York were eager to embrace the certainty and security of the church law of marriage. One question remains, however: were the courts sought equally by all or did they administer justice to a select group of people? The differences and similarities between medieval matrimonial litigation preserved in individual dioceses in the European past has received some attention in recent historiography, but the social and geographical parameters of such litigation has rarely been investigated. Charles Donahue and Andrew Finch have reached different conclusions in their analyses of differences in marital litigation patterns in France and England. Donahue argued that differences observed between the two countries indicate that French parents had more success than their English counterparts in controlling their offspring's choice of marriage partner.[1] Finch, on the other hand, found little difference between English and French material concerning marriages in difficulty and suggested that French and English litigants followed a similar path of increasing dissent before their marriages finally came to the attention of the courts.[2] Most other historians have concentrated on individual countries or dioceses. Most recently, P.J.P. Goldberg used the surviving fourteenth- and fifteenth-century York cause papers to argue for a marked decline in the economic activity of women and interpreted the decreasing numbers of fifteenth- and sixteenth-century matrimonial cause papers preserved in the York ecclesiastical archives

---

[1] Charles Donahue, Jr, "The Canon Law on the Formation of Marriage and Social Practice in the Later Middle Ages", *Journal of Family History*, 8 (1983), pp. 144–58.

[2] Andrew Finch, "*Repulsa Uxore Sua*: Marital Difficulties and Separation in the Later Middle Ages", *Continuity and Change*, 8 (1993), pp. 1–28.

as an index for an increasing dependence upon marriage among women in the fifteenth century.[3] Goldberg thus rejects the explanation for the same phenomenon given by Richard Helmholz in his classic study of the function of English ecclesiastical courts, in which he suggested that the decreasing case-load was due to an increased awareness of canon law rules of marriage and to "a gradual adoption of more settled attitudes and habits relating to marriage".[4]

Goldberg's findings rest on the assumption that the population which is visible in the selection of the York cause papers is a true reflection of Yorkshire's population in the period under investigation.[5] Although he identifies one important deviation from the kind of case-load to be expected in a provincial court – that there are no *ex officio* cases – he fails to come to grips with the social and geographical determinants of the population of litigants and deponents which appear in the cause papers.[6] Other scholars have commented on the composition of other populations of litigants, but they have rarely linked their observations to which kinds of courts they observed. In an aside, Richard Helmholz observed that members of the highest status groups and those of servile condition rarely used ecclesiastical courts to settle their marriage disputes.[7] His statement amplified the conclusions of an earlier study by Michael Sheehan, according to which the matrimonial litigation preserved in the Ely consistory court register for the period 1374–82 included a fairly representative cross-section of fourteenth-century Cambridgeshire population, with the possible exception of the highest status groups of that population.[8]

The apparent contradiction between the two studies by Goldberg and Sheehan becomes less striking when one considers the nature of the courts under investigation. The Ely act book investigated by Sheehan documented the day-to-day business of an East Anglian diocesan court whose jurisdiction covered a geographical area which

---

[3] P. J. P. Goldberg, *Women, Work, and Life Cycle in a Medieval Economy: Women in York and Yorkshire, c. 1300–1520* (Oxford, 1992), pp. 339–40.

[4] R. H. Helmholz, *Marriage Litigation in Medieval England*, Cambridge Studies in English Legal History (Cambridge, 1974), p. 166.

[5] Goldberg, *Women, Work, and Life Cycle*, pp. 221 and 376–78.

[6] Ibid., p. 251 An *ex officio* case is a case which was initiated by the court. It is the opposite of an instance case which was initiated by one of the parties.

[7] Helmholz, *Marriage Litigation*, pp. 160–61.

[8] Michael M. Sheehan, "The Formation and Stability of Marriage in Fourteenth-Century England: Evidence of an Ely Register", *Mediaeval Studies*, 33 (1971), pp. 228–63.

was substantially smaller than that of the archdiocese of York. The jurisdiction of the archdiocese of York included all of northern England, from north of the dioceses of Lincoln and Chester to the Scottish border. It thus included most of the Lake District and the old West, North and East Ridings of Yorkshire and the two dioceses of Carlisle and Durham.[9] R.M. Smith concluded that the cases that were brought before the ecclesiastical courts in Ely and the Canterbury consistory court probably did not represent more than 1 or 2 per cent of the total number of marriages in these regions.[10] If litigation levels were the same in the fourteenth century as they were in the fifteenth – and there is little reason to think that they were not – the eighty-eight fourteenth-century marriage cause paper files which survive in York probably represent less than 3 per cent of the total number of cases heard at the consistory court during that century and they represent an even smaller proportion of the total number of marriages in the region at the time. Against this background, it becomes particularly important to analyse the York cause papers as a group to establish the individual features of York matrimonial litigation. The difference in area between Ely and York, for example, probably means that the litigation preserved in the Ely court book covers a higher percentage of marriages in that region and presents the results of a more thorough policing of the canon law rules of marriage. An appearance before the York court probably took more effort and more energy than an appearance before the court of Ely. The use of the York court is there-fore likely to have been limited by two factors: the litigants' ease of access to the city of York (or somewhere where the archbishop's court convened); and the litigants' willingness and ability to spend the time in court and the money that a successful plea required.

It is an open question whether the changes in litigation patterns over time which the modern historian observes are reflections of real changes in social relations or if they reflect changes in contemporary legal or archival practices. Helmholz ascribed the fall in marriage litigation which he observed in other English courts to a change in social conventions, while Martin Ingram suggested that the additional

---

[9] Walter Smith, *Monastic Britain*, map. The Director General of the Ordnance Survey, Southampton 1978.

[10] R.M. Smith, "Marriage Processes in the English Past: Some Continuities", in *The World We Have Gained: Histories of Population and Social Structure*, Lloyd Bonfield, Richard M. Smith and Keith Wrightson (eds) (Oxford and New York, 1986), p. 70.

factor of an increased unwillingness on the part of ecclesiastical judges
to pass sentence for a clandestine marriage may have caused the fall in
cases.[11] Goldberg argues that the observed decline in marriage litigation in the fifteenth century is a consequence of the male backlash
against the participation of women in the work force which had been
made possible by the sudden demographic recession caused by the
Black Death in the previous century.[12] However, Goldberg is looking
at the survival rate of cause papers, and the fall in their survival rate is
not corroborated by a comparable fall in the total number of cases
recorded in the York courts' act books. This may be explained by
external factors, such as a transfer of certain kinds of marriage cases to
the secular courts, an increase in the matrimonial litigation heard by
lower jurisdictions in the northern province or changes in record
keeping. Burns' analysis of the surviving fifteenth-century act books
and act book fragments in York indicates that the number of cases
recorded in the act books depended to a large extent on the registrar
who presided at the time.[13] Burns pointed out that individual registrars had different ways of recording cases. Some did not record recon-
ventual cases (cases in which the defence took the shape of a
countercharge) as separate cases, while others did. Likewise, some
registrars recorded summary proceedings, arbitrations and purgations,
while others did not.[14] Despite such variations in practice, the total
number of cases which the registrars recorded varied little and
remained within the same maxima throughout the fifteenth century
and shows no evidence of a falling case load.[15] These variations in the

---

[11] Martin Ingram, "Spousals Litigation in the English Ecclesiastical Courts, *c.* 1350–
1640", in *Marriage and Society: Studies in the Social History of Marriage*, R.B.
Outhwaite (ed.) (London, 1981), pp. 38–57. Helmholz identified a decline in
matrimonial litigation in Canterbury, Rochester, Lichfield and Hereford. He
abstained from making comments about York, Helmholz, *Marriage Litigation*, p.
161.

[12] Goldberg, *Women, Work, and Life Cycle*, pp. 201–66.

[13] See K. F. Burns, "The Administrative System of the Ecclesiastical Courts in the
Diocese and Province of York", i, "The Medieval Courts", unpublished
manuscript (York, 1962). Only six complete act books, survive from the fifteenth
century. However, Burns's comments are based on a examination of all surviving
act book fragments.

[14] Burns, "The Medieval Courts", pp. 165–66.

[15] Burns calculated these figures for the case load of the consistory court using the
six surviving complete years. In the count of cases in Hilary term 1417 Burns
included cases from the preceding year and for this reason arrived at a figure of
139 cases for the entire year. If this is compensated for by substituting the number

recording of cases in the act books carry a further warning to the historian: archival practice – and therefore the survival chances of certain types of cases or certain types of documents – varied over time. It is arguable that the observed changes in the composition of the surviving cause papers reflect such changes rather than real secular changes in litigation patterns. Some registrars were doubtless more meticulous than others in preserving case files, while certain types of cases which would have been thrown out by one registrar may have survived in the archiepiscopal archives because of the whim of another. The cases recorded in the act books also make it clear that the cause paper material represents only a fraction of the business conducted by the court. No complete act books survive from the fourteenth century and only six years (1417–20, 1425 and 1486–87) are covered by surviving fifteenth-century act books.[16] During these six years, the registrar of the court recorded 533 cases, more than twice the total number of preserved fifteenth-century cause paper files, and there is no reason to believe that the annual average of about ninety cases heard by the court varied over the two centuries under investigation here. If the same number of cases were heard annually in York in the fourteenth and fifteenth century, the courts would have dealt with 18,000 cases in this period. Out of all the cases heard before the consistory court only some 600 cause paper files survive.

Chance probably played a large part in determining which cause paper files survived. This seems to be the only explanation possible for the sudden and otherwise inexplicable fall in litigation in the decade 1370–79. This fall becomes even more enigmatic when non-matrimonial is separated from matrimonial litigation. The rest of the fourteenth century saw a gradual increase in the survival rates of non-matrimonial cause paper files, rising from five in 1300–9 to twenty-two in 1360–69. For the decade 1370–79, the number of non-matrimonial cause paper files dipped to a low of eight cases, before recovering in a sharp rise to twenty-eight and fifty cases during the last two decades of the century. The number of matrimonial cause paper files preserved from each decade of the fourteenth century shows no such deviations, except for the same sharp increase from twelve surviving cause paper files in 1380–89 to twenty-eight in the decade

of cases observed in Hilary 1417 with the average number cases heard during that term in the other years for which act books survive the total number of cases in 1407 falls to 104.

[16] Burns, "The Medieval Courts", p. 167.

1390–99. This fluctuation in survival rates can only be explained by chance: there are no recorded plagues or epidemics in this period and the fact that matrimonial litigation remains at the same level in the decade in question only strengthens the claim that what we see is a simple chance deviation in survival rates rather than a significant reflection of a changing case-load.

Unrecorded changes in the organisation of the court may also have influenced the frequency of marriage litigation at the consistory court in York. We know from the cause paper files that archdeacons' and deacons' courts in Yorkshire dealt with matrimonial litigation.[17] But we have no way of ascertaining the volume of litigation these courts examined, nor can we say for certain that the observed fall in matrimonial litigation preserved among the cause papers in the fifteenth century is not due to an increased efficiency on the archdeaconal level or to an increased willingness among the laity or the official's court in York to accept the decision of the lower courts. This point is all the more important since the boundaries between the two levels of jurisdiction were vague throughout the period. The consistory court only reserved for itself the right to hear "major cases".[18] Such an ambiguous definition of its jurisdiction allowed the consistory court considerable discretion in its choice of which cases to claim. The observed fall in matrimonial cases in the cause papers can therefore possibly be explained by an increased willingness on the part of the consistory court to let minor cases be dealt with by the lower courts. Furthermore, R.M. Smith has suggested that observed changes in marriage litigation patterns could have been due to the introduction of new remedies in the secular courts to deal with such litigation.[19] Even

---

[17] The following fourteenth-century cases were heard by archdeacons' courts before the York consistory court: CP, E 23, 25, 71, 102, 137, 178, 191, 223, 241b and 257. The dean of the Christianity of York heard three cases before they were heard by the consistory court: CP, E 82, 159 and 198. For comparisons with other jurisdictions see Helmholz, *Marriage Litigation*, pp. 145–77; Ingram, "Spousals Litigation", pp. 42–44; Sheehan, "Formation and Stability", pp. 232–33.

[18] See Archbishop Giffard's letter to Ruffinus, archdeacon of Cleveland: "Intellegimus enim quod cognitionem habetis causarum ... nisi quod officiales nostri quandoque ... ad majores querelas ... rescripserunt ... vobis jurgiis et nobis causis majoribus ... reservatis." (Burns, "The Medieval Courts", p. 170).

[19] R.M. Smith, "Marriage Processes", draws attention to the fact that common law courts began to allow the sucessful plaintiff a possibility of recovering damages from the defendant for breach of promise. See also S. F. C. Milsom, *Historical Foundations of the Common Law*, (London, 1969), p. 289.

before analysing the preserved cause papers, we must therfore question how representative they are of litigation patterns, especially for general marriage patterns. Unrecorded changes in the internal organisation of the court in York, an increased willingness to accept the arbitration of a lower court, and changes in jurisdiction between the official's court and courts at the diaconal level or between common law courts and ecclesiastical courts, can easily be confused with changes in the survival patterns of the cause papers that indicate a change in marriage litigation.

The first question that must be asked when approaching the cause papers is whose litigation is preserved in these sources. The answer provides three important insights into the social setting of the court. First, that people who lived near main roads which led to a town where an ecclesiastical court convened were more likely to litigate than those who did not enjoy such easy access to the courts. Secondly, the wealthier a litigant was, the more likely he or she was to litigate in York. It is no surprise that all but one litigant claimed to be of free status. It is surprising that their claimed status was only challenged in three cases, particularly considering the fact that exceptions to libels or witnesses were frequent and often little more than recorded shouting matches.[20] Irregularities in the composition of the group of witnesses who were interrogated by the courts must also be considered in this connection. These suggest that it is an open question whether the witnesses represented the cross-section of society that some scholars seem to believe. The sex ratio of the witnesses is certainly not representative of society as a whole and their age-distribution suggests that there was a bias against using female witnesses of more than fifty years of age. It will also be suggested that the litigants were biased

---

[20] *Drifield* c. *Northdalton*; *Wright* c. *Byrkys*; and *Gudefelawe* c. *Chapman*. CP, E 28, 103 and 137. Only in *Wright* c. *Byrkys* is it likely that there was any truth in the allegation of the litigant's unfree status. One witness specified the degree of difference between the plaintiff and the defendant saying: "quod dictus [reus] est potentior et ditior in bonis sed est servilis conditionis et nativus domini duci Lancastriensis et habet in bonis majoribus suis. [Pars actrix est] libere conditionis ut [dicit ista jurata". CP, E 103 (1368).

Common objections to witnesses include that they were *viles et plebes* (e.g. *Walkington* c. *Bradley*), that they were bribed (e.g. *Cragger* c. *Chapelayn*), that they were mortal enemies of one of the litigants (e.g. *Walkington* c. *Bradley* and *Redyng* c. *Boton*), or – at the more extreme end of the spectrum – that a female witness was a procuress (*Walkington* c. *Bradley*) and that a witness was mentally deficient (*Redyng* c. *Boton*). CP, E 82, 92, 82, 92.

against a large section of the population – the unfree – who were open to such exceptions that litigants may have felt that to produce an unfree witness could actually jeopardise the successful outcome of their cases. It is certainly the case that only a few unfree witnesses appear in the surviving fourteenth-century cause papers. Thirdly, litigation papers show marginal experiences of marriage, since the marriages in question had to be either notorious in the local community or offer sufficient rewards to the litigants to motivate them to seek the arbitration of the church to settle their marriage disputes. In this chapter we shall investigate the first two propositions in detail. The third point will be considered later.

Both Judith Bennett and Michael Sheehan have drawn attention to the importance of easy access to the church courts. They also warn that the ready availability of *de facto* divorces made it easy for potential litigants to settle their marital disputes without ever appearing before the courts.[21] The York material emphasises these concerns. Plaintiffs are usually not recorded as giving their motives for going to court, but it is a common feature of the plaintiffs that they had easy access to the courts. Forty-one of eighty-eight fourteenth-century cases were initiated by litigants who lived less than twenty miles from York;[22] no less than sixty-two out of the eighty-four identified surviving cases came from within a forty mile radius from York.[23] Considering that the archdiocese of York included most of northern England and that the court in York heard appeals against the decisions of the courts within its archiepiscopal jurisdiction – which included most ecclesiastical courts from the southern border of the archdiocese of York to the Scottish border – one would have expected to see more cases originating at a greater distance from the ecclesiastical courts in York. Litigation preserved in the cause papers originated almost exclu-

---

[21] Sheehan, "Formation and Stability"; Judith M. Bennett, "Medieval Women, Modern Women: Across the Great Divide", in *Culture and History, 1350–1600: Essays on English Communities, Identities and Writing*, David Aers (ed.) (New York and London, 1992), p. 170.

[22] Twenty-five lived in the city of York or its environs (CP, E 14, 36, 82, 87, 89, 111, 116, 121, 126, 138, 150, 155, 157, 158, 159, 161 175, 198, 216, 221, 238, 239, 242, 245 and 248); three came from within a radius of ten miles (CP, E 25, 148 and 153); and a further thirteen lived within a radius of ten to twenty miles (CP, E 6, 18, 40, 84, 85, 92, 95, 97, 113, 181, 188, 191 and 210).

[23] Plaintiffs from villages within a thirty mile radius: CP, E 6, 18, 28, 37, 76, 92, 103, 106, 124, 178, 181, 186, 210, 211, 236 and 274. Plaintiffs from villages within a forty mile radius: CP, E 33, 61, 69, 79, 102, 114 and 212.

sively in the archbishop's personal jurisdiction or in the peculiars which were enclosed within the geographical boundaries of this jurisdiction. This trend is even more marked when the distance to the first court to hear the case is computed. Under these circumstances, we find that sixty of the eighty-eight cases were initiated in courts less than ten miles from the plaintiff's normal place of residence and seventy-five cases were initiated within a forty mile radius of the local court.

A further aspect of the geography of the cases deserves mention. When the litigants' home villages are plotted against a map of known medieval roads, it becomes clear that the vast majority of cases originated in villages that had good access to the courts. Only a few cases originated outside the Roman road network, and only a small number of cases originated in locations with no known major roads. Perhaps it is not surprising, then, that most appeals from other episcopal or peculiar jurisdictions that were heard in the York courts originated in courts located along the old Roman road going from London to the Scottish border.[24] Virtually no litigation originated from across the Pennines: litigants from this area would have had to go north of the Pennines almost as far as Carlisle and then follow the Roman road to York or go south as far as Chester and Stoke before turning north towards York. The litigation preserved in the cause papers therefore originates within a limited area which was heavily influenced by an urban economy. Those cases that did not originate in an urban environment usually came from a village settlement in the economic hinterland of a city. Rural litigation – litigation that originated in parishes with little access to an nearby urban centre – is virtually absent in fourteenth-century York cause papers. When it does appear, such as in the case of *Staindrop* c. *Dale*, one of the litigants was often an apprentice in a town who had decided to marry a woman in his former rural community.[25]

Firm evidence about the litigants' wealth is difficult to come by. This is particularly true for the majority of plaintiffs, who, being female, are notoriously under-enumerated in the surviving poll tax lists.[26] Women were also more likely than men to die intestate since

---

[24] Brian Paul Hindle, "Roads and Tracks", in *The English Medieval Landscape*, Leonard Cantor (ed.) (London and Canberra, 1982), pp. 193–218.

[25] CP, E 215.

[26] P. J. P. Goldberg, "Urban Identity and the Poll Taxes of 1377, 1379 and 1381", *Economic History Review*, 2nd series, 43 (1990), pp. 194–216.

married women's estates would not be distributed upon their death.[27] Similarly, the Freemen's Rolls of York – which have been used with great success by Barrie Dobson to show the occupational structure of the city – provide little evidence beyond the fact that a person with the same name as a (male) litigant was admitted to the freedom of the city.[28] However, evidence about litigants' *status* can be found in about two-thirds of the cause papers themselves. Although status is not a firm measure of economic ability, it does allow the historian to place most of the litigants in their social context. In the following, I have estimated the status of individual litigants using a system of five status groups numbered 1–5, 1 being the highest and 5 the lowest. Interpreting status, I have tried to use status groups as they were defined in documents from the fourteenth and early fifteenth century. I have, among others, consulted such documents as the Sumptuary Laws of 1363, which regulated the clothes members of different social groups were allowed to wear; the Statute of Labourers, which defined the terms and duration of service including wages; a list of trades in York drawn up by the common clerk, Roger Burton, in 1415; and a settlement between Nicholas Blackburn, mayor of York, and Archbishop Bowet from 1411, which described the order of precedence to be observed between various officers of the court and civic officials in civic and ecclesiastical processions.[29] Only one condition – in cases where a litigant had a member of the clergy in his or her family – has not followed any of these lists of status. Members of the laity with clerical family members have, however, been arbitrarily placed in the same status group as citizens, artisans and craftsmen. This system of status groups may give a false impression of precision in the placement of individual litigants. The status groups do not necessarily reflect the economic power of the litigants, nor is it intended as an index of their

---

[27] Michael M. Sheehan, *The Will in Medieval England: From the Conversion of the Anglo-Saxons to the End of the Thirteenth Century*, Studies and Texts (Toronto, 1963); Michael M. Sheehan, "The Influence of Canon Law on the Property Rights of Married Women in England", *Mediaeval Studies*, 25 (1963), pp. 109–24.

[28] R.B. Dobson, "Admissions to the Freedom of the City of York in the Late Middle Ages", *Economic History Review*, 23 (1973), pp. 1–22.

[29] Modernised texts of the Statute of Labourers and the Sumptuary Laws can be found in A.R. Myers (ed.), *English Historical Documents, 1327–1485* (London, 1969). Roger Burton's list of York crafts are found in R.H. Skaife, "Civic Officials of York", unpublished manuscript, York City Archives, York City Library and the agreement between Nicholas Blakburn and the archdiocese is paraphrased in Burns, "The Medieval Courts", p. 158.

income. They are intended to give a general impression of the litigants' relative position in the social hierarchy of the fourteenth century. It therefore includes more factors than pure economic ability, such as the office which the person held and his or her family background and claim to titles in land. The placement of individual litigants in particular status groups can be discussed, but the important point is that the status groups give a broad indication of the status of the people who used the ecclesiastical courts to settle their marriage disputes in the northern province. It will also be seen that among the litigants in the cause paper material there is a very large proportion of wealthy people and virtually no paupers or unfree. These are the five medieval status groups used:

1. Landowning nobility, owning land in more than one county; members of noble families with a permanent seat in parliament.
2. Landowning nobility or gentry with possessions in one county; holders of royal commissions; parliamentary representatives and holders of civic offices; citizens owning land outside the city; members of the clergy in York.
3. All other citizens, artisans and craftsmen; landowners not identified as *dominus* or *domina* in cause papers; people who have a priest in their family.
4. Small-scale farmers; servants; labourers, who are not identified as unfree; people possessing goods worth more than one mark.
5. Paupers; minors; people of servile status; people possessing goods worth less than one mark.

Whenever possible, the cases have been categorised according to the status of the plaintiff, since the plaintiff made the initial approach to a member of the court. If they informed the court of their occupation, women have been put in the corresponding category. If no other evidence is available, women are put in their fathers' or *de facto* husbands' status groups. The same has been done in the case of unmarried men whose status could not be identified in other ways. I have identified the litigants' status by three means. The simplest identification is the one that the litigants made themselves. Litigants frequently informed the courts about their status by quoting their title, their occupation, their income or the value of their belongings. Another means of firm identification of status group is contained in the evidence of witnesses. The witnesses regularly commented on the suitability of a marriage by referring to the relative incomes of the parties or recorded the value of a marriage settlement. Thirdly, circumstantial evidence has been used. For example, when a witness said that a litigant planted a field as a dowry for his alleged wife and other witnesses claim that she "behaved as his wife in matters of selling and buying corn" the man in question was undoubtedly a farmer.[30] Using the evidence of witnesses and the evidence of other surviving cause paper material for social classification of the litigants will tend towards a precise assessment of higher status groups and towards an over-enumeration of members of the lowest status groups. A member of the highest classes will insist on the mention of his or her title and will therefore always be recorded as status group 1 or 2 when such a person appears before the court. On the other hand, the members of status group 5 are likely either to request the protection of the archbishop or to be cited as paupers in their opponents' replies to the libel or in their exceptions to witnesses. If anything, the method of identification used here will tend to exaggerate the numbers of members of status group 5 that sought the help of the church courts.

Sixty-eight of the eighty-eight surviving marriage cases can be classified with reasonable certainty, i.e. either the plaintiff informed the court of his or her occupation, a witness mentioned the plaintiff's occupation, income or status in his or her deposition, or the case contains enough circumstantial evidence about status to make an identification. Thus a firm classification can be made in around two-thirds of the surviving cases. Although the remaining third of the cases do not contain enough evidence to establish their provenance firmly, it is unlikely that they have originated in the marginal status groups. A close reading of them certainly did not bring any evidence to light that they may have originated in the lowest status group. Helmholz commented that it was his impression that litigants in the York cause papers were wealthier as a group than the litigants in marriage cases preserved in other dioceses in England.[31] An analysis of the social backgrounds of the litigants in the cause papers partially substantiates this claim: in those forty cases where one or more of the litigants identified their social background they tended to come from status groups 1–3.[32] Sixteen of these forty cases involved people who

---

[30] CP, E 85.

[31] Helmholz, *Marriage Litigation*, pp. 160–61.

[32] Status group 1: CP, E 12, 14, 46, 108, 179, 259; status group 2: CP, E 15, 18, 62, 76, 79, 87, 89, 113, 175, 245, 248; status group 3: CP, E 26, 36, 37, 61, 69, 113, 124, 138, 153, 159, 161, 188, 198, 216, 221, 235, 238, 239, 242 257, 263;

insisted on using their titles or who were related to a member of the *Curia Eboracensis* or to another high-ranking cleric (for instance to a proctor of the *Curia Eboracensis,* or to the guardian of the hospital of St Giles in Beverley).[33] The words *dominus, nobilis vir, miles* or *nobilis mulier, domina* were used to describe at least one of the litigants in five enforcement cases,[34] in six cases of annulment of marriage[35] and in five other cases.[36] Twelve of these cases have been classified as belonging to status groups 1–2 – where such occupational descriptions should belong – the classification is made on the basis of the status of the plaintiff. At the other end of the social scale we note that only one plaintiff can be positively identified as unfree, that none of the plaintiffs informed the court that they were of unfree status and that the free status of a plaintiff was rarely contested. The free status of one defendant was contested and he was proven to be unfree.[37] Positive evidence about status is available for a number of litigants either in the cause papers themselves or in supplementary sources. Among the plaintiffs belonging to social group 1 is Katherine, the daughter of Sir Ralph Paynell, who pleaded for an annulment on the

status group 4: CP, E 23, 25, 70, 77, 82, 84, 85, 92, 102, 111, 113, 114, 121, 126, 137, 150, 155, 159, 181, 215, 223, 236, 241v, 242, 256. A further five cases may be classified as status group 4 by occupational surnames: CP, E 1, 6, 135, 223, 255. One case definitely originated in status group 5 (CP, E 103) and a further two cases may have involved a litigant from the same status group: CP, E 28 (the status group 5 litigant was the defendant) and *Gudefelawe* c. *Chapman,* in which Master Thomas Ponteland, a witness for the plaintiff, gave the following reason for his appearance as a witness in the case: "Et dicit idem juratus quod quidam Willelmus de Hesylryg venit ad ipsum et rogavit eum quod videret dictam Julianam, filiam tenentis sui, justitiam habere. Et dicit quod ipsam juvabat et ipsam fovebat in causa". CP, E 137.

[33] *Welewyk* c. *Midelton, and Garth and Newton* c. *Waghen.* CP, E 79 (1358–60) and E 245 (1391)

[34] CP, E 18, 89, 175, 179 and 188.

[35] CP, E 46, 69, 76, 87, 257 and 259.

[36] *Percy* c. *Colville* (non-payment of dowry); *Hiliard* c. *Hiliard* (validity of parents' marriage); *Welewyk* c. *Midelton and Frothyngham* (validity of vows, multiparty); *Garth and Newton* c. *Waghen* (multiparty over the proctor William Cawod's daughter). CP, E 12, 108, 79, 245.

[37] *Wright* c. *Byrkys* and *Sturmy* c. *Tully.* CP, E 103 (1368) ; 235 (1396). The unfree status of the defendant John Byrkys emerged during the interrogation of witnesses over his exceptions to the plaintiff's witnesses, "interrogata dicit quod dictus Johannes est potentior et ditior in bonis sed est servilis conditionis et nativus domini duci Lancastriensis et habet in bonis majoribus suis [Cecilia est] libere conditionis ut [dicit ista jurata]." CP, E 103.

grounds of her husband Nicholas Cantilupe's impotence in 1368. She was of the Paynell family who came over with William the Conqueror.[38] Her ancestors refounded the priory of the Holy Trinity, York, between 1090 and 1100[39] and further endowed it in 1166–79. [40] Katherine's father, Ralph Paynell, was a sheriff of Yorkshire and the Paynell family owned land in several counties.[41] Katherine Hiliard, the widow of Sir John Hiliard, who appeared in a plea for her dower to be assigned to her from her stepson, Peter, claimed that the dower consisted of one-third of twenty-four messuages, one mill, sixteen bulls, twenty-one bovates, five and a half acres of meadows, eight shillings in rents, and pasture for 300 sheep with the things that relate to them, in the villages of Arnall, Dripole, Riston, Preston, Sutton, Hedon and Carton. The villages, which can be identified today, are all located in Humberside. She has, however, been placed in status group 1 because she and her husband paid a canon called John Esthorp to go to the papal curia where he stayed for three months trying to obtain a dispensation for their consanguinity.[42] John Carnoby described himself as an *armiger* and claimed to have an annual income of more than one hundred marks.[43] His claim was contradicted by the defendant Johanna Monceaux's witnesses, who claimed that he was living on a paltry ten marks annually. Johanna's exceptions to John Carnoby were probably influenced by the fact that she was trying to prove to the court that she was too rich and powerful to have consented to marry him. Since the two appear to have settled the case out of court and to have married, the case has been put in status group 1.[44] Johanna Monceaux was doubtless one of the wealthiest and most

---

[38] The family's history is outlined in Charles Travis Clay (ed.), *Early Yorkshire Charters: Based on the Manuscripts of the Late William Farrer*, Yorkshire Archeological Society Record Series, extra series, i (1936).

[39] J. Raine (ed.), *The Register, or Rolls, of Walter Gray, Lord Archbisop of York: With Appendices of Illustrative Documents*, Surtees Society, 56 (Durham, 1872), p. 110.

[40] Clay (ed.), *Early Yorkshire Charters*, pp. 76–77 and 84–85.

[41] Charles Travis Clay (ed), *Early Yorkshire Charters: Based on the Manuscripts of the Late William Farrer*, Yorkshire Archeological Society Record Series, extra series, iii (1939).

[42] *Hiliard c. Hiliard*. CP, E 108 (1370).

[43] He was the plaintiff in *Carnoby c. Monceaux*. CP, E 179 (1390).

[44] Johanna Monceaux's will is dated 16 August 1426, Borthwick Institute of Historical Research, probate register, vol. 2, fol. 495.

influential female litigants in York. She was not only the *domina* of Barmston Manor and in possession of an annual income of more than 300 marks (which put her in the highest income bracket in the Sumptuary Laws of 1363); but, according to several of her witnesses, she was also related to the royal family through her father. The Monceaux family founded the hospital of St Mary, Bridlington,[45] and a certain John Monceaux represented the county of Yorkshire in parliament in 1351–52 and served several times on commissions of *oyer et terminer*.[46] Family relations and circumstantial evidence from the cause paper file itself place the plaintiff Alice Welewyk in CP, E 79, 1358–60 in status group 2. She was related to the prior of Warter and to the guardian of the hospital of St Giles in Beverley and worth a bribe of twelve marks to the defendant, Robert Midelton. Family and independent evidence places Agnes Huntington, who sued for a divorce from Simon Munkton in CP, E 248, in status group 2.[47] She was the stepdaughter of Hamo Hessay, the parliamentary representative for the city of York at the parliaments of 1337–38, 1339, 1352 and 1353.[48] Her deceased father, Richard Huntington, owned land outside the city, which he left her in his will.[49] Internal evidence shows that William Aungier, the plaintiff in *Aungier* c. *Malcake*, was from a wealthy family like Alice Welewyk.[50] Although none of the witnesses attempted an estimate of how much he owned, he was so wealthy that his wardship was purchased by the steward of the duchess of Hastings at a price of ten marks. He was brought up by the steward's brother, who was a priest in Elsing in Norfolk, where there

---

[45] William Page (ed.), *Victoria County History of England*, iii, *Victoria County History of the County of Yorkshire* (London, 1913), p. 305.

[46] Page, *VCH, Yorkshire*, p. 305; Myers, *English Historical Documents, 1327–1485*.

[47] As seen above in Chapter 2, the earliest surviving document in this case is Simon Munkton's plea for restitution of marital rights which he presented before the archbishop's court of audience on 21 August 1345. However, a letter from the commissary general dated 30 October 1345 shows that Simon's wife, Agnes Huntington, had initiated proceedings at the official's court before Simon made his plea to the archbishop. For this reason the case has been identified as a case with a female plaintiff.

[48] *Return: Members of Parliament, Part 1: Parliaments of England, 1213–1702* (London, 1878), pp. 117, 118, 120, 127, 152 and 154.

[49] York Dean and Chapter Wills, i, fol.14.

[50] CP, E 76 (1357–58).

was a school which William attended. William Aungier is categorised as status group 2. Among the clerics whose names appeared in connection with marriage litigation, we find two proctors of the *Curia Eboracensis*: William Calthorn (*Fossard* c. *Calthorn*) and William Cawod (*Garth and Newton* c. *Waghen*).[51] William Calthorn's opponent, Johanna Fossard, was of a wealthy York family enfeoffed to York property by the earl of Mortain.[52] She was the plaintiff and consequently the case is categorised as a status group 2: had William Calthorn been the plaintiff, the case would have been reduced to status group 3. The widowed daughter of William Cawod,[53] Agnes Waghen, was the object of the litigation by two male *competitores*: an apothecary and an *armiger*. She appeared as the defendant but all three parties in the case belong in status group 2. Twenty-five male litigants identified themselves to the court by their trade. Three of them were saddle makers,[54] three were tailors,[55] two were tanners[56] and there was a representative for each of the trades of masons, potters, rope-makers, barkers and drapers. All these have been categorised as group 4.[57] Although he was doubtless much wealthier than any of the above, Simon Munkton – who was the defendant in *Huntington* c. *Munkton* – should be counted among the artisans: he was a goldsmith. But since his wife – the above mentioned Agnes Huntington – initiated the case, I have counted the case as a group 2.[58] Tradesmen were also common among the litigants in the cause

[51] CP, E 175 (1390) and E 245 (1391).

[52] R.B. Pugh (ed.), *The City of York: The Victoria County History of England: A History of Yorkshire* (London, 1961), p. 50; William Farrer (ed.), *Early Yorkshire Charters*, i, *Early Yorkshire Charters: Being a Collection of Documents Anterior to the Thirteenth Century Made from Public Records, Monastic Chartularies, Roger Dodsworth's Manuscripts and Other Available Sources* (Edinburgh, 1914), p. 154; William Farrer (ed.), *Early Yorkshire Charters*. Yorkshire Archaeological Society Record Series, Extra Series (Edinburgh, 1916), pp. 454–57.

[53] Cawod's career spanned most offices in the legal system in York: He became a bachelor of canon law in 1376, he was the dean and chapter *auditor causarum* 7 November 1382 to 10 December 1389, a licentiate in canon law 1393, he was a vicar general 1397, and served as the official of Archbishop Bowet 1417–19. See Sandra Brown, "The Peculiar Jurisdiction of York Minster during the Middle Ages" (unpublished Ph.D. thesis, University of York, 1980), p. 35.

[54] CP, E 121, 159 and 223.

[55] CP, E 150, 235 and 263.

[56] CP, E 36 and 121.

[57] CP, E 138, 111, 138, 82, 198 respectively.

[58] CP, E 248.

papers in York. Two male litigants described themselves as travelling merchants, another as a spicer, and another as an apothecary in York. A final litigant from the city of York was a mercer. These would be members of status group 4,[59] as would the five litigants who informed the court that they were serving as servants.[60] The status of those litigants who did not explicitly identify their status can be guessed at from circumstantial evidence. One such plaintiff clearly worked the land, and therefore she is classified as a member of status group 4. During the course of the case it transpired that her alleged husband had sown two bovates of land for her,[61] In another case it transpired that the woman "treated him as her husband in all matters concerning the selling and buying of corn". [62] Another litigant was an apprentice, since he persuaded his fiancée to postpone the solemnisation of their marriage until the end of his apprenticeship. Although this is not made explicit in the cause paper file, it appears that Margaret Graystanes, the plaintiff in the original case – *Graystanes* c. *Dale* – before the official of Durham, was a servant in the household of the original defendant's aunt.[63] Therefore the case has been categorised as belonging to group 4. The distribution of cases across status groups 1–4 is reasonably close to what one would expect: a over-representation of the wealthy and a solid base of the middling status groups. Unfortunately, reliable computations of the relative numbers of income or status groups in the fourteenth century, which could show us whether the number of cases from each status group is in proportion to the size of that status group in the population at large, are not available. The volume of litigation which originated in status groups 1 and 2 must, however, be out of all proportion to the relative numbers of its members. Taken together, these two status groups initiated 21 per cent of all litigation in York. The number of cases initiated by these status groups probably also reflects their familiarity with the legal process. Well-educated, confident and wealthy people were more likely to litigate. They knew the rules of litigation and they had the money to go to court. Poorer people needed to make a special effort

[59] Chapmen: CP, E 92, 102; spicer: E 241v; apothecary: E 245; mercer: E 216.

[60] CP, E 121, 181, 238 and 242. The last case, CP, E 242 (1396), is a multiparty case between two servants and a third person whose trade is unspecified.

[61] "seisiret ipsa Alicia in duabus bovatis terre". CP, E 85 (1362–63).

[62] "a tempore quo dicti Willelmus et Alicia sic contraxerunt ut prefertur ipsa Alicia ipsum Willelmum definivit sicut vir suum in venditione et ventilatione bladorum suorum et in aliis que pertinunt ad matrem familiam". CP, E 84 (1361).

[63] CP, E 215 (1383–84).

to go to the courts; though the cause papers do not contain any identified *ex officio* litigation, some causes were appealed to York by appel-
lants who had been compelled to appear before a lower court.[64] This
is the situation for status groups 1–4, but, as pointed out before, there
is only one identified plaintiff who was a member of status group 5.
Another case – *Sturmy* c. *Tuly* – allegedly involved an unfree defendant, but during the case he proved that he was of free status.[65]

This lack of litigants in status group 5 is perhaps the most striking
fact of the cause papers, and it is all the more surprising since, as was
pointed out above in Chapter 4, Archbishop Greenfield's statutes of
1311 were designed to ensure equal access to the courts for all, regardless of their economic background. Even if all unidentified cases were
to have originated in status group 5, this status group would only
account for 23 per cent of preserved marriage litigation.[66] Canon law
allowed paupers, widows and orphans the archbishop's special protection and general access to the arbitration of the ecclesiastical courts
was guaranteed to almost every subject of the archbishop. In an
attempt to encourage his subjects' use of the courts, Archbishop
Greenfield fixed litigation costs at a uniform level in the statutes of the
court of 1311. The prologue informs us the statutes were drawn up to
achieve two aims: first, to eliminate the possibility of delays in cases
heard in the court; and, secondly, to limit the expense of conducting a
case for the litigants.[67] Only one cause paper file mentions the cost of
litigation. The case was initiated as a case of abjuration *sub poena
nubendi* before the dean of Beverley. When the defendant, Thomas
Midelton, a chapman from Beverly, tried to settle the case out of
court, he inquired of the plaintiff, Margery Merton, who was a
weaver:

how much she had spent on prosecuting said case. To which she said fifty-

---

[64] CP, E 6, 97, 102, 103, 111, 114, 135, 150, 191, 102, 211 and 263.

[65] CP, E 235 (1396–97).

[66] It is more likely that this litigation originated in the middle status groups: where
exceptions to the libel or to the plaintiff's witnesses exist among the unidentified
cases they do not quote the poverty or the status of the plaintiff as an objection.

[67] David Wilkins (ed.), *Concilia magna Britanniae et Hiberniae a synodo Verolamiensi
AD CCCCXLIV ad Londinensem AD MDC*, ii, *Concilia Magna Britanniae et
Hiberniae a synodo Verolamiensi AD CCCCXLIV ad Londinensem AD MDC*
(London, 1737), p. 409.

five shillings. And then he said: "I will pay you back. Have twenty shillings now in part payment".[68]

This tells us two things about these litigants. First that a weaver was willing to spend the equivalent of two months' wages on a case, which she had initiated, according to her own statement, because she did not like "being made a fool of" by her lover. Secondly, we see that the amount of 20s. in cash was easily available to Thomas Midelton. Margery Merton and Thomas Midelton are members of status group 4, the lowest status group found among the litigants. This suggests that, to most people who appeared before the courts in York, the cost of prosecution was not prohibitive even though the amounts involved in pursuing their cases could be substantial. The lack of status group 5 members in the cause papers, however, contradicts the idea of equal use of the courts by all status groups. There is no obvious reason why this might be: canon law claimed the right to examine all cases involving marriage and provided a kind of legal aid under which a pauper paid nothing to conduct his case. This policy of providing a means of litigating at the ecclesiastical courts for the poor is provided for in York by Archbishop Greenfield's statutes. Although it was possible for anybody to litigate in the courts in York, and although we have evidence that litigation was not prohibitively expensive, we have seen that an expected section of the population simply did not appear before the courts. Among the cause paper litigants we meet servants and labourers, farmers and citizens, but only one serf.

It has been common among historians to assume that one gender was more likely to initiate marriage litigation before ecclesiastical courts than another.[69] As it happens, an analysis of plaintiffs' gender

---

[68] Et tunc idem Thomas interrogavit dictam Margeriam quantum expendiderat in prosecutione dicte lite. Que dixit quod quinqueginta quinque solidi, et tunc ipse dixit "de hoc satisfacam te et habe hic xx solidos in partem." CP, E 102 (1365–67).

[69] For example, in his analysis of the documents produced by the court in matrimonial cases Richard Helmholz implies that an enforcement of marriage case was always brought by a woman: "The libel ended with the demand that the defendant be adjudged the plaintiff's legitimate *husband* and be required to treat *her* with marital affection". Helmholz, *Marriage Litigation*, p. 13. When discussing the repudiation of spouses or the abandonment of one spouse by another, which he calls "self-divorce": "Rarely did *men* claim the right to repudiate their *wives* without an excuse that was at least vaguely canonical. Almost always they had a

confirms that women initiated many more cases, both in York and at the first instance courts. Just over two-thirds – or fifty-nine – of the surviving matrimonial York cause papers were initiated by women at the first instance of the court.[70] Only twenty-nine cases were initiated at the first instance by men.[71] Among the twenty-eight cases which had more than one plaintiff,[72] eighteen women appeared in the first instance of the court to claim a man in marriage.[73] Fifteen of these women tried to persuade the court to annul a marriage which the documents identify as *de facto* and to enforce their marriages to the male defendant.[74] In three of these twenty-eight cases, two women were competitors for the same man.[75] In four multi-party cases, two men claimed a woman in marriage before she had set up a household with any man.[76] Thus the latter four cases did not involve the dissolution of a *de facto* marriage. Of the remaining six multi-party cases,

reason for the validity of their first marriage. But it was the *man* himself that worked out the divorce", ibid., p. 59 (my italics) Helmholz assumed that it was always the man who wished to obtain a divorce and that it was only men who abandoned their wives. At least one fourteenth-century self-divorce investigated by the official's court in York was initiated by a woman, see D.M. Owen, "White Annays and Others", in *Medieval Women*, Derek Baker (ed.), Studies in Church History, Subsidia 1 (Oxford, 1978), pp. 331–46.

[70] D.M. Smith lists cause papers by the plaintiff or appellant in York, *Ecclesiastical Cause Papers at York: The Court at York, 1301–1399*, Borthwick Texts and Calendars, 14 (York, 1988), p. viii. The following cases were initiated by women at the first instance court: CP, E 1, 6, 25, 28, 33, 36, 37, 40, 69, 70, 71, 77, 79, 82, 84, 92, 95, 102, 103, 105, 106, 108, 111, 113, 114, 116, 121, 126, 135, 137, 140, 150, 157, 158, 159, 161, 175, 178, 181, 191, 198, 202, 210, 211, 213, 215, 216, 221, 223, 235, 236, 239, 241b, 241i, 255, 256, 257, 259 and 263.

[71] CP, E 12, 14, 15, 18, 23, 26, 46, 61, 62, 76, 85, 87, 89, 97, 124, 138, 148, 153, 155, 179, 186, 188, 212, 238, 241v, 242, 245, 248 and 274.

[72] CP, E 25, 36, 37, 71, 77, 79, 87, 95, 103, 106, 113, 124, 126, 138, 148, 153, 155, 158, 159, 161, 175, 186, 188, 210, 215, 236, 242 and 256.

[73] CP, E 25, 36, 37, 71, 77, 79, 95, 103, 106, 113, 126, 158, 161, 175, 210, 215, 236 and 256.

[74] CP, E 25, 36, 37, 71, 77, 79, 103, 106, 113, 126, 161, 175, 210, 236 and 256.

[75] CP, E 113, 126 and 159. In these three cases; it is unclear whether the man had set up a household with one of the female plaintiffs. For example, in *Spuret c. Hornby*, Margery Spuret and Thomas Hornby first appeared before the dean of the Christianity of York who dismissed the case when Margery could not produce witnesses for her case. Four months later she initiated the present case again this time with witnesses: at this stage Thomas Hornby was also sought by Beatrice Gylling. CP, E 159 (1394)

[76] CP, E 138, 186, 188 and 242.

three were cases of precontract, all of which were brought by men in the first instance.[77] The plaintiff cannot be identified in three multi-party cases.[78]

If we break down the figures further into types of cases, this gendered trend remains among the largest groups of surviving litigation. The three major types of litigation – matrimonial and divorce, vows, and annulment cases – all demonstrate an approximate two-third majority of female plaintiffs. The unusual types of cases from a gender distribution point of view are *sub poena nubendi*, divorce *a mensa et thoro*, and alimony and restoration of marital rights cases. These four types of cases are entirely gender-specific. The causes of these irregularities are probably different for different types of case.[79] Women only were the litigants in the five surviving *a mensa et thoro* divorce cases. Given that these cases always dealt with severe cruelty between the spouses it is not surprising that men should not bring these cases to the *Curia Eboracensis*. Male violence towards women has always been more visible. It also tended to fall into the kind of categories that the courts could establish by proof: to use Mr Justice Devlin's famous phrase in summing up *R. v. Duffy* (1947), these men experienced "a sudden and temporary loss of self-control". The cases in York conform to this pattern. Although the libel in these cases always claims a long-lasting dissent among the spouses, the courts required, and often obtained, proof of single instances of violence. The man's violence was not always unprovoked. In two cases, a woman had either threatened to murder her husband when he was

---

[77] *Dronesfield* c. *Donbarre* (1364), *Elme* c. *Elme* (1389), *Thekilthorp* c. *Enges* (1374). CP, E 87, 153 and 155. I distinguish a precontract from a matrimonial and divorce case by the fact that we either have positive proof in the cause papers that the alleged spouse was not present in court or that we have no attestation that he was quoted to appear before the court.

[78] *Topclyff* c. *Erle* (1381), *Newport* c. *Thwayte* (1387), and *Sporet* c. *Hornby* (1394). CP, E 124, 148 and 159.

[79] Tove Rasmussen, "Jeg tager dig til min ægtemand ... .: kvinder og kirkeret i 1300–tallets Yorkshire" (*Hovedfagsopgave* [MA thesis], Copenhagen, 1985), pp. 41–48 comes to much the same results. However, we differ in the way that we compute the figures. Rasmussen counted the number of female plaintiffs when the cases were heard in York and subdivided the cause papers into three groups (enforcement, multi-party and divorce cases). I have computed the number of female plaintiffs in the court of first instance in nine categories.

asleep, or indeed actually tried to poison him.[80] Cases for the restitution of marital rights and cases dealing with alimony were brought exclusively by men. The three cases classified by D.M. Smith as alimony cases were all appeals against either the size of an awarded alimony,[81] or depositions about disputed payments of an awarded alimony. In *Colville c. Darell*, the court in York investigated whether the alimony awarded by the court three years earlier had been paid.[82] *Maynwaring c. Tofte* (1324) and *Thurkelby c. Paynton* (late fourteenth or early fifteenth century) were appeals against the size of alimony awarded in previous litigation, at the court in Lincoln and at the court of Arches in London. In one case – the appeal against a decision of the court of Arches in London – William Maynwaring of Lichfield claimed that he was too poor to pay the twenty marks annually awarded as an alimony to his wife, Margaret Tofte, and that the court of Arches was prejudiced against him because of the influence of the Tofte family in the south.[83] The other claimed that an alimony of twenty marks had been wrongfully imposed by the court of Lincoln on John Thurkilby, a spicer of York, while an appeal was in progress at the Apostolic See.[84] Both of these cases appealed not against the actual award but objected to the size or the enforcement of the alimony. The two restitutions of marital rights cases identified by D.M. Smith were also brought by men.[85] Both cases are relatively straightforward cases of a man, abandoned by his wife, who sought the help of the courts to reassert his rights over her (and her property). *Hadilsay c. Hadilsay* was successful,[86] *Huntington c. Munkton* was abandoned after seventeen months of litigation.[87]

Two-thirds of all the cases in the major types of case were therefore brought by women and their litigation was proportionately successful: approximately two-thirds of the preserved sentences were passed in favour of women. Women were nevertheless also more likely to

---

[80] *Appleton c. Hothwayt* (1389) and *Nesfield c. Nesfield* (1396). CP, E 150, 221.

[81] *Maynwaring c. Tofte* (1324) and *Thurkilby c. Paynton* (late fourteenth or early fifteenth century). CP, E 15, 241v.

[82] CP, E 14 (1324).

[83] CP, E 15.

[84] CP, E 241v.

[85] *Huntington c. Munkton* (1345–46) and *Hadilsay c. Hadilsay* (1395). CP, E 248 and 274.

[86] CP, E 274 (1395).

[87] CP, E 248 (1345–46).

initiate an appeal. Four-fifths of the appeals heard by the *Curia Ebora-censis* were brought by women. This is substantially more than the two-thirds over-representation of women among the first instance litigants, but it is impossible to suggest any reasons for this: the possibilities include the two explanations that women simply litigated more often or that the lower courts showed a bias in favour of men. Whatever the reason may be, it can be argued that women stood to lose or gain more than men from successful litigation. If the abandoned woman with children lost her case she would be left in her community as a single mother with the sole responsibility for her children. On the other hand, if she won her case she was guaranteed the security of a husband who was bound to look after their family. The relative success rate of women in the courts certainly indicates that the court was a powerful ally for women in their attempts to enforce their rights against reluctant husbands: the courts clearly judged cases on their merits. If one interprets the proportion of women who chose to litigate in York as an index of women's economic opportunities in Yorkshire in the fourteenth century, it would appear that the numbers contradict Goldberg's thesis that the fourteenth century was a time of economic opportunity and marked freedom for women. Women can be seen to have been keen to establish or preserve marriage, and their preponderance among the plaintiffs suggests that there was considerable pressure on women to marry. Men, on the other hand, rarely stood to gain from marital litigation. In most cases they were of the same status as the woman and of comparable or superior wealth.[88] In two cases, however, the male plaintiff's main motivation for bringing the case appears to have been their desire to acquire or maintain rights over properties belonging to the woman they sought in marriage.[89] The overwhelming majority of female plaintiffs is reflected in their success rate: thirty-five sentences by a first instance court were passed in favour of the woman,[90] and

---

[88] Only one of the women sought by a man in marriage – Johanna Monceaux, the defendant in *Carnoby* c. *Monceaux* – defended herself with the argument that she was far too wealthy to have consented to the marriage. CP, E 179 (1390). Men, on the other hand, often used this argument to try to discredit the woman's claim on them.

[89] *Canoby* c. *Monceaux* and *Huntington* c. *Munkton*. The latter was a case of divorce *a mensa et thoro*, the former is analysed in detail in Chapter 2.

[90] CP, E 1, 15, 18, 23, 28, 37, 40, 69, 71, 82, 84, 92, 102, 103, 105, 111, 113, 114, 116, 121, 124, 126, 135, 157, 178, 181, 188, 198, 202, 215, 213, 236, 255, 259 and 263.

twenty sentences in the first instance favoured the man's position.[91]
Women were also more likely to appeal the decision of the court.
Thirteen of the twenty appeals heard by the *Curia Eboracensis* were
made by women.[92] Women were thus more likely to use the courts to
settle their disputes with men and the courts seem to have been a
useful ally in their attempts to assert their rights.

The age distribution of the witnesses who appeared in the cause
papers gives us some further insights into the social setting of the
court in York. The most noticeable feature of this population is that
the sex ratio we observed in the population of litigants is inverted
among the witnesses. Out of 565 witnesses who are identifiable by
gender, 389 were men and 176 women.[93] Approximately half of these
witnesses, 265, or sixty-eight women and 197 men, informed the
court of their age. As one would expect, there is an under-representation of members of the age group 0–19 years. A witness had to be
legally competent in civil cases – he could usually not be less than
fifteen years of age.[94] For reasons of clarity, witnesses of less than
twenty years of age have been left out in the comparisons between
model age-structure tables and the York population in the graphs that
follow.[95] The age distribution of the male population of witnesses in

---

[91] CP, E 6, 26, 76, 77, 79, 85, 87, 89, 95, 97, 106, 137, 138, 155, 191, 211, 221,
235, 238 and 241v.

[92] CP, E 1, 6, 25, 26, 71, 82, 114, 137, 178, 215, 223, 241b, and 263.

[93] Goldberg, *Women, Work and Life Cycle*, p. 221, comes to much the same results.
Goldberg analysed the gender of 943 deponents who appeared before the court in
the period 1303–1499, dividing them into urban and rural cases. 401 of these
appeared before the court in the period 1303–99. The criteria which Goldberg
applied to select his sample are not explicitly stated in his book, but the sample
does not appear to have been enlarged from that used in his 1987 unpublished
Cambridge thesis "Female Labour, Status and Marriage in Late Medieval York and
Other English Towns" (Cambridge, 1987). The highly selective criteria for the
earlier sample are outlined in the thesis, p. 56.

[94] C.4 q.3 c.1–19; D. 22 c 5 Paul Fournier, *Les officialités au moyen âge: étude sur
l'organisation, la competence et la procédure des tribunaux ecclésiastiques ordinaire
en France, de 1180 à 1328* (Paris, 1880), p. 185; Helmholz, *Marriage Litigation*,
p. 155.

[96] Age distribution tables are taken from Ansley J. Coale, Paul Demeny and Barbara
Vaughan, *Regional Model Life Tables and Stable Populations*, Studies in Population
(New York and London, 1983). A model age distribution table is a mathematically
derived distribution of age groups according to varying demographic regimes. The
variables used in the equations are the population's mortality and fertility. On the
basis of these variables a distribution of members in different age groups is calcu

the cause papers shows an almost perfect fit, particularly among the older witnesses. Although this is perhaps a little surprising since it is often argued that high age was a positive factor when the courts evaluated evidence, the population of male witnesses could be a random survival representing the age structure of society at large. However, the comparison is to a stationary population and it was probably not the case that the fourteenth-century population was stationary, especially not in the later part of the century during which period almost three-quarters of the observed population appeared before the courts.[96] This may explain the somewhat different picture that emerges by a comparison of the female population to a level 4 stationary age-distribution table. Again, like the men, there is a good fit for individuals up to fifty years of age, but a marked decrease in the proportion of older women. Some explanations can be proposed. One is that the sample reflects some particular event in women's lives, such as marriage or childbirth, both of which would tend to limit women's mobility in the local community, and therefore also their opportunities for attending or accidentally overhearing exchanges of vows. This possibility must be rejected, though, since the fall in the representation of female witnesses occurs around the age when one would have expected to see an increase in women's mobility as their children were no longer so dependent on the presence of their mothers. Another explanation may be that the proposition that we are dealing with a stationary population is wrong. The age-distribution of the female population is commensurate with a growing population and therefore we may actually be seeing an over-representation of older males among the witnesses in the cause papers. Whatever the cause, this difference in the age distribution of male and female witnesses suggests that other selection criteria than pure chance are at work. The fact that there is such a good fit between the male population of witnesses and a reasonable age distribution table, and a correspondingly poor fit between the same age distribution table and the female population of witnesses, should warn us not to trust the cause papers too much as a random survival of court cases. The demographic distri-

---

lated. A comparison of the model age distribution table to the age distribution in an observed population may show if the age distribution of the observed population is commensurate with a random sample. The model age distribution table used for both sexes in this study is a west level 4 stationary population.

[96] Goldberg, *Women, Work, and Life Cycle*, pp. 7, 345–50, amongst others, argues that this period saw a strong recovery from the plague.

bution of witnesses in cause papers does not represent a typical or even common distribution of the population of the people of the northern province.

While it can be said that the typical plaintiff was a woman, the opposite is true about the witnesses: the typical witness was a man. Among the 565 witnesses there were 389 men and 176 women. In total, 265 witnesses informed the court of their age: sixty-eight women and 197 men. As one would expect there is an under-representation of members of the age group 0–19 years. This is largely because a witness had to be legally competent in civil cases.[97] The court in York appears not to have adhered strictly to this rule. The two youngest witnesses heard by the court were Cecilia de Shipton and Emmota Norice Hoby, aged thirteen, who were interrogated by the court in *Marrays c. Roucliff*.[98] The case concerned the marriage of a minor. The distribution of older witnesses is unusual too, and may indicate that a higher age was considered a benefit in a witness.[99]

Only a quarter – or 140 – of the witnesses informed the *Curia Eboracensis* about their occupation. By far the largest group among these witnesses is that of clerics: seventy-one people were related to the church in one capacity or other. Twenty-two of these were chaplains and twenty-one were unspecified *clerici*. The reason for this preponderance of clerics is likely to be that both the litigants and the court felt that their estate carried a certain value, especially in the kinds of cases that we are investigating here. In a manner of speaking, they were expert witnesses. Their training sensitised them to the meanings of the vows that they witnessed, and in some cases they were even called by the parties or by their parents to recite the words of the vows that made a marriage legally binding so that the parties could contract their marriage in a legally binding manner. Correspondingly, none of the preserved decisions of the court went against marriage if a priest or notary public claimed that he had been present at an exchange of vows that established marriage by *verba de presenti*. If a cleric testified to his knowledge of celebrations of marriage, that marriage was only dissolved by the *Curia Eboracensis* if the marriage

---

[97] C.4 q. 3 c. 1–19; D22 c5; Fournier, *Les officialités*, p. 185.

[98] CP, E 89 (1365).

[99] I have tried to match the age distribution for the York sample against a large number of the model life-span tables in Coale, Demeny and Vaughan, *Regional Model Life Tables and Stable Populations*. The best fit is to a model west, stable population, mortality level 1, which shows a reasonable fit for the age groups twenty to fifty years, but an over-representation of age groups sixty to ninety.

could be shown to be invalid for other reasons, such as force and fear, consanguinity or legal incapacity. The existence of a marriage can thus be said to have been taken for granted by the court if testified to by a cleric.

Among the remaining twenty-six persons in this group we find six parish priests, six notary publics and a number of nuns, monks and members of the courts.[100] Among the seventy lay witnesses who gave their occupations to the court the largest single group consisted of twenty-two servants. The term *serviens* with the name of their master, which was used by these people to describe themselves, in most cases meant that they were employees of their master rather than that they were his serfs. Most of them make it clear that they are on a contract of employment which is of limited duration. Eight people inform the court that they are *literati*. It is unclear what this description is supposed to convey: the normal dictionary definition is "lettered" or "liberally educated",[101] but they appear in cases where their ability to read is not an issue and they are not called to witness a written contract or appeal. All eight appear to be wealthy men, but apart from that it is impossible to characterise them further. In contrast, the four witnesses who characterise themselves as laymen *(laici)* are called to witness that a plaintiff has handed in a written appeal against a sentence of a lower court.[102] Among the rest of the witnesses who informed the court of their occupation we find craftsmen of various kinds from goldsmiths to butchers and tailors and a summoner and a runner for the archdeacon of Burton.[103] Although many people of lower rank undoubtedly appeared before the court, only a few of the

---

[100] The list of seventy-one clerics contained twenty-two chaplains, seventeen unspecified *clerici*, six vicars, six notaries public by apostolic authority (five of whom also described themselves as clerics, but are not counted among that group), three clerks, three vicars choral, two guardians of hospitals (St Mary's, Bootham; St Giles, Beverley), two nuns, two monks, one canon, the abbot of St Mary's Abbey, York, one clerk of the vestibule, one former official of the East Riding, one *janitor*, one *magister*, one *presbyter* and one registrar of the court.

[101] Charlton T. Lewis, *A Latin Dictionary Founded on Andrews' Edition of Freund's Latin Dictionary Revised, Enlarged, and in Great Part Rewritten* (Oxford, 1987), s.v. "litteratus".

[102] *Elewyk c. Midelton and Frothyngham* (1365) and *Huntington c. Munkton* (1345–46). CP, E 102 and 248.

[103] The complete list of occupations is: twenty-two servants, eight *literati*, six saddle-makers, four *laici*, four goldsmiths, two butchers, two ropemakers, two barbers, two spinners, two apothecaries, two tailors, one potter, one *grenster*, one *domina*, one *bociler*, one weaver, one fletcher, one draper (*tapiter*), one *wright*, one tanner,

witnesses describe themselves as agricultural labourers or farmers. We learn from depositions over the exceptions lodged against their testimony that a further two witnesses were paupers and in one of these cases a beggar.[104] Only about a quarter of the witnesses informed the court of their occupation, and by no stretch of the imagination can the group be said to be representative of the distribution of trades and occupations in fourteenth-century Yorkshire. An outstanding feature of this group of witnesses is the predominance of clerics among them. Almost half served the church in one function or another, whether as priests, notaries, nuns or monks.

That the witnesses do not represent a random sample of Yorkshire people is clear from a consideration of their social status. As was the case among the litigants, members of status group five are virtually absent from the list of witnesses. Only twenty-one of around 580 witnesses can be positively identified as members of status group 5.[105] The under-representation of status group 5 is perhaps explained by the rules of canon law governing the production of witnesses. The decretalists formulated the rule that anyone could give evidence in a case before an ecclesiastical tribunal, subject to certain important qualifications. If a witness could be shown to be inadmissible, his or her evidence would be suspect. If, furthermore, that witness was one of only two witnesses to overhear an exchange of vows, and if there was no supplementary proof of the existence of a contract, his disqualification could mean the difference between winning and losing the case. It was therefore in the litigants' interests to ensure whenever they could that their witnesses were not open to legal exceptions. A consideration of the rules of academic canon law may have informed their decision about whom to call to support their case.

Among the reasons for disqualification given by academic lawyers we find that in law a witness could be disqualified if it was demonstrated that he was under-aged, a serf, mentally retarded, a mortal enemy of one of the litigants or an excommunicate at the time of his

---

one fur-seller, one forester, one runner for the archdeacon of Burton, one summoner and one "citizen of York".

[104] *Bradley* c. *Walkington* (1355) and *Redyng* c. *Boton* (1366). The former case contains marvellously detailed descriptions about how the woman in question made her living cleaning for others in the neighbourhood of All Saints' North Street in York. CP, E 82 and 92.

[105] Their evidence is found in CP, E 89, 92, 113, 114, 155, 181, 198 and 235.

deposition.[106] Mental illness and status as a pauper was argued in *Redyng c. Boton*, enmity in *Hobbesdaughter c. Skipsea* and excommunication in *Huntington c. Munkton*.[107] Among the remaining cases with exceptions to witnesses, the objections were of a more general kind: that the witness's character was such that he could easily be persuaded to tell a lie or that the witnesses could be expected to lie because of their employment in the household of the other litigant. Thirty-five matrimonial causes paper files contain such exceptions to witnesses.[108] The evidence of an unfree person was thus open to many exceptions, some of which could invalidate his or her testimony. Against this background it is not surprising that litigants should want to avoid using serfs as witnesses whenever possible. Whatever the reasons for their absence may be, the fact that there are so few members of status group five among the witnesses must make us wary of using the cause papers as evidence for medieval demographics.

This analysis of the status of the litigants shows a disproportionately large group of litigants from the higher status groups, which indicates that status was intimately related to the wish to litigate. The cause papers contain a sample of the northern population which is biased towards the wealthiest and more confident segment of the population. Furthermore, the geographical distribution of the cases also showed marked anomalies: people who lived close to a court were more likely to litigate than those who did not. It must be admitted that the cause papers establish a poor foundation for an analysis of the underlying demographic structure of the society that produced this litigation. In addition, with regard to the witnesses, the age and status distribution of the witnesses who were interrogated by the courts raise questions

---

[106] The rules for proof by witness in the church courts are compared to practice in Charles Donahue, Jr, "Proof by Witnesses in the Medieval Courts of England: An Imperfect Reception of the Learned Law", in *On the Laws and Customs of England: Essays in Honor of Samuel E. Thorne*, Morris S. Arnold, Thomas A. Green, Sally A. Scully and Stephen D. White (eds), (Chapel Hill, North Carolina, 1981), pp. 127–58 and in Helmholz, *Marriage Litigation*, p. 133. James A. Brundage has some comments of value on this problem in *Law, Sex and Christian Society in Medieval Europe* (Chicago, 1987), pp. 345, 411.

[107] CP, E 92 (1366), 202 (1392) and 248 (1345–46).

[108] CP, E 6, 14, 15, 23, 33, 61, 77, 82, 89, 92, 102, 103, 111, 114, 116, 124, 135, 138, 150, 157, 159, 175, 179, 188, 191, 198, 202, 213, 216, 221, 223, 235, 238, 248 and 263.

about whether the witnesses represent a cross-section of medieval English society. A large section of the population – the unfree – was not perceived as desirable as witnesses. Their relative absence must also support the allegation that the cause papers do not represent a random sample of the population of medieval Yorkshire. Thus, both the litigants and the witnesses who appeared before the court in York were not representative of the total population, and the use litigants made of the courts was determined by their status and their distance to the courts. The York material in particular is therefore prone to present marginal and unusual aspects of the experience of marriage in the fourteenth century.

Although the matrimonial litigation papers show such marginal experiences of marriage, it is possible to learn a good deal about marital contracts and relationships from them as long as one does not attempt to apply these experiences equally to the total population. Instead, any analysis of the surviving cause paper material must establish the location and the status of the litigants and their witnesses. It is clear that the majority of litigants had easy access to the court; or that their marriages were either notorious in the local community; or offered sufficient rewards to one of the litigants to motivate them to seek the arbitration of a faraway church court to settle their disputes. The evidence contained in ecclesiastical court papers is at its best when used as evidence for the development and application of the law, but must be used for evidence of events outside the sphere of the law with the highest caution. For the reasons presented above, this study will not attempt to further quantify the evidence of the cause papers. If this is done with circumspection and tempered by a knowledge of the dynamics of the courts and of the application of canon law, these court records are capable of yielding important insights into the structure and practice of married life in the middle ages despite the methodological problems they pose.

10

The Courts and Medieval Marriage

The medieval church successfully claimed the right to pass judgment in cases where the salvation of the litigant's soul might be at stake. As the high middle ages wore on, marriage disputes became one of the commonest categories of dispute that thus fell under the church's jurisdiction. The church's legal position on marriage was first systematically treated by Gratian around 1140, who laid the foundation for the church's treatment of disputed marriages. His clarification of the basic legal consequences of marriage remained virtually unchallenged throughout the middle ages, but his definition of the moment when a marriage became legally binding was quickly seen to be unworkable. Over the next century the popes, decretists and decretalists continued to wrestle with the questions about the legal status of marriage. The eventual outcome was a distinction between marriages contracted by present or future consent. This vested unprecedented power over marriage in the parties themselves and removed the need for parental consent or even for any kind of ceremony or the presence of witnesses at the establishment of a marriage. This emphasis on individual choice meant a very real need for a way in which justice could be seen to be done in cases of disputes over the legality of marriage.

As part of the ongoing restructuring of the church that had begun with the Gregorian reform movement, the church therefore began to provide courts, which met regularly under the presidency of legally trained officers of the church, to hear and determine cases which the church claimed for its own. This new development took place all over Europe in the last half of the thirteenth century; and, though the early sources are sparse, it has been shown that the English church enthusiastically participated in this process. What has not been emphasised before is that the process of providing courts to settle marriage disputes met a need in the laity, that lay people enthusiastically embraced the new clarity offered by the church's rules, and that they relished the opportunity of having settled, once and for all, their disagreements over individual marriages.

This book has investigated the success of the implementation of the canon law rules of marriage in the church courts of one of the provinces in the fourteenth century. The relatively new law of marriage was clearly already well known by the early fourteenth century and the archdiocese of York provided a reliable and solid structure for the dispensation of the canon law. As a part of this dispensation of justice, the court maintained a full record of its activity. Two main impressions are gained from a study of these records. One is that the laity was well aware of and trusted the church courts; the second is that the church courts exercised their jurisdiction over marriage in an atmosphere of cooperation: the litigants had long since accepted the courts' right to decide matrimonial disputes and had no wish to challenge it. It is a measure of the success of canon law that the litigants defined themselves as married or not according to its rules.

The surviving fourteenth-century documents from the *Curia Eboracensis* represent its activity both as a first instance court and as an appeal court for the people living in peculiars which fell within the cognisance of the province of York. What is striking about the material is its social, legal and geographical diversity: although the last chapter of this book argued that the material is seriously biased in favour of litigation originating among higher status groups, the documents include litigation from people in all walks of life, from the lowest to, perhaps not the *highest*, but certainly the *higher* status groups of northern English society. They include people from the ranks of paupers, beggars, cleaners, day labourers, thieves and braggards and from the ranks of the nobility, such as the Colvilles, the Percys and the Cantilupes, some of whom, such as Nicholas Cantilupe, were related to practitioners of law and, more distantly, to a bishop; others, such as Johanna Monceaux, claimed to be related to the royal family. What they all had in common was that they sought the expertise of a church court to settle their marital disputes and that they were eager to use the opportunity to present their disputes to a professional body, although they may not necessarily have wanted to take the case through to its final sentence (as appears to be the case in *Carnoby* c. *Monceaux*). Nevertheless, the most enduring impression one gains from the analysis of the church courts is the vigour with which the laity pursued their cases in the legal system.

Every case in the cause papers is an instance case, initiated by a member of the laity, even the *sub poena nubendi* cases were heard by the court in York as instance cases pleading for the enforcement of conditional vows. When the laity sought the judgment of the court in their disputes over marriage, they conformed to the procedure of the courts. They appointed proctors to represent them and were rarely absent when summoned before the court. This is perhaps not so surprising as may at first appear. Throughout the cause paper material this book has identified attempts at out-of-court preparation for the courtroom procedures and argued that the courts functioned within a larger system of conflict resolution that included *ad hoc* lay tribunals. The cause papers show that such tribunals, formal and informal, investigated the cases before they appeared in the cause papers. These tribunals functioned in the "shadow of the law" and left dim trails and therefore it is impossible to say how common they were.[1] But where they leave traces in the courts' documentation they effectively helped prepare a case before it was heard by the proper court. Even in cases where it has been argued that the court officials themselves interfered in the process of litigation, the manipulations that have been suggested took place to strengthen the position of one of the litigants, rather than to enhance the power of the courts. In other words, the litigants craved the respectability that an apparently canonical resolution to their conflict imparted.

This cooperation between the courts and the litigants was probably due to two factors: one was that the personnel of the courts were well acquainted with the law and were seen to apply its rules impartially; the other that the laity understood the basics of the law and knew where to obtain advice to clarify the rules that were unclear to its members. Bishop Greenfield's court statutes of 1311 required the judges to have a degree in law and the proctors of the court to undergo a year's apprenticeship before being admitted to practice. These rules, and the court's annual recitation of its oath of office, which emphasised the common search for the truth over a competitive ethos, ensured that the court was also *seen* to be impartial. In addition, the litigants themselves knew the rules of canon law and accepted that the most effective place to settle matrimonial disputes was in the courts. It is clear from an analysis of the cases heard by the courts that the litigants had good reason to trust the courts. Though it has been argued that the courts sometimes interfered in the cases to try and encourage the outcome its members thought was the right one, as far as one can tell from the preserved material the court's officials

---

[1] I first came across this evocative phrase in Michael Grossberg, *A Judgment for Solomon: The d'Hauteville Case and Legal Experience in Antebellum America*, Cambridge Historical Studies in American Law and Society (Cambridge, 1996).

were impartial in their treatment of the cases when they came before them sitting in tribunal. They passed judgment according to the merits of the case as it was presented by the evidence in the court room. This, at least, is the conclusion one must draw from the fact that the numerical superiority of female plaintiffs is reflected in the number of sentences passed in favour of the woman's position. A few cases alleging partiality or misconduct did appear before the court in York, but their relative rarity can in fact be seen as indicators that, when the courts deviated from the impartiality expected of them, they were quickly brought to book by the laity, who knew that they could argue a case of misconduct in the *Curia Eboracensis*.

Although it did happen in a few cases, the litigants rarely referred to being intimidated outside the court room. Only one case, *Lovell* c. *Cantilupe*, CP, E 259 (1368–9), documents a direct attempt to interfere with the right of another litigant to seek the courts' decision in a marriage case. In another case (*Maynwaring* c. *Tofte*, CP, E 15) the male defendant argued that he felt that he could not travel in safety to the court of Arches in London to attend meetings of the court, because the journey took him through areas where his wife's family might attack him. But he did not prove that this intimidation actually took place. In the last case where a litigant interfered with the exercise of the courts' jurisdiction (*Huntington* c. *Munkton*, CP, E 248,), the wife, who had received a command from the archbishop's court of audience to restore her husband to his marital rights, was attacked by her husband in Stonegate: a misguided attempt to execute the command of the archbishop's court. These latter two cases, however, were not cases of direct interference in the exercise of justice: one litigant expressed his fear of what might happen before it actually happened and the other tried to implement a decision of the court believing that this decision gave him the right to force his wife to cohabit with him.

The courts showed a preference for maintaining the *status quo*, particularly in the *causae matrimonii et divortii*. As a consequence, the courts tended to uphold the marriage in which cohabitation was already established by the time the case came to the cognizance of the court. Only in cases where it was incontrovertibly shown by the testimony of several witnesses that vows established a legally binding marriage prior to the exchange of vows in the *de facto* marriage did the court pass sentence for the prior marriage. Only one type of case did not follow this trend. As a rule, *sub poena nubendi* cases were successfully prosecuted by the plaintiffs in York. In the nine surviving cases, five plaintiffs persuaded the court that intercourse had taken place after their forced exchange of promises to marry and the court passed sentence in favour of the existence of a marriage between the litigants. Once again, the cases received their sentence on their merits, it having been proved by at least two witnesses that intercourse had taken place. A presumption of intercourse was not enough to secure a favourable outcome for the plaintiff in a *sub poena nubendi* case.

Apart from evidence showing how the courts applied the rules of the canon law of marriage, the cause papers also show us that the litigants understood these rules even before they came into contact with the courts. Although the witness accounts cannot always be taken on face value, they demonstrate a central feature of lay people's knowledge of marriage ritual in the fourteenth century. Both the witnesses and the litigants agreed that the constituent moment in a marriage was when words of consent were spoken. Among the witness accounts one can find examples of rituals being performed in connection with marriages, but these rituals are always additional to the exchange of a spoken vow. A solemnisation of marriage at the church door, the exchange of rings or kisses through a garland of flowers, or the blessing of the marriage bed, were indications of the parties' consent to the marriage after the vows were spoken. These actions, however, were never mentioned as the constituent action in marriage, whether by the witnesses in their depositions or by the litigants in their articles. There can be no doubt that the church had successfully implemented the ideal of freedom of choice that was made a part of the canon law of marriage in the twelfth century.

The litigants' consistent use of the correct formulae for the exchange of promises to marry and their witnesses' precise recollection (or alleged recollection) of the words used indicate that when lay people appeared before the courts they understood when a situation could possibly establish a marriage, and that they knew, used and applied the canon law rules of marriage to their own lives. They frequently insisted on the presence of a priest to help the contracting parties recite precisely those words which established a union with the desired legal consequences. It is clear from the cause papers that the litigants knew that not only could they contract marriage without solemnising the union at the church, but that they also knew that a marriage contracted under such conditions could be prosecuted in the ecclesiastical courts. It could be argued that the witnesses may have been instructed by the litigants or their proctors before they gave their testimony, but this argument does not disprove the fact that the witnesses displayed an understanding of canon law in their testimony, regardless of when they had learned its rules.

The level of knowledge of the law among the laity was variable, as might be expected. Specifically, there was some uncertainty among the litigants about the exact words to be used to make a marriage legally binding – a fact ably exploited by the more unscrupulous among the litigants. Some of the litigants knew the general rules about marriage vows but had been misled by an ambiguous wording at an exchange of vows. Others showed a much more sophisticated understanding of the rules, which led them to exchange promises to marry hoping to be able to have premarital intercourse without the legal consequences which they knew were normally associated with that action. Unfortunately, the cases in which these attempts appear suffer from flaws in the presentation of the evidence which means that the sentences preserved with the cause papers reflect the court's weighing of the evidence as it was presented. They are not a decision on the admissibility of the actions of the litigants.

Although it has been pointed out that the cause papers contain many cases prosecuted by litigants from the propertied classes, the statutes of the courts in York provided the opportunity of prosecution to most people in the northern province, whether they were rich or poor, employers or employees, landowners or traders. There is still one question, however, about lay people's access to the courts which remains unanswered. It is impossible to say anything about whether the unfree used the courts at all. Only one case (*Sturmy* c. *Tuly*, CP, E 235), which concerns a man's alleged unfree status, shows any kind of concern for the status – unfree or otherwise – of a person who appeared in court. The free status – or lack of it – of all the other litigants who appear in the cause papers cannot be established. Most of the litigants came from the propertied classes, or served with a master in the cities, or were themselves masters of a trade. Thus it is quite possible that the unfree were able to employ the services of the courts in York, but this problem cannot be illuminated by a study of the surviving York cause papers.

Interpreting the motives of the litigants when they presented their cases to the court is difficult on the basis of the cause paper material. In a few cases, however, educated guesses can be made and in one instance a litigant explained why: she did not want to be made look a fool. Other litigants were not so forthright and only guesses can be made concerning their motives. It is probable that some female litigants tried to better their situation by bringing a case before the court in York, either as a divorce case to stop the husband's sale of their land or in the hope of establishing a marriage with a man well above their own status. It should be pointed out that attempting to better social standing through such a dubious means as a possibly false claim of marriage was not confined to women but that men tried to bring these kinds of cases too. It is also clear, however, that a number of cases were simply part of a larger attempt by the parties to either mend or break their marriages. Some, such as Alice Palmer in *Palmer c. Palmer and Southburn* did so successfully by providing perjured witnesses to previous marriages,[2] others, such as John Carnoby in *Carnoby c. Monceaux*,[3] simply brought his case before the court in an attempt to force it to enforce his dubious union to Johanna Monceaux. Agnes Huntington in *Huntington c. Munkton* had quarrelled with her husband about the alienation of her ancestral land – a problem wtih which the church courts could not help her.[4] Her response was to reformulate her original complaint in such a way that it became possible for the courts do so. The true extent of the practice of "repackaging" can never be known. Occasionally, some light shines through less than perfect seams in the resultant narratives. We can only describe these cases as they appear in the surviving documentation and make educated guesses at the real issues at stake.

In sum, the litigants relied on the court and its personnel to give them the right answer in their disputes. As in any gamble, the answer might not be the one they wished for, but the litigants used their knowledge of canon law and the courts to sort out problems with their private lives. A small proportion of the litigants had a better knowledge of canon law and sought to abuse the legal process so that their marriages or dissolutions appeared to others to be canonically valid. Medieval people thus formulated their doubts about marriage in terms the canon law could understand. They attempted to live their lives according to its complex rules, and in this attempt they show how successfully these rules were implemented. It is impossible not to think that the reason for its success was that the canon law provided the answer to their problems.

[2] CP, E 25 (1355–56).
[3] CP, E 179 (1390).
[4] CP, E 248 (1345–46).

Bibliography

Adams, Norma, and Charles Donahue, Jr, "Introduction", in *Select Cases from the Ecclesiastical Courts of the Province of Canterbury, c. 1200–1301*, Selden Society, 95 (London, 1981), pp 1–120.

Aers, David, "Criseyde: Woman in Medieval Society." *Chaucer Review*, 13 (1979), pp. 177–200.

Alessandro, John A., *Gratian's Notion of Marital Consummation* (Vatican City, 1971).

Baildon, W. Paley, *Feet of Fines for the County of York from 1347 to 1377: 21–51 Edward III*, Yorkshire Archaeological Society (London, 1915).

Bellomo, Manlio, *The Common Legal Past of Europe 1000–1800*, trans. Lydia G. Cochrane (Washington, DC, 1995).

Bennett, Judith M., "Medieval Women, Modern Women: Across the Great Divide", in *Culture and History 1350–1600: Essays on English Communities, Identities and Writing*, ed. David Aers (New York; London, 1992).

Benson, C. David, ed., *Critical Essays on Chaucer's Troilus and Creseyde and his Major Early Poems* (Milton Keynes, 1991).

Berman, Harold J., *Law and Revolution: The Formation of the Western Legal Tradition* (Cambridge, Massachusetts, and London, 1983).

Brentano, Robert. *York Metropolitan Jurisdiction and Papal Judges Delegate, 1279–1296* (Berkeley, 1959).

Brewer, Derek, "Review of Henry Ansgar Kelly, *Love and Marriage in the Age of Chaucer*", *Review of English Studies*, 28 (1977), pp. 194–97.

Brown, Sandra, "The Peculiar Jurisdiction of York Minster during the Middle Ages" (unpublished Ph.D. thesis, University of York, 1980).

Brown, William, ed., *The Register of Thomas of Corbridge, Lord Archbishop of York, 1300–1304*, i, Surtees Society, 138 (Durham, 1925).

Brown, William, ed., *The Register of William Wickwane, Lord Archbishop of York, 1279–1285*, Surtees Society, 114 (Durham, 1907).

Brown, William, and A. Hamilton Thompson, eds, *The Register of William Greenfield, Lord Archbishop of York, 1306–15*, i, Surtees Society, 145 (Durham, 1931).

Brown, William, and A. Hamilton Thompson, eds, *The Register of William Greenfield, Lord Archbishop of York, 1306–15*, ii, Surtees Society, 149 (Durham, 1934).

Brundage, James A., *Law, Sex and Christian Society in Medieval Europe* (Chicago, 1987.

Brundage, James A., *Medieval Canon Law* (Harlow, 1996).

Burns, K. F. " The Administrative System of the Ecclesiastical Courts in the Diocese and Province of York", i, "The Medieval Courts", unpublished manuscript (York, 1962).

Bériou, Nicole, and David L. d'Avray, "Henry of Provins OP's Comparison of the Dominican and Franciscan Orders with the 'Order' of Matrimony", *Archivum Fratrum Praedicatorum*, 49 (1979), pp. 513–17.

Calendar of Inquisitions Post Mortem and Other Analogous Documents Preserved in the Public Record Office Prepared Under the Superintendence of the Deputy Keeper of the Records, xiii, 44–47 Edward III (London, 1954).

Cantor, Leonard, ed., *The English Medieval Landscape* (London and Canberra, 1982).

Carlson, Lizzie. *"Jag giver dig min dotter"*: *trolovning och äktenskap i den svenska kvinnans äldra historia* (Lund, 1965).

Cheney, C. R., "Rules for the Observance of Feastdays in Medieval England", *Bulletin of the Institute of Historical Research*, 34 (1982); reprinted in *The English Church and Its Laws, 12th-14th Centuries*; item no. 10, Variorum Collected Studies.

Cheney, C.R., and B.E.A. Jones, eds, *English Episcopal Acta* (London, 1986).

Chobham, Thomas, *Thomae de Chobham Summa confessorum*, ed. F Broomfield, Analecta medievalia Namurcensia (Leuven, 1954)

Clay, Charles Travis, ed., *Early Yorkshire Charters,* iv, *The Honour of Richmond, Part 1*, based on the manuscripts of the late William Farrer, Yorkshire Archeological Society Record Series, Extra Series, 1 (1936).

Clay, Charles Travis, ed., *Early Yorkshire Charters*, vi, *The Paynell Fee*, based on the manuscripts of the late William Farrer, Yorkshire Archeological Society Record Series, Extra Series, 3 (1939).

Coale, Ansley J., Paul Demeny and Barbara Vaughan, *Regional Model Life Tables and Stable Populations*, Studies in Population (New York and London, 1983).

d'Avray, D. L., "The Gospel of the Marriage Feast of Cana and Marriage Preaching in France", in *The Bible in the Medieval World: Essays in Honour of Beryl Smalley*, ed. Katherine Walsh and Diana Wood, Studies in Church History (Oxford, 1985), pp. 207–24.

d'Avray, D. L., and M. L. Tausche, "Marriage Sermons in *Ad Status* Collections of the Central Middle Ages", *Archives d'histoire doctrinale et literaire du moyen âge* (1981), pp. 71–119.

Dahlerup, Troels, *Studier i Dansk senmiddelalderlig kirkeorganisation*, Kirkehistoriske Studier, 2nd series, 18 (Copenhagen, 1963).

Dahlerup, Troels, *Viborg Stifts Officialer*, Kirkehistoriske samlinger, 4th series, 7 (Copenhagen, 1964).

Darmon, Pierre, *Trial by Impotence: Virility and Marriage in Pre-Revolutionary France*, trans. Paul Kegan (London, 1985).

Dauvillier, Jean, *Le mariage dans le droit classique de l'église, depuis de Décret de Gratien (1140) jusqu'à le mort de Clément V (1314)* (Paris, 1933).

Davies, G.R.C., *Medieval Cartularies of Great Britain: A Short Catalogue* (London, 1958).

Decretales domini Gregorii papae IX: V ae integritati una cum glossis restitutae (Venice, 1591).

Decretum Gratiani emendatum et notationibus illustratum una cum glossis, (Venice, 1591).

Dobson, R.B. "Admissions to the Freedom of the City of York in the Late Middle Ages", *Economic History Review,* 2nd series, 23 (1973), pp. 1–22.

Donahue, Charles, Jr, " 'Clandestine'" Marriage in the Later Middle Ages: A Reply", *Law and History Review,* 10 (1992), pp. 315–22.

Donahue, Charles, Jr, "Proof by Witnesses in the Medieval Courts of England: An Imperfect Reception of the Learned Law", in *On the Laws and Customs of England: Essays in Honor of Samuel E.* Thorne, ed. Morris S. Arnold, Thomas A. Green, Sally A. Scully and Stephen D. White (Chapel Hill, 1981), pp. 127–58.

Donahue, Charles, Jr, "The Canon Law on the Formation of Marriage and Social Practice in the Later Middle Ages", *Journal of Family History,* 8 (1983), pp. 144–58.

Donahue, Charles, Jr, "The Policy of Alexander the Third's Consent Theory of Marriage", in *Proceedings of the Fourth International Conference of Medieval Canon Law,* ed. Stephan Kuttner, Monumenta Iuris Canonici, 5 (Città del Vaticano, 1976), pp. 251–81.

Elvey, G.R., ed., *Luffield Priory Charters Part 1* (Northampton, 1968).

Farrer, William, ed., *Early Yorkshire Charters,* i, *Early Yorkshire Charters: Being a Collection of Documents Anterior to the Thirteenth Century Made from Public Records, Monastic Chartularies, Roger Dodsworths Manuscripts and Other Available Sources* (Edinburgh, 1914).

Farrer, William, ed., *Early Yorkshire* Charters, iii, *Early Yorkshire Charters: Being a Collection of Documents Anterior to the Thirteenth Century Made from Public Records, Monastic Chartularies, Roger Dodsworths Manuscripts and Other Available Sources,* Yorkshire Archaeological Society Record Series, extra series (Edinburgh, 1916).

Finch, Andrew, "Parental Authority and the Problem of Clandestine Marriage in the Later Middle Ages", *Law and History Review,* 8 (1990), pp. 189–204.

Finch, Andrew, *"Repulsa Uxore Sua*: Marital Difficulties and Separation in the Later Middle Ages", *Continuity and Change,* 8 (January 1993), pp. 1–28.

Firth, C. B., "Benefit of Clergy in the Time of Edward IV", *English Historical Review,* 32 (1917), pp. 175–91.

Fournier, Paul, *Les officialités au moyen âge: étude sur l'organisation, la competence et la procédure des tribunaux ecclésiastiques ordinaire en France, de 1180 à1328* (Paris, 1880).

Fransen, Gérard, "La formation du lien matrimonial au moyen âge", *Revue de droit canonique*, 21 (1971), pp. 106–26.

García y García, António, ed., *Constitutiones concilii quarti Lateranensis una cum commentariis glossatorum*, Monumenta iuris canonici, Series Glossatorum, 2 (Città de Vaticano, 1981).

Gibbs, Vicary, *The Complete Peerage of England, Scotland, Ireland, Great Britain and the United Kingdom: Extant, Extinct or Dormant* (London, 1913).

Goldberg, P. J. P., "Female Labour, Status and Marriage in Late Medieval York and Other English Towns" (unpublished Ph.D. thesis, University of Cambridge, 1987).

Goldberg, P. J. P., "Urban Identity and the Poll Taxes of 1377, 1379 and 1381", *Economic History Review*, 2nd series, 43 (1990), pp. 194–216.

Goldberg, P. J. P., ed. and trans., *Women in England, c. 1275–1525: Documentary Sources*, Manchester Medieval Sources (Manchester, 1995).

Goldberg, P. J. P., *Women, Work, and Life Cycle in a Medieval Economy: Women in York and Yorkshire, c. 1300–1520* (Oxford, 1992).

Greenaway, George W., *English Historical Documents, 1042–1189*, ii, ed. D.C. Douglas (London and New York, 1981).

Grossberg, Michael, *A Judgment for Solomon: The d'Hauteville Case and Legal Experience in Antebellum America*, Cambridge Historical Studies in American Law and Society (Cambridge, 1996).

Hanawalt, Barbara A., "The Power of Word and Symbol: Conflict Resolution in Late Medieval London", in *Of Good and Ill Repute: Gender and Social Control in Medieval England* (Oxford, 1998), pp. 35–52.

Helmholz, R. H., "Abjuration *Sub Poena Nubendi* in the Church Courts of Medieval England", in *Canon Law and the Law of England* (London, 1987), pp. 145–56.

Helmholz, R. H., "Ethical Standard for Advocates and Proctors in Theory and Practice", in *Canon Law and the Law of England* (London, 1987), pp. 41–58.

Helmholz, R. H., *Marriage Litigation in Medieval England*, Cambridge Studies in English Legal History (Cambridge, 1974).

Hindle, Brian Paul, "Roads and Tracks", in *The English Medieval Landscape*, ed. Leonard Cantor (London and Canberra, 1982), pp. 193–218.

Ingram, Martin, "Spousals Litigation in the English Ecclesiastical Courts, *c.* 1350–1640", in *Marriage and Society: Studies in the Social History of Marriage*, ed. R.B. Outhwaite (London, 1981), pp. 38–57.

Kelly, Henry Ansgar, *Love and Marriage in the Age of Chaucer* (Ithaca, New York, 1975).

King, H.P.F., J.M. Horn and B. Jones, eds., *John Le Neve: Fasti Ecclesiae Anglicanae* (1962–67).

Kuttner, Stephan, *Harmony from Dissonance: An Interpretion of Medieval Canon Law* (Latrobe, Pennsylvania, 1960).

Lasch, Christopher. "The Suppression of Clandestine Marriage in England: The Marriage Act of 1753", *Salmagundi*, 26 (1974), pp. 90–109.

Latham, R.E., ed., *Revised Medieval Latin Word-List from British and Irish Sources* (London, 1965).

Leclercq, Jean, *Monks on Marriage: A Twelfth-Century View* (New York, 1981).

Lewis, Charlton T., *A Latin Dictionary Founded on Andrews' Edition of Freund's Latin Dictionary Revised, Enlarged, and in Great Part Rewritten* (Oxford, 1987).

Liebermann, Fritz, ed., *Die Gesetze der Angelsachsen*, i (Halle, 1960).

Longley, K.M., "Towards a History of Archive-Keeping in the Church of York: II. The Capitular Muniments", *Borthwick Institute Bulletin*, 1 (1976), pp. 103–19.

Macfarlane, Leslie, "The Primacy of the Scottish Church, 1472–1521", *Innes Review*, 19 (1968), pp. 111–29.

Milsom, S. F. C., *Historical Foundations of the Common Law* (London, 1969).

Morris, C., "From Synod to Consistory: The Bishop's Court in England, 1150–1250", *Journal of Ecclesiastical History*, 22 (1971), pp. 115–23.

Murray, Jacqueline, "Individualism and Consensual Marriage: Some Evidence from Medieval England", in *Women, Marriage and Family in Medieval Christendom: Essays in Memory of Michael M. Sheehan*, ed. Joel T. Rosenthal and Constance Rousseau, Studies in Medieval Culture, 36 (Kalamazoo, 1998), pp. 121–51.

Murray, Jacqueline, "On the Origins and Role of 'Wise Women' in Causes for Annulment on the Grounds of Male Impotence", *Journal of Medieval History*, 16 (1990), pp. 235–49.

Murray, Jacqueline, "Trial by Congress", *Lawyers Weekly*, 6, no. 44 (20 March 1987), pp. 20–21, 31.

Myers, A.R., ed., *English Historical Documents*, iv, *1327–1485* (London, 1969).

Noonan, John T., "Marital Affection in the Canonists", *Studia Gratiana*, 12 (1967), pp. 479–509.

Noonan, John T., "Gratian Slept Here: The Changing Evidence for the Identity of the Father of the Systematic Study of Canon Law", *Traditio*, 35 (1979), pp. 145–72.

Owen, D.M., "White Annays and Others", in *Medieval Women*, ed. Derek Baker, Studies in Church History: Subsidia (Oxford, 1978) pp. 331–46.

Page, William, ed., *Victoria County History of England*, iii, *Victoria County History of the County of Yorkshire* (London, 1913).

Pollock, Frederick, and Frederic William Maitland, *The History of English*

Law before the Time of Edward I, revised by S. F. C. Milsom, 2 vols (2nd edn, Cambridge, 1968).

Powicke, F.M., and C.R. Cheney, eds, *Councils and Synods with Other Documents Relating to the English Church*, 2 vols (Oxford, 1964).

Pugh, R.B., ed., *The City of York*, Victoria County History of England (London, 1961).

Purvis, J.S., *The Archives of the York Diocesan Registry: Their Provenance and History*, St Anthony's Hall Publications 2 (London, 1952).

Raine, J., ed., *Testamenta Eboracensia: or Wills Illustrative of the History, Manners, Language, Statistics, &c. of the Province of York from the Year MDCCC. Downwards*, Surtees Society, 4 (Durham, 1836).

Raine, J., ed., *The Register, or Rolls, of Walter Gray, Lord Archbishop of York: With Appendices of Illustrative Documents*, Surtees Society, 56 (Durham, 1872).

Rasmussen, Tove. "Jeg tager dig til min ægtemand....: kvinder og kirkeret i 1300-tallets Yorkshire" (Copenhagen, 1985).

Return. Members of Parliament, i, *Parliaments of England, 1213–1702* ([London], 1878).

Rymer, Thomas, *Foedera, conventiones, littera et eiusconque generis acta publica, inter reges anglae et alios quosvis imperatores, reges, pontifices, principes, vel communitates; ab ingressu Gulielmi I in Angliam, AD 1066 ad nostra usque tempora habita aut tractata* (London, 1827).

Sayers, Jane, *Papal Judges Delegate in the Province of Canterbury, 1198–1254* (Oxford, 1971).

Searle, E., ed., *Chronicle of Battle Abbey* (Oxford, 1980).

Sheehan, Michael M., "Choice of Marriage Partner in the Middle Ages: Development and Mode of Application of a Theory of Marriage", *Studies in Medieval and Renaissance History*, 1 (Vancouver, 1978), pp. 1–33.

Sheehan, Michael M., " 'Maritalis Affectio' Revisited", in *The Olde Daunce: Love, Friendship, Sex and Marriage in the Medieval World*, ed. Robert R. Edwards, Stephen Spector and Paul E. Szarmach (Albany, New York, 1991), pp. 32–43, 254–60.

Sheehan, Michael M., "Marriage and Family in English Conciliar Legislation", in *Essays in Honour of Anton Charles Pegis*, ed. J. Reginald O'Donnell (Toronto, 1974), pp. 205–14.

Sheehan, Michael M., "Marriage Theory and Practice in the Conciliar Legislation and Diocesan Statutes of Medieval England", *Mediaeval Studies*, 40 (1978), pp. 408–60.

Sheehan, Michael M., "The Formation and Stability of Marriage in Fourteenth-Century England: Evidence of an Ely Register", *Mediaeval Studies*, 33 (1971), pp. 228–63.

Sheehan, Michael M., "The Influence of Canon Law on the Property Rights of Married Women in England", *Mediaeval Studies*, 25 (1963), pp. 109–24.

Sheehan, Michael M., *The Will in Medieval England: From the Conversion of the Anglo-Saxons to the End of the Thirteenth Century*, Studies and Texts, 6 (Toronto, 1963).

Sheehan, Michael M., "Theory and Practice: Marriage of the Unfree and the Poor in Medieval Society", *Mediaeval Studies, 50* (1988), pp. 457–87.

Sheehan, Michael M., and Jacqueline Murray, comps, *Domestic Society in Medieval Europe: A Select Bibliography* (Toronto, 1990).

Simpson, A.W.B., *A History of the Land Law* (Oxford, 1986).

Skaife, R.H., "Civic Officials of York", unpublished manuscript, York City Archives (York City Library).

Smith, D.M., *A Guide to the Archive Collections in the Borthwick Institute of Historical Research*, Borthwick Texts and Calendars: Records of the Northern Province (York, 1973).

Smith, D.M., *Ecclesiastical Cause Papers at York: The Court at York, 1301–1399*, Borthwick Texts and Calendars, 14 (York, 1988).

Smith, R.M., "Marriage Processes in the English Past: Some Continuities", in *The World We Have Gained: Histories of Population and Social Structure*, ed. Lloyd Bonfield, Richard M. Smith and Keith Wrightson (Oxford and New York, 1986).

Smith, Walter, *Monastic Britain*, map, Director General of the Ordnance Survey (Southampton, 1978).

Storey, R. L., *Diocesan Administration in Fifteenth-Century England*, Borthwick Papers) 16 (2nd edn, York, 1972).

The Catholic Encyclopedia, vi (New York, 1907).

Tierney, Brian, *Medieval Poor Law: A Sketch of Canonical Theory and Application in England* (Berkeley and Los Angeles, 1959).

Whitelock, Dorothy, Martin Brett and C.N.L. Brooke, eds, *Documents Relating to the English Church, AD 871–1204* (Oxford, 1981).

Wilkins, David, ed., *Concilia magna Britanniae et Hiberniae a synodo Verolamiensi AD CCCCXLIV ad Londinensem AD MDC*, 2 vols (London, 1737).

Winroth, Anders, "The Two Recensions of Gratian's Decretum", *Zeitschrift der Savigny-Stiftung für Rechtsgeschichte: Kanonistische Abteilung, 83* (1997), pp. 22–31.

Woodcock, B.L., *Medieval Ecclesiastical Courts in the Diocese of Canterbury* (London, 1952).

Index